SECURITY POLITICS IN THE COMMONWEALTH OF INDEPENDENT STATES

Also by Mehdi Mozaffari

AUTHORITY IN ISLAM

Security Politics in the Commonwealth of Independent States

The Southern Belt

Edited by

Mehdi Mozaffari
Department of Political Science
University of Aarhus
Denmark

First published in Great Britain 1997 by
MACMILLAN PRESS LTD
Houndmills, Basingstoke, Hampshire RG21 6XS and London
Companies and representatives throughout the world

A catalogue record for this book is available from the British Library.

ISBN 0–333–66892–8

First published in the United States of America 1997 by
ST. MARTIN'S PRESS, INC.,
Scholarly and Reference Division,
175 Fifth Avenue, New York, N.Y. 10010

ISBN 0–312–17459–4

Library of Congress Cataloging-in-Publication Data
Security politics in the commonwealth of Independent States : the southern belt / edited by Mehdi Mozaffari.
p. cm.
Includes bibliographical references and index.
ISBN 0–312–17459–4 (cloth)
1. Asia, Central—Foreign relations—1991– 2. Asia, Central––Economic conditions. 3. National security—Asia, Central.
I. Mozaffari, Mehdi.
DK859.57.C57 1997
327.58'009'049—dc21 97–1718
CIP

This book is printed on paper suitable for recycling and made from fully managed and sustained forest sources.

10 9 8 7 6 5 4 3 2 1
06 05 04 03 02 01 00 99 98 97

Printed in Great Britain by
The Ipswich Book Company Ltd
Ipswich, Suffolk

Contents

List of Tables

List of Figures

Notes on Contributors

M. Babaev is a counsellor at the European Bank for Reconstruction and Development in London. He joined the bank in July 1991 as counsel in the General Counsel's Office and since February 1992 has been a counsellor with special responsibilities for Central Asia. He is a graduate of Kiev University where he obtained an MA in public international law and a PhD in international law. His previous positions include Foreign Associate, Cleary, Gottlieb, Steen & Hamilton, New York, USA, and Professor of International Law, Baku University School of Law.

E. Boikova is a graduate from the Moscow Institute of International Relations. Her speciality is foreign affairs. She holds the Russian academic degree of PhD (History). Her present position is at the Institute of Oriental Studies, Russian Academy of Sciences where she specializes in modern history and the culture of Mongolia and Soviet/Russian–Mongolian relations. She is the author of more than 30 articles on different aspects of Mongolia's internal affairs and its foreign relations, a monograph on the foreign policy of Mongolia in the 1960–1970s and a bibliography of Mongolian studies in the USSR in 1987–1991.

M. Dillon is a lecturer in modern Chinese history in the Department of East Asian Studies at the University of Durham, UK. He has a BA in Chinese and a PhD in Chinese history from the University of Leeds and his main research interests are the history of the Muslim Hui people of Gansu and Ningxia in northwestern China and the Uyghurs of Xinjiang and current social and political change in China and Central Asia. He has carried out research in China, Kazakhstan and Mongolia.

A. Ehteshami is a reader in international relations and the Director of Postgraduate Studies at the Centre for Middle Eastern and Islamic Studies, University of Durham. He received his PhD in politics from the University of Exeter where he was appointed a lecturer in politics (1989–1993) and Director of the Middle East Politics Programmes (1992–1993). Among his most recent publications are *Islamic Fundamentalism* (co-editor) (Westview Press, 1996), *After Khomeini: the Iranian Second Republic* (Routledge, 1995) and *From the Gulf to Central Asia: Players in the New Great Game* (editor) (University of Exeter Press, 1994).

R. Freitag-Wirminghaus, D. Phil., studied Islamic Studies, Turkology and Ethnology at Hamburg University. In 1986–1987 he was an academic member of the Orient Institute of the Deutsche Morgenländische Gesellschaft. Since 1989 he has been working for the German Orient-Institute, Hamburg. His subjects of research are Turkey, Transcaucasus and Central Asia.

A. Hyman is an associate editor of the journal *Central Asian Survey* (London) and he was a senior fellow of the SSRC-MacArthur Foundation (New York) on Peace and Security in a Changing World, 1991–1993, and a visiting fellow at Queen Elizabeth House, University of Oxford, 1991–1992. He is the author of *Afghanistan under Soviet Domination 1964–91* (Macmillan, London, 1992, third edition). He also edited *Pakistan. Zia and After* (Asia Publishing House, London, 1989) and has written chapters in various books including *The Cambridge Encyclopedia of the Middle East,* edited by Trevor Mostyn and Albert Hourani (Cambridge University Press, 1988). He is currently writing a book focusing on nationalism and independence in the Central Asia region.

S. M. Kasimov is the Director of the Institute of Economy, Business, and Retraining under Tashkent State Economic University, Head of the 'Small and Medium Size Business' Department and works in the field of applying economic mathematical methods in small and medium sized businesses. He has published 81 scientific articles and monographs. He acts as a consultant in connection with creating effective and medium sized enterprises and the privatization of state enterprises. He has experience in organizing and conducting scientific, practical seminars on market relations principles.

M. Mozaffari is Dr d'Etat en Science Politique (Sorbonne-Panthéon). He is the former head of the Department of International Relations at Tehran University and the University of Aarhus, a former professor of Political Science at Tehran University, a former associate professor at the Sorbonne, and a Docent of International Relations at the University of Aarhus (Denmark). He is the author of a number of books and articles within the following fields: theories of international politics, the Middle East, Islam and the Commonwealth of Independent States.

I. Tiouline is a professor of political science and the first vice-rector of the Moscow State Institute (University) of International Relations (MGIMO). From 1970 till 1992 he was Assistant to the Rector, General Secretary, Director of the Center of International Studies, Vice-Rector and Director of Research of the MGIMO. He is a member of several international boards and the author of many publications published in the USA, UK, France and Russia on the problems of international relations, security, diplomacy and Russian foreign policy.

G. M. Winrow is an associate professor in the Department of Political Science and International Relations at Bogazici University, Istanbul, Turkey. He was educated at Oxford, Lancaster and Manchester Universities and has also worked at Leicester University. His publications include *The Foreign Policy of the GDR in Africa* (Cambridge University Press, 1990); *Where East Meets West: Turkey and the Balkans* (Institute for European Defence and Strategic Studies, 1993) and *Turkey in Post-Soviet Central Asia* (The Royal Institute of International Affairs, 1995). He is also co-editor of *Turkey: Economic, Social and Foreign Policy Challenges for the 1990s* (E.J. Brill, 1995). He has also had various book chapters and articles published on East German and Turkish foreign policy. These articles have appeared in journals such as *The World Today*, *Africa International Review*, *Il Politico*, *Journal of South Asian and Middle Eastern Studies* and *European Security*. He is a member of the Royal Institute of International Affairs, London. He is currently developing a research interest in the security issues of the Black Sea and the Mediterranean.

Preface

The collapse of the Soviet Union was undoubtedly one of the most crucial events of the current century. The bipolar system which emerged as the result of the Second World War disappeared, at least for a while, without producing a new system. During this transitional period, the former Soviet republics and territories underwent a tremendous and unprecedented change. Some of them obtained independence for the first time in history and without asking or struggling for it. Some others waited patiently to finally become independent (the Baltic countries). A few of them are still fighting for their independence (Chechnya). Russia is still the centre of the disintegrated internal empire, but without enthusiasm and without the necessary will and capabilities, compared to what it had before, because Russia is hesitating about its own identity and status (superpower, great power, Western or Eurasian).

The Commonwealth of Independent States (CIS) still represents a diffuse and weak cooperation network which can be used for different purposes. The predominant ambition is to construct a model similar to the European Union (EU). However, everything seems to indicate that this goal will not be reached any time soon. The CIS could also be used as a platform for building a new empire. All these horizons and directions in their varieties and all the unsettled scenarios make the study of the CIS highly stimulating.

This book aims to provide both a theoretical and an analytical framework for the study of the CIS' southern belt, with a special focus on Central Asia. The book's feature is interdisciplinary with political science and international politics approaches as the main disciplines. The book is divided into three parts. The first part deals with security and foreign policy. In this connection, the first chapter provides a theoretical framework for a better understanding of the security issues in both Central Asia and Caucasus; this is always in relation to Russia's security concerns and ambitions. Why are the Central Asian and the newly independent Caucasian republics seeking Russian protection, despite the fact that – for more than a century – they have been dominated by Russia? Why is Russia willing to construct – together with these new states – a new security system, in spite of the fact that the southern regions of the late Soviet–Russian empire are considered a serious handicap to its own development and progress? And what has motivated the former USSR republics (except the Baltic states and Chechnya) to build up a new security system despite the absence of any tangible threat? The aim of Chapter 1 is precisely to provide appropriate explanations for these questions.

The second chapter examines Russian diplomacy in the transitional period. Ivan G. Tiouline presents an analysis of the Russian formulation of foreign policy, through the Foreign Ministry. He also studies the evolution of the Foreign Ministry, the characteristics of the diplomats and their difficulties at the present time. Special attention is paid to the period under Andrei Kozyrev as foreign minister, with a short evocation of his dismissal and replacement by Evgenii Primakov.

The third chapter looks at Mongolia's national security which puts Central Asia into a broader perspective. Elena V. Boikova focuses on the process of democratization in Mongolia, the first Asian country of the socialist world to initiate democratization. This chapter carefully studies the complicated Russia–Mongolian relations as well as the role of China and Japan in the future of Mongolia which is not a member of the CIS.

In the fourth and last chapter of Part I, Rainer Freitag-Wirminghaus undertakes the task of studying Turkmenistan's place in Central Asia and the world. Turkmenistan represents one of the world's richest countries in terms of natural gas. Its geographical position (between the Caspian Sea, Iran and Uzbekistan) provides it with both privileges and inconveniences. Furthermore, Turkmenistan did not adhere to the CIS' Collective Security System. Turkmenistan remained neutral. The security issues as well as the questions related to the transportation of Turkmen gas are discussed.

The external powers' position, policy and relations with the Central Asian republics constitute the second part of the book. For this purpose four countries (Iran, Turkey, Afghanistan and China) have been chosen. This choice is motivated by these countries' geographical and cultural closeness with Central Asia. While China, Afghanistan and Iran border directly on this region and are *nolens wolens* deeply implicated in its political and economic life, Turkey, by virtue of its cultural affinities with Central Asia, stands as one of the most influential powers in this region. Anoushiravan Ehteshami focuses his study (Chapter 5) on Iran and Central Asia. He demonstrates the deep impact of the sudden creation of new states on the northern Iranian borders and on Iranian policy with respect to issues such as security, economy and oil. Ehteshami, who is familiar with the study of Iranian diplomacy also pays attention to Iranian diplomatic trends and nuances, but also to the difficulties Tehran's regime is facing in this region. In the following chapter, Gareth M. Winrow continues on the same path; this time on Turkish policy in Central Asia. He begins his study with the clear statement that Turkey's first priority in foreign policy is to be admitted as a full member of the EU. Therefore, relations with Central Asia do not really constitute a foreign policy priority for many officials in Ankara. On the other hand, he emphasizes that no state is a monolithic entity. There exist in Turkey some notable pro-

Pan-Turkic forces (within the government also). He also explains the importance of economic and educational relations between Turkey and the Turkic states (including Azerbaijan). Chapter 7 deals with Afghanistan and Central Asia. Anthony Hyman explains the exceptional closeness between these two entities. Geography, history and culture are of course among the factors which play a major role in this closeness. However, one must not forget that members of all five major nationalities of the former Soviet Central Asia are represented in the Afghan population. The Afghan crisis had and still has a direct influence on both Tajikistan and Uzbekistan. Hyman also discusses the military dimension of the relations between Afghanistan and Central Asia. The last chapter of Part II concerns China's relations with Central Asia with particular reference to Kazakhstan. Michael S. Dillon draws our attention to the consequences that China's new economic reforms could have for the economic future of Central Asia. Besides the economic factor, the historical and human contacts between the population of the Chinese provinces (Xinjiang, Urumgi and Kashghar) on one side and the population of the western parts of Kazakhstan and Kyrgyzstan on the other could lead to political exploitation. Kazakhstan's nuclear capabilities represent another highly sensitive issue which is studied in Chapter 8.

In Part III, four chapters deal with economic issues. Chapter 9 starts with a theoretical discussion on two different concepts: regional cooperation and integration. It is also a comparative analysis of the CIS and EU and their differences and similarities. The different scenarios for the CIS' future have been submitted to reflection and assessment. After identification and a description of the CIS' three different dimensions and institutions, the discussion continues on regional cooperation networks. The Economic Cooperation Organization (ECO), the Caspian Sea Organization (CSO) and the Black Sea Economic Cooperation Zone (BSEC) have been studied. An important issue, the role of the EBRD in Central Asia, constitutes the topic of Chapter 10. Mahir Babaev who is himself the EBRD's counsellor shows his expertise on this matter and explains the role of the European Bank for Reconstruction and Development during the difficult period of transition. He arrives at the conclusion that the bank's priorities in this region is the development of the financial and banking sectors. Finally, Chapter 11 examines the role of oil and gas in the Caspian region. Questions related to the ownership, production and transportation of oil and gas, as well as the role of both regional and international actors in this vital question figure among the main issues of this chapter. Finally, in the last chapter, Saidakhrol M. Kasimov demonstrates the deep and broad impact of the disintegration of the Soviet Union on the economic structures and orientations of Uzbekistan, the most populous republic in Central Asia. Animated by a quite optimistic spirit, Kasimov – after retracing the path of Uzbekistan's economic situation before and after independence – analyses the Uzbeks' move from being a producer of a single raw material (cotton) to being an exporter of mainly finished products. Such a radical transformation, which needs time, patience and favourable conditions, will, in Kasimov's view, most likely be realized on an evolutionary path where economics should take precedence over politics and the state should play the role of the principal agent of reform. At the end of his chapter, Kasimov, who is an economist, sets up a series of proposals with regard to preserving and improving Uzbekistan's economy in a changing world.

This book contains updated versions of the most relevant papers that were presented at the conference on Central Asia in Transition held in August 1995 in Copenhagen and sponsored by the European Seminar on Central Asian Studies. Some other papers are also based on presentations made at the Pan-European International Relations Conference in Paris, September 1995. One of them was presented at the Central Asian Geopolitics Seminar in Chandigarh (India, December 1995).

As editor of this book, I would like to thank the members of the workshop on Central Asia's Place in the World for their wonderful cooperation and friendship. My special thanks go also to Jens-Christian Sørensen of the Nordic Institute of Asian Studies (Copenhagen) who deployed extraordinary efforts to make the Copenhagen conference a successful enterprise. Michael Vale kindly read some of the manuscripts and made precious improvements. I am also indebted to the Department of Political Science of the University of Aarhus for providing me with marvellous accommodation and support. I am of course grateful to T.M. Familoe, Macmillan Publishing Director, a gentleman, for his advice and his patience. Some maps, tables and figures reproduced in this book are borrowed from British Petroleum, *Financial Times*, *The Economist* and others. The sources are indicated and I thank them all. Finally, I would like to thank my son Hamed, whose moral and intellectual support has always been of enormous significance to me.

MEHDI MOZAFFARI
University of Aarhus

Part I
Security and Foreign Policy

1 The CIS' Southern Belt: a New Security System

M. Mozaffari

INTRODUCTION

Under the supervision of Russia, a new security system is progressively being established in Central Asia and Caucasus. The final form and modality of this new security system has not yet emerged; it is still in the 'moulding'. However, two things are clear: (1) the emerging security system differs quite markedly from its predecessor, under which the Central Asian and Caucasian republics were still an integral part of the USSR and (2) the process is a direct result of the unprecedented transformations that have occurred within the former Soviet Union. The Soviet–Russian empire had three different dimensions: (1) it was a superpower, second only to the USA, in political and military terms, (2) it had an external empire which roughly embraced the Warsaw Pact countries and (3) it was in possession of an internal empire, that is all the non-Russian parts of the Soviet Union which were – to different degrees – submitted to Russia's domination. In this chapter, I shall only deal with two parts of the internal empire: Central Asia and Caucasus. Central Asia and Caucasus are facing a huge range of complex problems including such things as nation state building as well as ethnic, economic, political and environmental issues. In the following, I shall focus only on their security concerns. I will try to answer the following questions. What impact did the Soviet Union's collapse have on the political evolution of the newly independent republics of Central Asia and Caucasus? This point is important, because the manner in which they became independent – and, consequently, full international actors – has undoubtedly influenced their security strategy choice. How did the Central Asian and Caucasian republics manage their security issues after independence? How did Russia react to the Central Asian and Caucasian security concerns? And, more specifically, why are the Central Asian and the newly independent Caucasian republics seeking Russian protection, despite the fact that for more than a century they have been dominated by Russia? Why is Russia willing to construct – together with these new states – a new security system, in spite of the fact that the southern regions of the late Soviet–Russian empire are considered a serious handicap to its own development and progress? Finally, what has motivated the former USSR republics (except the Baltic states and Chechnya) to build up a new security system despite the absence of any external tangible threat? The aim of this study is to provide appropriate explanations for these questions. The analysis will focus on the following issues: change, the security complex and the security system. I shall begin with the phenomenon of Change.

CHANGE IN CENTRAL ASIA AND CAUCASUS

The unprecedented political changes that have recently occurred in Central Asia and Caucasus do not just constitute a change in degree, but are in fact a change in substance. Thus, the first characteristic of this transformation is that the political entities in Central Asia and Caucasus have, for the first time in modern history, become full international actors. They have shifted from what Friedrich Meinecke called a 'Kulturnation' to a 'Staatsnation' (Meinecke, 1908). The second characteristic concerns the issue of security. These new republics were part of the security logic of a superpower, but now they have become normal powers and as an integral part of a superpower they belonged to the global system, but now they merely constitute a subsystem. Another aspect of this change is visible at the regional level. The Central Asian republics are becoming more sensitive to events in Turkey, Iran and Afghanistan and vice versa. This rising reciprocal sensitivity has been interpreted by some scholars as an 'extension of the Middle East'!

Origin of change

The origin of the transformation is well-known, that is the fall and following disintegration of the Soviet–Russian empire.[1] The fall of an empire is in itself a dramatic event, but the decline of the Soviet–Russian empire seems particularly dramatic, at least in the scope of modern times. In the twentieth century alone, six empires have perished: the Austro-Hungarian, the Czarist Russian, the Ottoman, the British, the French and, finally, the Soviet–Russian (the Japanese, the Ethiopian and the Iranian 'empires' are not included in this list). The different changes that followed the decline of the first five empires certainly had a tremendous impact on international relations as well as on the global international system. Nevertheless, despite their importance, these changes are really not comparable with those produced by the fall of the Soviet–Russian empire, particularly with regard to their impact on the global system. The changes resulting from the fall of the five first empires all took place at the actor level, that is they all resulted in changes inside the system. In other words, the number of top actors changed, as exemplified by the movement from multipolarity to bipolarity that ensued after the Second World War, but the global system essentially remained unchanged, that is it remained anarchical. However, with the fall of the Soviet–Russian empire, the system itself has changed for the first time in modern history. Or, at the very least, it has raised questions about the nature of the system. Waltz (1993) believes that 'despite changes that constantly take place in the relations of nations, the basic structure of international politics continues to be anarchical' (p. 59). Moreover, according to Waltz (1993), 'Bipolarity continues because militarily Russia can take care of itself and because no other great powers have yet emerged' (p. 52). Nevertheless, he admits that 'some of the implications of bipolarity ... have changed' (Waltz, 1993, p. 52). However, if the system is no longer fully anarchical, it may have become something else: polyarchic, multiarchic, plurilateral (Cerny, 1993, p. 31), hegemonic, apolaire[2] or, simply, a 'new middle age' (Minc, 1993). Alternatively, the system may still be in transition, that is, it may not yet have reached its 'final' form. However, whatever the future form of the system, there can be no doubt that the current system differs from that which existed before the autumn of 1991. Nor can there be any doubt that this important transformation is a direct result of the decline of the Soviet–Russian empire.

Process of change

An important element in the current context is that the Soviet–Russian empire disintegrated without any revolution at the centre or in the 'periphery'. Moreover, in relation to the extraordinary character of the event, the rebellions and revolts were also relatively insignificant, except perhaps in the Baltic countries. In fact, the decline of the Soviet–Russian empire came about as a consequence of a deep crisis at the centre and not in the periphery. As a consequence, the republics of Central Asia and Caucasus attained independence sheltered from the distress of revolution, rebellion and even crisis, not to mention the wars of liberation that many Third World countries have had to undergo. The republics merely had to accept the changes that were commanded from the top, that is from the central Communist Party in Moscow. Perhaps this explains the somewhat restrained enthusiasm that greeted these new measures.

The fact that things happened relatively peacefully is significant, not least because it has had real impacts on the future evolution of both the centre (the Russian Federation) and the new independent republics. In particular, the crisis in which these new nations have found themselves (whether in the form of ethnic, confessional or national struggles) affirms their relative immaturity. It is astonishing that these crises (internal and regional struggles) have erupted after independence and not before; obviously discontent, frustration and even 'national' vindication existed in certain sections of the former USSR, but this never resulted in a concrete movement against the dominance of the centre. In short, these countries have undergone a revolutionary change without experiencing a proper revolution.

The extraordinary continuity of the communist political structure is one of the consequences of this non-violent and perhaps undesired independence. The existing structure has obviously changed its name; it is no longer called 'communist', but in reality things have largely remained unaltered. Thus, although all the independent republics have adopted political pluralism, it is still the old political apparatus that holds the real power. It is therefore not surprising that certain ultranationalist leaders (Abulfazl) Elchibey in Azerbaijan and Zviad Gamsakhurdia in Georgia) have had to hand back their power to former communist leaders (Heidar Aliev in Azerbaijan and Eduard Shevardnadze in Georgia) after initially having been elected into office by a huge majority of the votes. Unlike Caucasus, the Central Asian ultranationalist groups did not emerge as powerful forces; however, the 'liberal', 'democratic' and Islamist groups were repressed or eliminated by force. This is particularly the case with Kazakhstan and Uzbekistan, where the liberal groups were repressed, as well as in Tajikistan, where the war between the democratic–Islamic coalition and ex-communist bloc resulted in the return to power of the ex-communists.

Another consequence is that Russia has been successful in recuperating its influence over the whole region, thereby reintegrating it into a Russian *zone d'influence* (or in Russian terminology 'zone of responsibility').[3] Consequently, this change has had a real impact on the form of the future security system. One of the results of this change was the birth of new subsystems and security complexes.

THE BIRTH OF NEW SUBSYSTEMS AND SECURITY COMPLEXES

The study of subsystems and security complexes is important because they constitute an interposed space between the global and national levels which is different from both of these; subsystems and security complexes have their own distinct dynamic, logic and life. In fact, one could call a security complex a regional system, because it is necessarily connected to some geographical proximity. A security complex is defined as 'a group of states whose primary security concerns link together sufficiently closely that their national securities cannot be considered apart from one another' (Buzan, 1991, p. 190). A certain number of explicit and implicit points follow from this definition.

1. Security complexes are a product of the anarchical character of the global system. In particular, in a hierarchic and purely hegemonic system there can only be one security system.
2. Security complexes are anarchical by nature, that is the presence of different autonomous actors (that is, different 'national securities') is imperative to the identification of security complexes.
3. 'The security complexes emphasize the interdependence of rivalry as well as that of shared interests' (Buzan, 1991, p. 190).
4. The concept of security does not just embrace military and political security concerns, but (in our time more than ever) also the economic and environmental dimensions of security, which are equally important.
5. Membership of a specific security complex does not preclude membership of another. Thus, Turkey is a member of both the European, Middle Eastern and the Caucasian security complexes.
6. The formation of a security complex requires some geographical proximity. Without the geographical proximity criterion, every national security would, in one way or another, be related to another national security, at least theoretically. This is obviously absurd.

Problem 1: do Central Asia and Caucasus constitute a security complex?

Undoubtedly the situation today in Central Asia and Caucasus differs from that which prevailed before the dissolution of the Soviet Union. Thus, under the previous state of affairs, these regions were an inherent and fully integrated part of a superpower and, as such, were protected by the Soviet security umbrella. This umbrella was not only tenacious enough to protect the regional republics from external threats, but also had a dissuasive impact on internal and interrepublic conflicts. The umbrella, however, disappeared with the fall of the Soviet Union and the existing network, the Commonwealth of Independent States (CIS), in which the republics are merely considered as the near abroad or, perhaps more accurately, as the new abroad in relation to the Russian frontiers, does not in itself constitute a framework capable of ensuring efficient protection. Security has thus, due to the anarchy which currently reigns, become pre-eminent. However, the republics' changed status, from superpower to subsystem, has meant that they, once independent, have had to undertake the responsibility for their security themselves.

Certain other factors lend credence to the proposition that Central Asia and Caucasus today each constitute a security complex. First of all, the Central Asian republics form a coherent region in geographical terms. Moreover, although each republic conducts its own specific national policy as determined by its own interests, their security policies are interconnected. Hence, Kazakhstan, being a nuclear power and having a large borderline with Russia, has different security and foreign policy stances from those of Tajikistan and Turkmenistan, who are neither nuclear powers and nor do they share any border with Russia. Nevertheless, Kazakhstan cannot afford to be and indeed is not (essentially for fear of a domino effect and ensuing regional instability) indifferent to events in Tajikistan or Uzbekistan and vice versa.

The same reasoning holds for Caucasus, only the interconnections and interdependence are even more pronounced and evident. Hence, any change in Armenian security automatically influences Azerbaijan and vice versa. The same considerations apply in the relationship between Georgia and the territories of Northern Caucasus (Chechnya,[4] Ossetia, Ingush, Daghestan and others). For example, an eventual creation of a 'Northern Caucasian Confederation' would undoubtedly have serious repercussions on Georgia's territorial (Abkhaz and Southern Osset) and political integrity. On the other hand, an eventual effective restoration of Georgian sovereignty over Abkhazia would reduce the likelihood of a political unification of Northern Caucasus and, by implication, reduce the likelihood of the further disintegration of the Russian Federation.

To conclude, the dissolution of the Soviet–Russian empire has resulted in the emergence of new security complexes.

Problem 2: are there one or two security complexes in Central Asia and Caucasus?

Central Asia and Caucasus differ geographically and to some extent also culturally. Thus, while Caucasus has access to open sea through the Black Sea, Central Asia only has access to the completely landlocked Caspian Sea. Moreover, Central Asia is more oriented towards Asia (China, Afghanistan, Russia, Mongolia and Iran), whereas Caucasus is orientated towards the Balkans and (through Turkey) Europe. Finally, the Caspian Sea constitutes a natural barrier between Central Asia and Caucasus.

Islam dominates in Central Asia and Christianity in Caucasus. Thus, two of the three independent countries of Caucasus (Armenia and Georgia) are Christian and virtually all of Central Asia is Muslim (Khazakstan's large Russian population being the main exception). Moreover, ethnically the Turks dominate Central Asia (the exception being Tajikistan which is of

Iranian ethnicity), whereas the only Turkish area in Caucasus is Azerbaijan and the Nakhichevan enclave. From a cultural point of view, Central Asia thus appears more homogeneous than Caucasus. The question, however, is whether the regions also differ from the point of view of security.

One may argue that, in reality, no tangible security connections exist between Central Asia and Caucasus. Each possesses its own dynamics, preoccupations and opportunities. Thus, what goes on in Tajikistan or Uzbekistan does not really matter to the security of Georgia, Armenia and Azerbaijan. And, vice versa, the Armenian–Azeri conflict over Nagorno–Karabak does not concern the security of the Kazakhs, nor the Kyrgyzs.

Central Asia and Caucasus also have a lot in common. Thus, until quite recently, as integrated members of the Soviet Union, they shared the same destiny and, although their 'new' destinies are not necessarily identical, they are nevertheless still tied together. Their security ties are not linked together directly but curiously enough go through 'extra' regional powers, of which Russia is the most important. The Russian Federation still dominates the area and will probably continue to do so for a long time. Furthermore, all the Central Asian and Caucasian republics are members of the CIS and, as we shall see later on, most of them have signed bilateral security treaties with Russia. The regions are thus interconnected through Russia. Despite the pre-eminent importance of Russia, three or four other 'extra'-regional powers (China, Iran, Turkey and Afghanistan) also influence and have an impact on the security issues of the region. We shall return to this issue later on.

As far as the issue of a security complex is concerned, the situation in Central Asia and Caucasus resembles that of the Persian Gulf and the rest of the Middle East. The Middle East, which represents a subsystem, is essentially divided into two different but interconnected security complexes: (1) the Persian Gulf region and (2) the rest of the Middle East. The former essentially obeys the imperatives of the oil and gas 'order', while the latter is deeply burdened and influenced by the Arab–Israeli conflict. However, at the same time, these issues are closely connected with one another. The difference between the two Middle Eastern security complexes and the Central Asian and Caucasian security complexes arises from the way they are connected: in the Middle East the connection is direct and internal, whereas between Central Asia and Caucasus the connection is indirect and external.

In short, Central Asia and Caucasus constitute two separate but 'extra'-connected security complexes. The connection is not assumed by the national actors of the regions but by 'external' regional powers, namely Russia, Iran, Turkey and, to some extent, Afghanistan.

THE ESSENTIAL STRUCTURE OF CENTRAL ASIA AND CAUCASUS

The diffusive character of the security issue at the global level obstructs the global system from constituting a single security complex. Security complexes are thus proper to subsystems. Each subsystem has its own security complex, because the ordering principle (in Waltz's (1979) jargon) of each security complex is unique. Waltz's (1979, p. 81) ordering principle is the same as Buzan's (1991, p. 21) essential structure. The essential structure of every subsystem has the four following components.

The linkage between a subsystem and global system

Not all subsystems and regions are viewed alike by the global system. Some are considered more important than others. Thus, the Persian Gulf region is more important to the global system because of its huge oil and gas reserves than is the Balkan region. Consequently, the global system is more sensitive towards the former than the latter. In principle, there is a direct relation between the degree of anarchy of a specific region (security complex) and its vulnerability towards the outside world; the more immature a region, the more it risks being exposed to external intervention and the like.

With regard to Central Asia and Caucasus, the question is how sensitive the global system is towards these subsystems? To answer this question, we must, *a priori*, have a proper definition of the global system. As mentioned above, scholars of international politics have not yet reached a consensus on the issue of the nature of the existing global system (anarchical, fully anarchical, less anarchical, hegemonic, pluralistic and so on). However, if the global system is taken to be adequately defined by US hegemony, then one may conclude that the linkage is still weak; the USA has other priorities than Central Asia and Caucasus, for example the Persian Gulf, Japan and Europe. The weakness of the linkage is, to a large extent, explained by changes on the general policy agenda or map of preferences of the USA. With the deterioration of the Soviet nuclear threat, security no longer occupies the most prominent place on the American agenda. Other issues, such as the economy, unemployment and the environment, now figure high on the agenda. This explains the USA's relatively high sensitivity towards the Persian Gulf region as compared to Central Asia and Caucasus.

However, as noted above, this analysis is only valid when the global system and US hegemony are considered identical. In reality, the global system is broader than US hegemony and, therefore, other actors should be included in our definition of the global system. One could argue that the global system is designed by the Big Five (USA, Russia, China, France and the UK, the permanent members of the UN Security Council). The new role attributed to the UN (in, for example, Kampuchea, Somalia, Iraq and Yugoslavia) lends credence to this argument. Yet, despite the gravity of the situation in Central Asia and Caucasus, these regions have not attracted the attention of the Big Five (apart from the shipment of a small number of UN observers to Georgia). For the time being, neither the USA nor the EU are very interested in the area. Gennadii Burbulis (co-author of the official report on Russian foreign policy) puts it like this: 'There is a logic that will bring [the former Soviet republics] back again our way. Europe will not take them as they are.'[5] And even if Western powers

> choose to organise chaos, [they] won't be able to do it. The resources of the West are limited in every sense, and it is not in position to canalise them into continental Eurasia. The projection of military power is practically impossible in this case: The West went to war in the Gulf, relying on a ramified system of alliances in the region; it has none in mainland Eurasia (Pleshakov, 1993, p. 22).

While the linkage to the USA (taken as a hegemon) is weak, the linkage with the Russian Federation is particularly strong and, to some extent also, those with the neighbouring states of China, Turkey, Iran and Afghanistan. The sensitivity of Russia may be explained by the fact that millions of Russians live in the area (see Table 1.1).

The situation in Kazakhstan is particularly sensitive because almost half of the population is Russian (Kazakhstan's ethnic composition is 41 per cent Kazakh, 37.8 per cent Russian, 5.8 per cent Germans, 5.4 per cent Ukrainian and 10 per cent others).[6] Kazakhstan is, *de facto*, considered semi-Russian, because any threats to it, whether societal or external, directly jeopardize the security of Russians. Other countries also feel exposed to the region: Turkey, which is composed of Turks and Kurds, fears a serious Kurdish separatist movement, Iran, which is a mosaic of different ethnicities and tribes, fears a possible Azeri and Turkmen expansion and Afghanistan, with its 3 million Afghani Tajiks, fears the installation of a hostile regime in Tajikistan.

In this section we have seen that the sensitivity of the global system (whether US hegemony or world pluralism) towards Central Asia and Caucasus is remarkably low at the moment. Consequently, the plausibility of a US or EU military intervention in the area would also seem to be low, for which reason the region is presumably more likely to follow the regional dynamics (Russia in particular) than those of the global system.

TABLE 1.1 *Indigenous and non-indigenous people in the population of Central Asia**

Republics	*Total population*	*Indigenous population⁺*	*Non-indigenous population*	*Non-indigenous population (%)*	*Main non-indigenous peoples and their number: People*	*Thousand*
Kazakhstan	16 464	6 893	9 751	58.1	Russians	6 228
					Germans	958
					Ukrainians	896
Uzbekistan	19 810	16 593	3 217	16.2	Russians	1 653
					Tatars	468
					Crimean Tatars	189
Kyrgyzstan	4 258	2 851	1 407	33.0	Russians	917
					Ukrainians	108
					Germans	101
Tajikistan	5 093	4 465	628	12.3	Russians	388
					Tatars	72
					Ukrainians	41
Turkmenistan	3 523	2 942	581	16.5	Russians	334
					Tatars	39
					Ukrainians	36
Central Asia *in toto*	49 148	33 744	15 404	31.3	Russians	9 520
					Ukrainians	1 234
					Germans	1 135

* Composed from the national composition of the USSR population according to the All-Union Census of 1989 (Moscow, 1991).
⁺ Kazakhs, Uzbeks, Kara-Kalpaks, Kyrgyz, Tajiks and Turkmens.
SOURCE *Central Asia Today*, no. 1 (1994).

The anarchical quality

All regions are not necessarily equally penetrable and vulnerable, that is there is no direct causality between the importance of a region and its degree of vulnerability. For example, during the Cold War, Western Europe, as a region and a subsystem, was very important to the global system, but it was neither very penetrable nor very vulnerable. In particular, penetrability and vulnerability depend on the degree of anarchical maturity or immaturity. In an earlier study of structural changes in the Persian Gulf I proposed four kinds of anarchy: immature, semi-immature, semi-mature and mature (Mozaffari, 1994). These different types of anarchy form a scale or a continuum of sorts. Immature anarchy refers to a situation in which everybody is against everybody (chaos). Semi-immature anarchy occurs when relations between states are rather strained, but a slight possibility of establishing amicable bonds remains. Semi-mature anarchy applies to a situation in which the regional actors concerned cooperate in order to resolve their disputes peacefully and thereby avoid war (a security regime). Finally, mature anarchy pertains to a situation in which states have reached a level of understanding such that they have not only agreed to resolve differences peacefully, but have also managed to extinguish all fears as regards their military and political relations (security community).[7] The semi-immature anarchy that prevailed ineluctably played an important role in the regional complications and conflicts (in Caucasus, the Nagorno-Karabak conflict between Armenia and Azerbaijan, as well as the Georgia-Abkhazia conflict and in Central Asia, the turbulence in Tajikistan). Today, however, both Central Asia and Caucasus have moved towards semi-maturity by pursuing peaceful solutions. An important step in this direction was the joining of all the republics of Central Asia and Caucasus in the CIS (Ashkhabad Summit, December 1993) as full members. Under this union, military and economic force between members is prohibited.

On the distribution of power

Waltz (1979, p. 98, 1986, p. 93) believes that under anarchy the distribution of power among actors is an attribute of the system. In other words, the global system determines the power relations of subsystems. As mentioned above, the global system, whatever its ordering principle, has a number of preferences and demands as regards subsystems. These demands and preferences differ from subsystem to subsystem and are indicators of the sensitivity of the global system. In our context, the fact that the global system's sensitivity towards Central Asia and Caucasus has been demonstrated to be low implies that the global system is almost indifferent to the distribution of power in these regions (with the exception of Kazakhstan's military nuclear capabilities). In a sense, the distribution of power is delegated from the global system to the regional system. In other words, the region becomes more dynamic and more dependent on the regional game. The Russian Federation, which is capable of intervening directly or indirectly, militarily or politically according to its interests and preferences, is still the main actor in these regions. In some instances, Russia supports one state against another (Armenia versus Azerbaijan), whereas in other instances it supports one leader against another (Eduard Shevardnadze versus Zviad Gamsakhurdia). It also uses its influence and military capabilities to 'punish' dissidence, as illustrated by its indirect but nevertheless effective support for the Abkhazia rebels in their struggle against Georgia. (A 'punishment' motivated by Georgia's initial refusal to adhere to the CIS.) Russia also supports certain political groups and parties against other political formations, as for instance in Tajikistan. Thus, Russia is manipulating the power relations both within and between states. Turkey, Iran and the Arab countries of the Persian Gulf also influence power relations and capabilities in the region. However, rather than being exerted through direct military intervention, it comes in the form of economic, financial and cultural support to certain carefully selected states and groups, as for instance Turkey's support of Azerbaijan against Armenia or Iran's discreet support of the 'Islamists' in Tajikistan against the 'Pro-Russians'.

Patterns of amity and enmity

The patterns of amity and enmity can generally be divided into two categories: conjunctural and structural. Conjunctural amity and enmity do not constitute patterns, since the situation may change at any time, according to the political evolution. Two states may be friendly today and enemies tomorrow and vice versa, depending on their interests and perceived threats. Central Asia and Caucasus differ in terms of structural amity and enmity. In Central Asia, structural enmity does not really exist. The existing disputes over minorities, territory and water resources (as between Uzbekistan, Kyrgyzstan and Tajikistan) are, after all, 'normal' political disputes. On the other hand, in Caucasus structural enmity exists between Armenia and Azerbaijan. Although ethnic and confessional complications are present, the main object of their enmity is territorial (Nagorno–Karabak). Nevertheless, it is the ethnic and confessional complications that have created the patterns of enmity in Armenian–Azeri relations. The same relations exist between Georgia and Abkhazia and Georgia and Southern Osset (Abkhazia and Southern Osset were formerly part of Georgian territory).

OPTIONS AND THE MANAGEMENT OF SECURITY

As the internal empire has become the near abroad, so has the imperial order been replaced by the anarchical order. Faced with the self-help principle, these new international actors, just as all other international actors, have had to choose the best possible option. States searching for security have *grosso modo* two options available: to be neutral or to build (or adhere to) an alliance with other states. Neutrality and alliance can each take a variety of forms. Thus, neutrality can be formal, recognized or informal and non-aligned. Alliance can be formal, informal or bandwagoning.

The question is what options were available to the Central Asian and Caucasian republics? Could they realistically be neutral? I shall argue that neutrality was not the best possible option for them. The essence of neutrality is undertaking the task of assuring security alone. Assuring security means being militarily able to defend the state's territorial integrity, the safety of its population and the survival of the state's political bodies (all together can be labelled as security basis needs). Such a strategy will result in a security dilemma in that others cannot distinguish between the defensive and offensive intentions of actors and the effectiveness of the offence versus the defence. Consequently, an escalating arms race may result. None of the Central Asian and Caucasian states have chosen to be neutral. Why? Simply because such a strategy did not – in their perception – constitute the best possible option. Suppose Uzbekistan had chosen to assure its own defence alone. In this case, every single Uzbek gesture to improve its military power (men and equipment) – even if the Uzbek intentions with such an improvement were only of a purely defensive nature – would immediately be interpreted by its neighbours, including Russia and Iran, as an offensive measure. If all the states of the region were to follow the Uzbeks, a prisoner's dilemma situation would arise resulting in an arms race coupled with mutual suspicion. Another reason for rejecting neutrality was obviously related to the fear of abandonment. The risk of abandonment was actually rather significant, especially during the uncertain period immediately after independence (multiethnic, latent regional conflicts over water, borders and so on). To conclude, the risk of a security dilemma coupled with the risk of abandonment was enough to dissuade the Central Asian and Caucasian republics from adopting neutrality.

Having rejected the different forms of neutrality, the newly independent states chose alliance as their security strategy. Alliance is defined as the 'formal or informal relationship of security cooperation between two or more sovereign states' (Walt, 1990, p. 1, note 1). The states formed an alliance (primary phase) or joined in the alliance (secondary phase) either to balance power or balance threat. The balancing of power occurs when 'the states join alliances to protect themselves from states or coalitions whose superior resources could pose a threat' (Walt, 1990, p. 18). The balancing of threat occurs 'when the most threatening state or coalition is significantly more dangerous than the second most threatening state or coalition' (Walt, 1990, p. 265) (see Figure 1.1).

The question is which of these two models was chosen. In reality, these models are not fully appropriate to explain the alliance formation of the CIS. In both models, an alliance formation is motivated by external threats. However, as argued above, no tangible nor even latent external threat existed. Nobody outside of the CIS intended to threaten the ex-Soviet republics. The threats, if there were any, were internal (= societal) and/or regional (among the Central Asian and Caucasian states themselves) and/or deriving from the Russian Federation. If one considers the Russian Federation as the source of danger, all non-Slavic requests for alliance with Russia look like bandwagoning, which precisely refers to an alignment with the source of danger. Walt (1990, pp. 28–32), in his attempt to understand when states bandwagon, concluded that the plausibility for bandwagoning will be high if the state is weak, if there are no available allies and if there is a war. The two first conditions were in place in Central Asia and Caucasus. They were both economically and militarily weak and there was no other available allies than Russia. Compared with the Eastern European countries (the Soviet Union's external empire), the states in Central Asia and Caucasus were rather more restricted to the opportunities available to them. 'The latter can use the available existing structures – the OSCE, NATO and WEU'. Therefore 'the Eastern European states are keen to pursue security policies by looking away from Moscow, avoiding alignment with any successor of the former Soviet Union or a Russian focused union' (Traistaru, 1993, p. 301). The situation was diametrically opposite in Central Asia and Caucasus, where there was no qualified available ally, apart from Russia.[8] By bandwagoning they hoped to moderate any possible aggressive intentions on the part of Russia. Because they bandwagoned in peace time, they would certainly also do so in war time.

Balance of Power Theory

cause

Imbalance of power ——————> alliances against the strongest state

Balance of Threat Theory

cause

Imbalance of threat ——————> alliance against the most threatening state

Source: S.M. Walt, *The Origins of Alliances* (Ithaca: Cornell University Press, 1990) p. 265

Figure 1.1 The Balance of Power and the Balance of Threat

Alliance is essentially a security regime. A security regime is defined as 'those principles, rules, and norms that permit nations [states] to be restrained in their behaviour in the belief that others will reciprocate' (Jervis, 1984, p. 173). Jervis (1984, pp. 176–8) spelt out four conditions necessary to forming a security regime.

1. The great powers must want to establish it.
2. The actors must also believe that others share the value they place on mutual security and cooperation.

3. One or more actors must not believe that security is best provided for by expansion.
4. War and the individualistic pursuit of security must be seen as costly.

The first condition corresponds to what Keohane (1984) labelled the theory of hegemonic stability, that is 'the view that concentration of power in one dominant state facilitates the development of strong regimes, and that fragmentation of power is associated with regime collapse' (p. 142). This theory which is a logical consequence of Keohane's (1984) constraint-choice analysis explains the emergence of the CIS and the dominant role of Russia. Conditions 2–4 have been tested several times since the beginning of the end of the Soviet Union and later since the creation of the CIS. The Azerbaijan–Armenian war over Nagorno–Karabak, and Azerbaijan and Georgia's attempt to pursue security individually (hence their delayed adherence to the CIS) has demonstrated the unproductivity of war and the advantages of cooperation.

How should the CIS security regime be classified? Following Young's (1984, pp. 98–100) typology, there are three kinds of international regimes: spontaneous, negotiated and imposed regimes. The CIS is definitively neither spontaneous nor imposed. It is not spontaneous, because it is a conscious coordination between participants. It is not an imposed order – as the Warsaw Pact was – because it involves the explicit consent of the participants. The CIS appears to be a negotiated order, because it is the expression of explicit consent on thc part of individual participants. This is, however, a truth with modifications, because we have to remember that the 'explicit consent' of the Asiatic members of the CIS in reality is the result of a significant degree of constraint. Thus, the CIS is an arrangement in between a negotiated and an imposed regime – not in the sense of Young's (1984) definition, but in Keohane's (1984) sense, that is 'a regime agreed upon within constraints that are mandated by powerful actors' (Keohane, 1984, p. 146).

THE EMERGENCE OF A NEW SECURITY SYSTEM

A security system is an institutionalized cooperation network between a group of states for the purpose of reducing the threats against its members to a minimum and providing the maximum possible freedom of choice for them.

Security complexes and security systems are two closely related, but not necessarily identical concepts. They are closely related because security is the central issue in both. In general (although not always), there is a security complex where there is a security system. Thus, 'Western' Europe forms a security complex and, at the same time, most countries in this area are also members of the NATO security system. There are, however, exceptions to the rule. For example, Turkey and Canada are both full members of the NATO security system, but do not belong to the same security complex (in geographical terms). Security complexes arise naturally, without negotiation (they are a matter of destiny), while security systems are artificial and, hence, negotiated, that is, the former is often determined by geography, whereas the latter is a matter of choice based on calculated decisions. Moreover, there is no causal relation between the existence (or non-existence) of a security complex and the establishment (or non-establishment) of a security system. For example, the 'security system' of the Persian Gulf, the Gulf Cooperation Council (GCC), is parochial and virtually insignificant; it does not constitute a general security system. Similarly, there is no security system for the North African security complex. Generally, security systems are created or at least initiated by super- and/or great powers. A great number of examples lend credence to this hypothesis: NATO, WARSAW, CENTO, SEATO and so on.

Security systems are motivated by the presence of a common threat. Security interdependence (= security complex) between states tends to accelerate the construction of a security system. However, as discussed above, there is no automatic relationship between security interdependence and security systems which are not global (not even NATO is global) and the evolution from security interdependence to security system depends on the configuration of the security complex. Security systems may also be forced upon groups of states by a superpower or a great power, as was the case with CENTO (Central Organization). Neither Turkey (as a full member of NATO and thus under US protection) nor Pakistan (with no common border with the Soviet Union) needed to join a regional security system such as CENTO. The 'logic' of the Cold War, however, compelled them to respond positively to US wishes. In exchange for joining, they could expect substantial (economic, military and political) rewards from the US. In general, the effectiveness (= dissuasive capacity) of a security system depends on whether a superpower, or a great power participates or not. 'Autonomous' security systems are virtually ineffective (for example, the GCC).

Are Central Asia and Caucasus covered by a comprehensive, institutionalized security system? Central Asia and Caucasus are members of the CIS, which embraces all of the former Soviet Union (apart from the Baltic countries). However, the CIS, *per se*, could not guarantee the security of its members. However, the Treaty on Collective Security, agreed on in Tashkent in May 1992, can and does. The security system took some time to realize.

The following three main phases towards the formation of the security system are worth noting.

1. The chaotic and slavic phase. In the initial phase, immediately after the break-up of the Soviet system, there was no security system at all. Moscow lacked a well-defined policy and chaos ruled. It was during this quite short phase (from the coup in Moscow in August 1991 to the signing of the pact of the Community of Independent States in December) that the Soviet republics proclaimed their independence.
2. The formative and Eurasian phase. This phase embraces the period from December 1991 (the formation of the CIS) to the winter of 1992, when the Tajik crisis,[9] in which Russia, Kazakhstan and Uzbekistan took part, began. All the Central Asian and Caucasian republics, apart from Azerbaijan and Georgia, became members of the CIS in this phase.
3. The affirmative and extensive phase: This is the most recent phase. Russia has gradually reaffirmed its military and economic dominance. This is illustrated by Azerbaijan and Georgia's recent adherence to the CIS and by the re-establishment of the rouble zone (Ashkhabad Summit, September 1993).

The assessment of threats

The assessment of threats is a necessary step in the process of achieving an adequate security strategy. However, before taking this step we must have a definition of security.

Security is an elastic concept covering an immense spectrum beginning with the foetus and ending somewhere in space. Thus, one could arguably consider foetal security as the departure point, while another could choose the integrative environment. Between these two extremes, a range of different securities exists including individual, familial, societal, national, regional and global security. Whatever the level of analysis, security means, roughly speaking, the absence of threats. Security can also be defined as the freedom to choose. Obviously, in the real world, complete freedom of choice and a permanent absence of threats is not possible. In the real world, there is security when there are no threats to vital interests. However, vital interests are a relative and changing concept that depend on perception. What is vital to one may not be vital to another. For instance, for some religion is considered vital, while for others the political regime (democracy) and yet others national cohesion is considered vital. Today, the economy and the environment are becoming an inherent part of security. In sum, security is both an extensive (more than purely military) and a relative (actor's perception) concept.

Consequently, everything that disturbs freedom of choice is considered a threat. Threats are different both in degree and in orientation. Every disturbance in the freedom of choice is not necessarily considered a threat. Only severe disturbance is a threat. An assessment of the degree of severity depends on the disturbed's perception. The threat can be external, internal or both. In general, strong states are more sensitive to external threats, while weak states are more vulnerable to internal threats.[10]

Threats may be military or non-military and may originate from one or several actors. The (internal or external) structure may, in itself, constitute a threat against one or more states (Petersen, 1990, p. 27). Thus, the Cold War was a structural threat to practically all states and the vacuum or the weak structure the end of the Cold War brought to certain regions (for example, Caucasus) is a structural threat to stability.

Now, is there any severe threat to the security of the newly independent republics of Central Asia and Caucasus which could justify the Treaty on Collective Security System in Tashkent (15 May 1992)? Obviously, there must have been at least a perception of it, otherwise the treaty would not exist. The question is what type of threat could motivate a commitment to the CIS and, consequently, to the Tashkent Treaty? In the following, I shall review the different, possible threats.

Military threats

Such threats could potentially come from NATO, China, Iran, Turkey and Afghanistan. The NATO threat ceased after the collapse of the Soviet–Russian empire. NATO and the individual constituent members have kept a low profile and have systematically retained themselves from any action that could be interpreted as an intervention. In any case, as argued by Pleshakov (1993) above, the West does not have the military capabilities to intervene in the southern parts of the ex-Soviet Union. Moreover,

> the West economic impact is minimal: its involvement in the economies of all the post-Soviet countries will remain at a miserable level for a long time yet. And its political influence? To exercise it, you have to be not just a strong and mighty power up hill and down dale, but to be deeply involved in the affairs of respective countries and to have a human infrastructure here, if I may put it this way (Pleshakov, 1993, p. 22).

China, with borders to Kazakhstan (1700 km), Kyrgyzstan and Tajikistan could play a crucial role in Central Asia. China could create serious problems for Russia if it wanted to challenge the whole construction of the CIS. However, viewed in the current international context and given the internal problems of China particularly in the Muslim-dominated Xinjiang province,[11] such a scenario appears unlikely. Even in the pandemonium of an eventual disintegration of China, resulting in the independence of the Xinjiang province, neither Russia's nor Central Asia's security would be jeopardized. The only hypothetical danger (and here only to Russia) would be a realization of the clash of civilizations (Huntington, 1993).[12] This hypothesis depends on the occurrence of, first, a definitive movement of the Slavic–Orthodox civilization (Russia, Ukraine and Belarus) towards the West and, second, the constitution of a coalition between the Confucian and Islamic civilizations. In this situation, China would extend its influence over the Central Asian republics in order to form (perhaps with the support of certain other Muslim countries) a bloc against the Western Slavic civilization (the pawn scenario). At present, however, relations between China, Russia and Central Asia are improving (the pivot scenario).

Iran, by virtue of its geographical position (it has borders with Armenia, Nakhichevan, Azerbaijan and Turkmenistan), provides a bridge between Central Asia and Caucasus, not to say 'between Central Asia and the rest of the world', as the Iranian Foreign Minister Ali Akbar Velayati noted.[13] It is also an unavoidable (geographical) link between the Arab countries in the Persian Gulf and the Central Asian and Caucasian republics. Moreover, it has strong cultural and linguistic affinities with Tajikistan. In the current context, Iran's geopolitical position can be compared to that of Russia. They are both animated by the same historical and political ambitions for these regions, part of which, incidentally, was Persian territory until the mid-1800s.[14] However, Iran's ambitions are seriously constrained by its rather limited military and economic capabilities. The only 'weapon' it disposes over is political Islamic extremism. Iran has, however (despite its Islamic rhetoric), followed a pragmatic approach in order not to perturb its relations with the regimes of the region. Islamic fundamentalism in Central Asia tends to be of the 'Wahhabi' or 'Afghan' variety, related to Saudi Arabia or Afghanistan and sometimes both.[15] This does not mean that Iran is uninterested in closer political relations with its northern neighbours. They are working on it. President Rafsanjani's visit (November 1993) to Central Asia demonstrates Iran's double game. Rafsanjani presented a political draft to his Central Asian colleagues. None of them signed it … Neither President Kerimov of Uzbekistan, nor President Nazarbayev of Kazakhstan (nor any of the three other Central Asian leaders, Kyrgyzstan's Aqaev, Turkmenistan's Niyazov and Tajikistan's Abduljanov) sympathize with Islamic fundamentalism. However, this has not prevented close economic cooperation and sound neighbourly relations with Islamic Iran. Thus, Iran does not appear to represent a threat to Central Asia. In fact, Iran has been very concerned, not to say apprehensive, about some of the events that have taken place across its northern frontiers.[16]

Turkey neither has the opportunity nor any interest in intervening or threatening the security of Central Asia. Turkey's geopolitical position is quite different from that of Russia and Iran. Turkey has no frontier with any of the Central Asian republics and, with respect to Caucasus, it only has borders with Armenia, Georgia and the enclave of Nakhichevan, but not with Azerbaijan (mainland). Not having a border with Azerbaijan is a major handicap, particularly as it has been chosen by Turkey as the first base for its economic, political and cultural expansion into Central Asia. Turkey is, culturally speaking, the dominant actor in the region. As noted above, all the Central Asian republics, with the exception of Tajikistan, as well as Azerbaijan (and Nakhichevan) in Caucasus, are of Turkish culture and language. This soft power provides Turkey a significant influence. However, cultural ties between Turkey and Central Asia are not the only explanation for their particular relationship. These cultural ties have been used by Turkey for its own economic expansion into Central Asia.[17] Turkey, however, seems to play a minor role in Central Asia in terms of security, essentially because it is severely constrained by both geography and economics, but also because it is primarily oriented towards the EU. The only place Turkey could intervene is Caucasus. This could happen in an attempt to defend Azerbaijan or to contain Georgia from disintegration. However, despite oral support and official protests in favour of Baku, the Turkish Government has not undertaken any military actions against Armenia. Ankara is, presumably, apprehensive of the negative impact a possible military intervention would have on the West (in particular the European Union which is mostly pro-Armenian). Moreover, the outlook of a possible Russian intervention is daunting. Thus, Turkey does not appear to pose any threat to the new security system either.

Afghanistan could potentially play an important, though limited, role in the security of Central Asia. The situation on the Tajik–Afghan border testifies to the critical role of Afghanistan. However, Afghanistan, with its limited capabilities, will not intervene in Central Asia unless Tajikistan's internal troubles oblige it to do so. Cooperation between the Islamic fundamentalists of Tajikistan and one or more of the fundamentalist Afghan groups is also a possibility.

In sum, the new security system would not seem to be motivated by threats from regional actors or NATO. However, what about structural military threats?

A structural military threat

A structural military threat against the security of Central Asia would imply total regional disintegration. However, this is not the case. In fact, the general tendency is towards integration, not disintegration. This is illustrated by the emergence of the Economic Cooperation Organization (ECO), the Black Sea Economic Community and the Caspian Sea Organization. Thus, there does not seem to be any structural military threat.

A non-military actor threat

A non-military actor threat could derive from Islamic fundamentalist groups, 'new' religious movements or human rights activists. There is, however, no indication that these groups should have undertaken actions that could threaten the security of Central Asia and Caucasus; certainly not threats that could motivate the creation of a new security system.

A non-military structural threat

It also seems illusory to believe that a non-military structural threat (ecology, lack of resources ...) could have incited the Central Asian and Caucasian republics to enter the new Russian-led security network.

What motives lie behind the establishment of the security system? As stated above, a security system emerges when a group of states perceive a common threat. The question therefore is what, if any, common threat could motivate the engineering of the new security system? We shall first discuss external threats against Russia, Central Asia and Caucasus.

Security motivations

The review of the different, possible threats demonstrated that security motivations could not adequately explain the Central Asian and Caucasus states' commitment to a collective security system. That being the case, what could be the real motives that led to this commitment? In my analysis a combination of five different motives represent the region's needs in terms of security.

Fear of uncertainty

Central Asia and Caucasus have been under Russian control (Czarist and communist) for over a century. For Central Asia, independence is an almost totally new experience. In fact, Central Asia has not been independent since the ancient dynasties of Sâmânid (874–999) and Timurid (1405–1507). The situation is somewhat (but not fundamentally) different for Caucasus. Both Armenia and Georgia have been independent, but that was a very long time ago. Azerbaijan has also known independence, but it was precarious and short-lived (1918–1920). Thus, in reality, none of these countries were prepared for their new destiny. Unlike the Baltic States which sought the independence that was so deeply rooted in their history, Central Asia and Caucasus did not really desire independence. They felt orphaned and the immediate reaction of most of the republics was to rejoin Russia. There was some resistance to such reintegration within Georgia and Azerbaijan. However, it was short-lived. Both were 'persuaded' to rejoin. One can justifiably ask what happened to the centrifugal force that usually appears when newly independent countries gain freedom? The answer is quite simple. First of all, the Soviet system was not colonial. Under the framework established by the Communist Party, the Soviet republics benefited from a significant degree of autonomy in internal affairs. Although almost 25 million Russians were implanted across the republics, they were all expected to act as *Homo sovieticus*. Of course, this does not mean that there were no tensions in the relations between the Russian population and officials, on the one hand and the local population and officials, on the other. However, this does not necessarily imply colonialism. Second, no other realistic option seemed to open up to the newly independent republics. No other country in the region had adequate capacities to assume the role of Russia. Moreover, one does business with someone one knows rather than with a complete stranger.

Fear of internal turbulence

Threats to the security of a society do not always come from the outside.

The organization of Central Asia and Caucasia around a state is quite a new phenomenon, for which reason they are facing huge difficulties related to the construction of their nation state. The bulk of these difficulties originates from societal threats, particularly those connected with ethnic, cultural and religious matters, rather than from outside. Political instability and chaos is another preoccupying possibility. We must not forget that during the process towards independence, as well as immediately afterwards, almost all the Central Asian and Caucasian republics were politically unstable. Thus, in Azerbaijan there was a feud for power between pro-Russians (under the leadership of President Ayaz Mutalibov) and anti-Russians (led by Abulfazl Elchibey of the Azerbaijan Popular Front, AzPF).[18] In Georgia, events turned dramatic in the autumn of 1991 and resulted in President Zviad Gamsakhurdia's fall from power on 5 January 1992 (he had been elected to office on 26 May 1991). Calm was not restored with Eduard Shevardnadze in power (he was elected to the office on 11 October 1992). Abkhazia has, *de facto*, separated itself from Georgia. In Tajikistan, a regular civil war broke out between the old communists, backed by Russia and the coalition of democrats and Islamists. It was the Tajik civil war that finally led to CIS military intervention and the creation of the Tashkent Collective Security Treaty. The Uzbek regime, under the leadership of President Kerimov (elected to office in December 1991), has had to fall back on repression to neutralize the considerable political weight of the Birlik[19] group. This is in the spirit of President Niyazov who eliminated the democratic group of Agzybirlik.

Fear of regional conflicts

Territorial demarcations have often been decided by third parties, often colonial or quasi-colonial powers. Therefore, disputes between newly independent states over territorial borders are not unusual. And Central Asia and Caucasus are no exception. Under Soviet rule, these conflicts were frozen, but not resolved. However, with the decline of the Soviet–Russian empire and the ensuing anarchy, these conflicts floated back to the surface. Thus, Tajikistan has substantial territorial claims on Samarkand and Bukhara, which are currently part of Uzbekistan, there are disagreements about the division of water resources between Kyrgyzstan and Tajikistan, Kyrgyzstan is apprehensive of Kazakhstan's territorial ambitions and so on. The territorial disputes in Caucasus are much more serious. The conflicts in Georgia (Abkhazia) and between Armenia and Azerbaijan (Nagorno–Karabak) have only cooled (relatively) down because of Russian intervention (Russia has intervened militarily in Georgia and has supported Azerbaijan's 'new' political regime). Thus, the extent and the gravity of the problem and the fact that the regimes in Central Asia and Caucasus were unable to resolve or at least to freeze their disputes on their own meant that Russia had to be called in for assistance.

The need for a regulator

Every interstate system has a regulator. The regulator may be a single state or an axis of several (generally two) states. Thus, the European Union is based on the Franco-German axis. The regulator's role is primordial to the functioning of the system. Without the regulator, the system breaks down. Hence, a European Union without France and/or Germany is inconceivable at present, but the withdrawal of any other member will not necessarily lead to a dissolution of the EU. The Russian Federation performs the role of regulator in Central Asia and Caucasus. Only Russia has the qualifications and determination to undertake this task. Not only is Russia militarily capable of protecting the area, whether by nuclear or conventional arms, but it is also able to put a lid on interstate conflicts. Moreover, all Central Asian and Caucasian societies, particularly the élite (who have for the most part been educated in Moscow, Leningrad or other ex-Soviet cities), are familiar with the Russian institutions, procedures, language and mentality. In fact, Central Asia, Caucasus and Russia share similar administrative, economic, financial and political structures. They have a lot in common. In any case, there was not much of a choice. As President Kerimov of Uzbekistan put it, 'Russia must be the *guarantor* of security in Central Asia. Because it is the logic of history.'[20] Nevertheless, Central Asia and Caucasus have repeatedly tried to escape from the claws of Russia. As early as June 1990 (in Alma-Ata), they tried 'to set up [an autonomous] mechanism for regional coordination for at least economic policy, but their efforts had few concrete results'[21] and again, in December 1991, during the Central Asian summit, 'faced with the question of whether to try to create a rival Central Asian or Muslim commonwealth, including Azerbaijan, Central Asia opted to demand membership in what, with their accession, became CIS'.[22] In April 1992, the Central Asian presidents met in Bishkek (Kyrgyzstan) 'in another attempt to organize mechanisms for regional cooperation; but already the five countries were visibly going their own ways'.[23] In fact, the only network for cooperation in which Russia does not participate is the Economic Cooperation Organization (ECO). The ECO, however, is a purely economic organism and, as such, not an alternative to the Russian-led security system. To conclude, Russia is the only power in the region able to play the role of regulator. It is the regional centre of gravitation.

Where does the 'light' come from?

Historically, Central Asia and Caucasus have been contained by their geography. The region could be described as a 'black hole', squeezed in between four empires: Russia to the north, China to the east, Persia to the south and the Ottoman empire to the west.

In this respect, the situation remains very much unchanged, except that they are no longer surrounded by empires. The novelty of the situation resides in another fact. Central Asia and Caucasus are in search of a development model that will allow them to effectively introduce a market economy and political modernization. For obvious reasons, neither China nor Iran can serve as a model. The Turkish model,[24] characterized by the separation of religion and state, the slow but certain introduction of a market economy and democracy *à la Turque*, might theoretically appear appropriate to adopt. However, Turkey is unable to provide for their security and, in any case, it is only a 'second-best' model. Russia, on the other hand, is not only able to guarantee the security of Central Asia and Caucasus, although the Russian experiment is far from over, but it may also represent a model fit for imitation. We must also remember the fact that when we talk about a common culture, we generally think of linguistic, religious and traditional aspects. However, a common culture could also include the political and administrative culture. In this respect, Central Asia and Caucasus have undoubtedly more in common with Russia than with the other regional powers. Moreover, in these regions the Russian language constitutes the lingua franca which provides another important link with Russia.[25]

After having reviewed the security needs of Central Asia and Caucasus, I shall now turn to Russia's interest in creating a new Russian-led security system.

Russia's interests in a new security system

Russia's policy towards its southern neighbours continues to be ambiguous. This is, however, not a deliberate policy, but a result of Russia's political situation. An unambiguous policy towards Central Asia and Caucasus would, *a priori*, necessitate that the Russians have a crystal-clear image of their own future position and role in the New World Order, which they do not have ... yet. What kind of power is Russia today? Russian scholars and leaders (at least those in office) agree that Russia is no longer a global power. A global power 'in modern times is, evidently, a country which is the mainstay of meta-structures (geopolitical, economic, humanitarian, etc.)' (Pleshakov, 1993, p. 21).[26] Thus, according to this definition, 'Russia has ceased to be a global power. Her influence and, what is more important, her interests in Southeast Asia, Africa and Latin America are not great' (Pleshakov, 1993, p. 21). If Russia is no longer a global power, then what is it? 'A normal great power', answers the former Russian Foreign Minister Andrei Kozyrev (Kozyrev, 1993, p. 3). 'A Eurasian power', a Russian scholar modestly says (Pleshakov, 1993, p. 21). Whatever the answer, one thing is sure, the Russian élite disagrees on this crucial question. Hence, Arbatov (1993, p. 8) identified three fractions: reformers, reactionaries and centrists. Without going through a comprehensive study of these fractions, let me just discuss the essence of their differences. First of all, they disagree on the definition of foreign policy. That is, they disagree on which regions and territories should be considered domestic and which external. In general, Central Asia and Caucasus are formally referred to as the 'near abroad'. This is obviously an ambivalent term, because it is not evident how near 'near' is or, for that matter, how abroad 'abroad' is. Moscow itself has no clear answer to this question. The elimination of the Ruskoi–Khazbulatov axis in October 1993, naturally contributed somewhat to clarifying Moscow's position. However, the uncertainty still lingers on, as exemplified by the title of a recent *Moscow News* article, 'Where Do Russia's Southern Borders Pass?' (12 November 1993). The second difference in opinion among the Russian élite concerns foreign policy priorities. While Arbatov (1993) felt that 'the first and highest foreign policy priority for Russia is its relations with other former republics of the USSR, and first of all with Ukraine and Kazakhstan' (p. 26), others tend to favour improving relations with the 'far abroad', in particular the West (the USA, EU and Japan), in order to build trust and 'overcoming the Cold War legacy' (Boris Yeltsin, Radio Mayak, 27 October 1993). Hence, 'there is a real sense in which the "far abroad" appears closer than the "near abroad", as Russia's leaders currently find it easier to deal with certain Western countries than they do with some of the newly independent states on Russia's periphery' (Lough, 1993, p. 22). It seems, however, that after a period of 'diplomacy of smiles' and the 'policy of yes', Russia is now more hesitant and that

> Russian foreign policy most probably will shift from the pro-Western paradigm that dominated during 1992–93 to a centrist or moderate–conservative position. It will become more assertive as to Russia's national interests, prestige and independent role in regional and global affairs (Arbatov, 1993, p. 41).

Significant signs of such a shift are already apparent in official statements and in the policy actions of Russia. Thus, the former Foreign Minister Kozyrev, who has been one of the prominent 'pro-West' figures, had begun – long before his resignation from office – to emphasize the differences of interest that exist between Russia and the West.

> Partnership and alliance [with the West], he said, never mean merger. Russia has and will have different, and moreover, concrete interests. This is true to any state, particularly so for a great power (Kozyrev, *Moscow News*, 22 October 1993, p. 4).

Despite this less pro-Western statement and some others in the same spirit, Kozyrev was replaced by Evgenii Primakov, a hard-line diplomat (10 January 1996). There are basically three reasons behind Russia's special interest in Central Asia and Caucasus. First of all, as mentioned above, almost 25 million Russians live in the newly independent states. Consequently, Russia has reserved a 'special role' for itself (Arbatov, 1993, p. 29) in this 'zone of responsibility' (Bogaturov, 1993, p. 42). Secondly, there is the question of security and stability. Today, Russia's role in Eurasia 'consists, above all, in stabilising herself and the continuous states whose equal and intensive cooperation ... will restore to the continent the missing "critical mass" of stability' (Bogaturov, 1993, p. 42). The demarcation of Russia's zone of 'vital interests' depends on Russia's own assessments and on the state of affairs in those particular sections of the former Soviet republics.[27] This may be said to be Moscow's version of the Monroe Doctrine. Finally, Russia is apprehensive of an eventual vacuum across its southern borders for fear of

'Asiaticism' (*sic*). 'We must prevent a drift to "Asiaticism" or we may risk, say, allowing Islamic fundamentalism or other extremists in the region to bring Central Asia under their sway' (Kozyrev, 1993, p. 4). There are three ways to achieve these objectives: (1) by manipulation, (2) by integration and (3) by manipulation and integration. The proponents of pure manipulation argue that Russia can only regain its dominance over all the territories of the former USSR

> by manipulation of various factors: the economic dependence of some republics, the presence of an ethnic Russian population and Russian armed forces on the territory of others, and in still others, ethnic and political tensions and border conflicts among them. By this kind of logic, the weaker and less stable the other republics, the stronger and better off Russia is (Arbatov, 1993, p. 30).

Others, however, believe that the hardliners may be underestimating the extent of nationalism in the southern states. They take the dangers of uncontrolled destabilization with its potential domino effects seriously by arguing for a peaceful integration. Their credo presupposes that 'the modern world is an interdependent world. And if you want to live the way they live in the EC [now EU], you've got to learn the art of integration' (Zagorsky, 1993, p. 46). In between the hawks and doves there are those (among them Kozyrev) who feel that the newly independent republics should be drawn 'into the OSCE process with all its lofty principles'; yet reserve 'the use of forcible methods; economic and military' (Kozyrev, 1993, p. 5).

CONCLUSION

This study of the changes in Central Asia and Caucasus has clearly demonstrated that, after a period of hesitation and resistance (towards Russia), these two regions are now willing to cooperate under the leadership of Russia. This cooperative network is not similar to the old Soviet system. It is based on mutual interests and needs rather than on a unilateral hierarchical arrangement. The independent former Soviet republics' acceptance of Russia's predominance is not only a necessary condition of Russia's commitment to provide protection, but also a framework in which Russia must respect the independence and territorial integrity of these republics. Nothing is free, not even hegemony! Otherwise, it would be, as Huntington (1993) stated, 'against Russia's long-term interests to reassert itself in a coercive way because that will inevitably inflame nationalism among the other peoples'.[28] Naturally, much depends on the general political situation in Russia and first and foremost in Moscow. If the Russian leaders succeed in producing stability in their own country, it will undoubtedly strengthen Russia's position in general and in particular towards the independent ex-Soviet republics. In this case, Russia will continue its efforts to establish a comprehensive, general security system, covering the major part of its old empire (apart from the ex-East European countries). In this model, 'Russia would play the role of first among equals in interstate relations in the CIS – rather like USA in Nato, or Germany in the European Union ... Russia will also have to continue to be a local peace keeper or peace enforcer'.[29] That is, the Central Asian and Caucasian republics will no longer constitute just a simple security complex, but will become members of a security system. Such an evolution inevitably reduces the regional dynamics in Central Asia and Caucasus. Consequently, it will also lead to a diminution of the reciprocal sensitivity between these regions, on the one hand and other regional powers such as Iran, Turkey and China, on the other. More specifically, a new constellation of Russia's southern republics will lead to a marginalization of China, Turkey and Iran, thus reducing their respective influence on Central Asia and Caucasus. In short, the establishment of a single security system implies a return of some sort to the *status quo ante* for these three powers. That is, presumably, they will again have to deal with a 'new' superpower.

NOTES

1. I have deliberately used the term Soviet–Russian empire to emphasize the difference between the ethnical empire (in this case purely 'Russian') and the Party (or communist) empire. Some scholars believe that the 'Soviet Union cannot legitimately be termed a "Russian empire", neither can Russians be called an "imperial people"'. To have an empire, Besançon explained, 'one must have a privileged people, an essentially military means of conquest, and limited goals. The Russian people has no privilege, it has "advantages" certainly, as the surest ally of communism, and party leaders are often drawn from its ranks, even in the national republics ... A Russian who enjoys privileges as a Communist owes his privileges to his communism, not to his Russianness', quoted by J. Dunlop, in I. Bremmer and R. Taras (eds) *Nation and Politics in the Soviet Successor States* (Cambridge University Press, 1993), pp. 45–6. On the contrary, some Russian authors argue that Russia is an empire 'apart from other empires of the past. I called it *organic* because it was held together by a common geopolitical area, a common economy and common security requirements. Its principal characteristic was the fact that it was a unique polyethnic cultural entity in which hundreds of ethnic groups, peoples and nationalities coexisted peacefully...', E. Pozdnyakov, 'Russia Today and Tomorrow', *International*

Affairs, No. 2 (1993), p. 23. I think that the term Soviet–Russian empire inaccurately indicates both the predominance of Russians and the total hegemony of the Communist Party.

2. The expression *apolaire* is Jacques Delors' (Former Head of the EU Commission), *Le Monde*, 7–8 November 1993.
3. A. Bogaturov, 'The Euroasian Support of World Stability', *International Affairs*, No. 2 (1993), p. 42.
4. On Chechnya, see 'Chechnia, Report of an International Alert finding mission' (Stefan Sullivan, London, International Alert, 1992), *Moscow News*, A. Avtorkhanov, 'The Chechens and Ingush during the Soviet Period and its Antecedents' in M.B. Broxup (ed.), *The North Caucasus Barrier* (London: Hurst & Co., 1992) and *Moscow News*, 26 November 1993.
5. In J. Checkel, *RFE/RL Research Report*, no. 41 (16 October 1992), p. 20.
6. Bulletin on Kazakhstan published by the Foreign–Economics Relations Board (DEIK) (Istanbul, April 1993).
7. This model is a variant of Hedley Bull's classic model. Bull makes a clear distinction between the state system and the society of states (in his jargon the international system and the international society at the global level). The state system refers to a plurality of sovereign states, forming a system, which does not, however, constitute a society of states:

   > There would be states, and interaction among them on a global basis, but the element of acceptance of common interests or values, and, on the basis of them, of common rules and institutions, would have disappeared. There would be communication and institutions among these states, but no commitment to a network of diplomatic institutions; agreements, but no acceptance of a structure of international legal obligation ... (Bull, *The Anarchical Society* (London: Macmillan, 1985), p. 249).

   The society of states emerges when the constituent members accept the essential rules that are to regulate their relations with each other. The current situation in Central Asia and Caucasus falls within a category in between the state system and the society of states (which I have called semi-immature), that is a situation in which the actors recognize each others existence, but not each others full legitimacy.
8. Since 31 January 1992 the Central Asian and Caucasian republics have been members of the CSCE. But until now the CSCE (now the OSCE) has demonstrated only a small interest in these areas. Its efforts to solve the Nagorno–Karabak conflict on a multilateral basis (independent of the Russian Federation) have failed. Even the constitution of the so-called Minsk Group under the auspices of the CSCE did not obtain any results. The return of peace, though relative, in Caucasus is due only to Russian pressure and intervention.
9. On the Tajik Civil War, see the interview with Anatoly Leonidovich, First Deputy Minister of Foreign Affairs of Russia, *Moscow News*, 13 August 1993. In this interview he stated that 'All cardinal political changes in Russian history – both progressive and reactionary – began with unsuccessful wars: The reforms of Alexander II in the 1860s; the First Russian revolution of 1905; the Bolshevik Revolution of 1917; and Mikhail Gorbachev's perestroika. If, following this pattern, another Russian foray into Central Asian murderous politics ends in

defeat, the consequences for Russia and the world are bound to be very sad'. See also 'Tajik Civil War', *RFL/RL Research Report*, 12 February 1993.

10. Following Buzan (1991), 'the principal distinguishing feature of weak states is their high level of concern with domestically generated threats to the security of the government ...' (p. 99).
11. Xinjiang is a 1 447 000 km^2 region with a population of 13 000 000 (60 per cent Chinese, 35 per cent Ouigours, 3.5 per cent Kazakh, 0.8 per cent Huis, 0.4 per cent Kirghizi, and 0.3 per cent Mongolians). See the interesting article by Isabelle Maltor and Dongfang Ouyang, 'Nouvelle donne régionale pour le Xinjang', *Le Monde Diplomatique*, November 1993.
12. Huntington (1993, p. 22) believes that 'conflict between civilizations will be the latest phase in the evolution of conflict in the modern world'. And in the future, 'The world will be shaped in large measure by the interactions among seven or eight major civilizations. These include Western, Confucian, Japanese, Islamic, Hindu, Slavic-Orthodox, Latin-American and possibly African civilizations'.
13. *Tehran Times*, 17 November 1993, p. 1.
14. As a consequence of two Iranian military defeats, in 1813 (Golistan treaty) and 1828 (Turkmentchay treaty), Russia has succeeded in conquering a large part of the Iranian kingdom by expanding into areas of Caucasus that were formerly Iranian territory.
15. *Le Monde*, 22 July 1993, p. 4. It should be mentioned that the expression 'wahhabi' does not automatically refer to Saudi Arabia and never to Iran. The term 'wahhabi' has been used by the official newspapers in Central Asia, indicating merely 'fundamentalism'; see Oliver Roy, 'Le renouveau Islamique en URSS', *Des éthinies aux nations en Asie Centrale* (Paris: Edisud, 1991), p. 137.
16. Iranian fear was motivated by certain statements from some Azeri officials. For instance, the Azeri President Abulfazl Elchibey stated, in connection with the Turkic Summit in Ankara in October 1992, that Iranian Azerbaijan should become independent and called for the overthrow of the Islamic regime in Iran, while vowing allegiance to Atatürk by describing himself as his faithful follower and soldier. Elchibey's statement provoked massive protestations from the Iranian deputies, especially those from Azerbaijan. *Tehran Times*, 9 November, p. 1 and 27 December 1992, p. 1. To neutralize Elchibey's ultranationalist influence on Iranian Azeris, the government immediately took two important measures. First, Tehran announced the creation of a new province named West Azerbaijan with Ardebil as the administrative centre. Thus, Iranian Azerbaijan, which was already divided into two provinces (the East with Tabriz as the capital the West with Rezaiyya (now Ourumiyya) as the capital), is now divided into three provinces. *Tehran Times*, 13 January 1993, p. 1. Second, the Iranian Home Office announced that henceforth the Ministry's permission would be required for marriage with foreigners. This measure aimed at improving the control over the migratory movements in the northern borders. *Tehran Times*, 28 January 1993, p. 4.
17. Philip Robins, 'Between Sentiment and Self-Interest: Turkey's Policy toward Azerbaijan and the Central Asian States', *The Middle East Journal*, vol. 47, no. 4 (Autumn 1993).

18. 'Anti-Russian sentiment in Azerbaijan was exacerbated by the intervention of the Soviet military in Baku in January 1990, allegedly to prevent the seizure of power by the AzPF, during which some 150 people, mostly innocent civilians, were killed', Elizabeth Fuller, 'Azerbaijan's Relations with Russia and CIS', *RFE/RL, 3* October 1992. The AzPF won the first battle when its leader, Abulfazl Elchibey, was elected president of Azerbaijan (7 June 1992). One year later, Elchibey had to flee from Baku to Nakhichevan (August 1993) leaving the power to Geidar Aliev, a well-known communist veteran and a former member of the Soviet Communist Party's politbureau.
19. The Birlik movement was a 'loose group of urban intellectuals who considered themselves proponents of Western-style democracy, and individuals from various backgrounds who were attracted by *Birlik's* programme calling for the restoration of the Uzbek cultural and religious heritage and the advancement of Uzbek national interests', Bess Brown, 'Tajik Civil War Prompts Crackdown in Uzbekistan', *RFE/RL*, 12 March 1992.
20. *Le Monde*, 7–8 March 1993.
21. Bess Brown, 'Regional Cooperation in Central Asia', *RFE/RL*, 29 January 1993, p. 32.
22. Ibid.
23. Ibid.
24. See Andrew Mango, 'The Turkish Model', which is a critical analysis of what has been said and written about the Turkish Model, *Middle Eastern Studies*, vol. 29, no. 4 (October 1993), pp. 726–57.
25. The economic dependence of Central Asia and Caucasus on Russia certainly constitutes another motive to keep very close relations with Russia. Under the Soviet regime, 'Kazakhstan and the republics of Central Asia received substantial sums of money in the form of income compensation, price subsidies and grants for social infrastructure ... In 1975, the total value of these grants was 305 million rubles (0.3 per cent of the total USSR budget), and by 1989 the value of the grants had risen to 5.9 billion roubles (2.6 per cent of the budget). In 1990 disbursements totalling 8.6 billion roubles were planned ...'. See Michael Bradshaw, *The Economic Effects of Soviet Dissolution* (London: Royal Institute of International Affairs, 1993), p. 20.
26. Actually, Pleshankov (1993) uses the term 'great power' instead of 'global' or 'superpower'.
27. Bogaturov (1993) argued that the fact that Latvia and Estonia border directly on Russia does not as such threaten the security of Russia. Unless 'it comes to threaten an uncontrollable refugee outflow or bloodshed'. Likewise, Russia's security is not directly affected by the conflict in Tajikistan. But this conflict will affect Russia's security if it spreads to Kazakhstan and turns into a regional conflict provoking armed intervention of powerful 'extraregional forces' like those of Pakistan and Iran. *International Affairs* (Moscow: February 1993), p. 42. See also Yevgeny Shaposhinko's article on 'A Security Concept for Russia', *International Affairs* (Moscow: October 1993), pp. 10–19.
28. Interview with Alexei Pushkov, *Moscow News*, no. 10 (11–17 March 1994) p. 6.
29. Sergei Karaganov in *Financial Times*, 21 March 1994.

REFERENCES

A.G. Arbatov, 'Russia's Foreign Policy Alternatives', *International Security*, vol. 18, no. 2 (Fall 1993), pp. 5–43.

A. Bogaturov, 'The Euroasian Support of the World Stability', *International Affairs* (Moscow: February 1993), pp. 32–44.

P.G. Cerny, 'Plurilateralism: Structural Differentiation and Functional Conflict in the Post-Cold War World Order', *Millennium*, vol. 22, no. 1 (Spring 1993), pp. 27–51.

S. Huntington, 'The Clash of Civilizations?', *Foreign Affairs* (Summer 1993), pp. 22–49.

R. Jervis, 'Security Regimes', in S.D. Krasner (ed.), *International Regimes* (Ithaca: Cornell University Press, 1984), pp. 173–94.

R.O. Keohane, 'The Demand for International Regimes', in S.D. Krasner (ed.), *International Regimes* (Ithaca: Cornell University Press, 1984), pp. 141–71.

A. Kozyrev *et al.*, 'What Foreign Policy Russia Should Pursue', *International Affairs* (Moscow: February 1993), pp. 3–21.

J. Lough, 'The Place of the Near Abroad in Russian Foreign Policy', *RFE/RL Research Report*, vol. 2, no. 11 (12 March 1993), pp. 21–29.

F. Meinecke, *Weltbürgertum und Nationalstaat: Studien zur Genesis des deutschen Nationalstaats* (Munich: Olendenbourg, 1908/1962).

A. Minc, *Le nouveau moyen âge* (Paris: Gallimard, 1993).

M. Mozaffari, 'Neorealism and Structural Changes in the Gulf', in Stuart S. Nagel (ed.), *Asian Development and Public Policy* (London: Macmillan, 1994), pp. 214–34.

J.S. Nye, Jr, *Bound to Lead* (New York: Basic Books, 1990).

N. Petersen, 'Trusselsopfattelser og sikkerhedsbegreber i international politik', in *Trussel eller tillid*? (Stockholm: Nordsam, 1990), pp. 17–33.

K. Pleshakov, 'Russia's Mission: The Third Epoch', *International Affairs* (Moscow: January 1993), pp. 17–26.

I. Traistaru, 'Options for a Security Regime in Eastern Europe after the Cold War', in F.R. Pfetsch (ed.), *International Relations and Pan-Europe* (Hamburg: LIT Verlag, 1993), pp. 297–313.

O.R. Young, 'Regime Dynamics: The Rise and Fall of International Regimes', in Stephen D. Krasner, *International Regimes* (Ithaca: Cornell University Press, 1984), pp. 93–113.

S.M. Walt, *The Origins of Alliances* (Ithaca: Cornell University Press, 1990).

K.N. Waltz, *Theory of International Politics* (Reading, Mass.: Addison-Wesley, 1979).

K.N. Waltz, 'Reflections on Theory of International Politics: Response to My Critics', in Robert O. Keohane (ed.), *Neo-realism and Its Critics* (New York: Columbia University Press, 1986), pp. 322–45.

K.N. Waltz, 'The Emerging Structure of International Politics', *International Security*, vol. 18 no. 2 (Fall 1993), pp. 44–79.

A. Zagorsky, 'The Commonwealth: One Year On', *International Affairs* (Moscow: February 1993), pp. 45–62.

2 Russian Diplomacy: the Problems of Transition

I. Tiouline

Domestic factors play an active role in the formulation and execution of a state's foreign policy. History provides ample examples of how fundamental changes on the home front can induce radical shifts in foreign policy and alter a country's international status.

It is evident that numerous interacting factors are at work in the formulation of foreign policy, which may be said to be a product of the coordinated effort of several agencies of the state.

First among these is of course the Foreign Ministry. An analysis, therefore, of the workings of the Foreign Ministry is crucial to a correct perception of Russian diplomacy in the period of transition. For many decades Soviet and Russian diplomatic services existed in a state of genuine symbiosis. Although the Ministry of Foreign Affairs (MFA) of the Russian Soviet Federative Socialist Republic (RSFSR) has existed since 1944, it performed only formal and decorative functions. Moreover, the Russian Ministry was broadly considered a dumping ground for incompetent or disgraced diplomats. Russia's declaration of sovereignty in June 1990 and the subsequent appointment of Andrei Kozyrev as minister did not change much in the traditional relationship between the Union and the republic MFAs. However, with the dissolution of the Union, interrepublic talks abruptly assumed a new guise as negotiations between the sovereign states and the role of the Russian MFA accordingly increased dramatically.

The Union MFA was disgraced due to the position adopted by its head A. Bessmertnykh and other officials and Soviet ambassadors during the August 1991 coup. The Minister was forced to resign on 23 August. His successor, B. Pankin, took drastic measures to re-establish control over the situation. Many high-ranking diplomats were fired in Moscow and abroad and the Union republics were encouraged to have a greater say in the formulation of foreign policy. On 13 September, Pankin convened the Council of Foreign Ministers of the USSR and the Republics and assigned it a 'key role'. The next day the new Foreign Ministry Collegium was formed and two new executive bodies were established to promote cooperation between the centre and the republics. One of these was the Executive

Secretariat for the Council of Foreign Ministers, the other was the Commission of Permanent Representatives of the Republics. In addition, Pankin announced his intention to support the application of any republic that wished to join the UN as well as to establish republic diplomatic missions within Soviet embassies abroad (Russia appointed her representative to Washington on 19 November) and to curtail KGB activity within the Ministry radically. Nevertheless, neither these steps nor the return of Eduard Shevardnadze to the position of the minister could check the disintegration of the Foreign Ministry. Each new day brought more censure from Russia. On 22 October Boris Yeltsin announced that after January 1992 Russia would finance only three Union ministries, the Union MFA not included. On 25 October Kozyrev opined that the Soviet MFA in its present form did not serve the interests of Russia and the other republics and called for its transformation into a body with coordinating and consultative functions only. The decisive blow was delivered by Yeltsin during the Congress of Russian People's Deputies on 28 October. He demanded a radical reorganization of the Union MFA that would transform it into a body for coordinating the international activities of the republics and proposed a tenfold reduction in its staff. Several days later the matter was submitted to the State Council of the USSR for deliberation. In a speech on that occasion, Gorbachev advocated a unified foreign policy which would enable the retention of Soviet international standing. Pankin approved a maximum of a 30 per cent reduction in the Soviet MFA's staff. The State Council concurred with Pankin, though it was clear that this was nothing more than a mere holding action. As a French expert Anne de Tanguy put it, 'the wind has already changed, and the boat deserted by many of its diplomatic crew was fast sinking'.[1]

To sum it up, the attempted coup became a turning point for the Russian diplomatic service. A truly new page in its history was turned when the Commonwealth of Independent States (CIS) was created in December 1991. President Yeltsin's Decree of 16 December 1991 entitled 'On the Diplomatic Service of the Russian Soviet Federal Socialist Republic (RSFSR)' charged the MFA with the following tasks: (1) to assume effective control over the disbanding of the Soviet MFA, together with its headquarters, buildings, property and educational institutions, as well as embassies, consulates and other representations abroad, (2) to prepare a new organizational and personnel chart for the Russian MFA within no later than 1 month, along with proposals for the future employment of the former staff of the Soviet MFA, (3) within no later than 1 month to conduct negotiations with the CIS members as well as with other ex-Soviet sovereign states for the purpose of establishing joint coordinating and consultative mechanisms in the field of foreign policy, (4) to elaborate a provisional act for the Russian diplomatic service before 1

January 1992 and (5) to establish a government protocol service to outline common protocol guidelines in the RSFSR.[2]

The Russian tricolour was hoisted over the Soviet embassies abroad. This symbolic act signified the emergence of a new state, the rebirth of an independent sovereign Russia, recognized by the world community as the successor to the USSR. However, it created forthwith a number of urgent problems for the Russian diplomatic service, in particular for its personnel both at home and overseas. Two aspects were most important: the human dimension, that is the staff structure and the infrastructural and organizational dimension.

It should be kept in mind that Kozyrev, who was appointed the Minister for Foreign Affairs of the RSFSR, inherited a staff dwarfed by the behemoth former Union MFA. Whereas the starting staff of the Russian MFA was 70 people, which later increased to 240, the Soviet MFA had 3500 at the central headquarters on Smolenskaya Square plus thousands overseas. Kozyrev therefore had cogent grounds for comparing the two ministries with David and Goliath, respectively, in a speech to the top executives of both MFAs on 23 December 1991 on the problem of integrating the two. After paying tribute to the high professional standards of the Union MFA and praising the revolutionary accomplishments of the Russian MFA, Kozyrev set forth the goal of creating an integrated structure derived from both to serve Russian democracy. Kozyrev outlined the following tasks: (1) to trim the staff and to cut back on spending without impairing the ability of the diplomatic service to function, (2) to co-opt junior and middle-level diplomats of both the MFAs in accordance with a plan that would not give the staff of the new Russian MFA a monopoly on the 'revolutionary' viewpoint, even as the old school would not be considered the sole proprietors of professionalism, (3) to select and appoint the appropriate persons for the top positions, namely deputies to the minister and department heads and (4) to reform the ministerial organizational structure, bearing in mind that retaining the Committee for Foreign Trade and Economy, which was established during the last months of the Union MFA, would be rather inappropriate.[3]

Some of the objectives outlined by Kozyrev were achieved within a short time. His speech also stressed that the day-to-day responsibility for managing the Russian MFA lay with his own deputies. Not one of the former Union MFA deputies to the minister were included in this group. Later, in winter 1992, the above-mentioned Committee for Foreign Trade and Economy became the independent Ministry of Foreign Economy of Russia.[4] However, other problems were much less easy to resolve. The most complex was that of the diplomatic staff.

Diplomacy is a major political institution of any country. Inasmuch as its task is to promote the national interest abroad, its loyalty to the government must be beyond dispute. However, creating a loyal and reliable institution is a long and demanding process, requiring the aim of selection and training of personnel who will be responsible for conducting foreign policy strategy on a day-to-day basis.

The formation of the Soviet diplomatic corps was an arduous task that took long to accomplish in its day.[5] To begin with, the overwhelming majority of Russian diplomats both in the ministry and abroad, being devoted to the throne and cherishing their honour, refused to cooperate with the new state. This explains why Soviet diplomacy began with sailor Markin, revolutionary functionaries such as Trotsky, Litvinov, Krasin and Raskolnikov, who drew on the experience of Chicherin, Maisky, Solovyev and other diplomats and officials of the old school. As time passed, however, the 'revolutionary' reserve began to dwindle and the first purges were inaugurated.

Practice showed that the diplomatic service required everyday attention and that something more than revolutionary zeal was needed to hammer it into appropriate shape. The very nature of diplomatic work ruled out the involvement of a large number of people, which therefore meant that each diplomat had to be trained in many fields and that success depended directly on the individual knowledge and collective experience of a staff kept deliberately small. Furthermore, the service needed people dedicated to the party's ideals and obedient to its will, which implied that all the Soviet diplomats had to be party members with an impeccable service record.

Thus, as early as the 1930s, the Soviet diplomatic service embarked upon a radical restructuring under the national slogan 'Everything depends on specialists'. Most of its recruits were graduates of the newly established Institute for the Training of Diplomatic and Consular Personnel under the USSR People's Commissariat of Foreign Affairs (PCFA). The institute admitted young specialists who already had a higher education in the social, political and other sciences and were 'mobilized' by the party for diplomatic work. Be that as it may, although the institute was renamed the Advanced School of Diplomacy (ASD, 1939) and later the Diplomatic Academy (1974), it provided the service with a backbone that lasted to one degree or another until the mid-1980s.

In 1937–1938, new diplomats assigned to the PCFA, which had just been through a wave of repression, found no-one in most departments but one or two typists. They found themselves straightaway burdened with enough assignments to occupy an entire department and were thus drawn into the whirlpool of diplomatic activity. Later on practically all the newcomers became deputy ministers, department heads or ambassadors. Many of them were really gifted even by today's standards.

During the war, when the contours of post-war diplomacy began to emerge, the decision was taken (in 1943) to embark on the training of a new generation of professional diplomats and to this end create a Department of International Relations at Moscow State University, renamed the Moscow State Institute of International Relations (MGIMO) in 1994. Most of the first students were young soldiers and officers, wounded or discharged, who had returned from the front. There was also a sprinkling of school-leavers. They were destined to become politicians, diplomats, scholars, journalists and intelligence officers known at home and abroad.

A rule in force at the time prohibited conferring the prime diplomatic rank of attaché on MGIMO graduates or giving them a diplomatic assignment immediately upon graduation. An interim of 1 or 2 years was required. Under perestroika this term was even lengthened to 4 years. Repeated attempts were made to prevent MGIMO graduates who had not done a course of study at the Diplomatic Academy being given the post of first secretary or counsellor notwithstanding the fact that most of them had a standard of education vastly superior to that of party 'reinforcements'. Military structures were invariably invoked as an argument, it being forgotten that military school graduates become lieutenants immediately and work in the field in a troop unit during their studies.

At the same time, the ASD continued training diplomats from people of an entirely different stripe as well. It was obliged to admit 'Party recruits', that is people who had held various jobs as Party or Komsomol functionaries, civil servants or managers in the economy executives and were 'recruited by the Party' to 'reinforce' the diplomatic service. Whereas before the war and in the early post-war years ASD graduates were normally appointed to primary diplomatic posts, in the Khrushchev and particularly the Brezhnev period people selected by the party became the main reserve of senior and leading diplomatic staff. In the period from 1954 through to 1988 the Diplomatic Academy alone supplied the Soviet MFA with over 800 former CPSU functionaries, plus dozens of other Party, Komsomol, Soviet and state enterprise officials who entered the diplomatic service without any formal training. They included people who had received a solid education and met high cultural standards and who had mastered the diplomatic profession in a short time. However, most of them remained outsiders to that environment. As they had no knowledge of either the problems or foreign languages, all that they were able to do was to sermonize and set 'guidelines'. They were unfit for creative work and found themselves at sea in the various departments concerned with global affairs and the delicate problems of relations with the

Western world. They found a niche for themselves at best in developing countries and above all in socialist community countries, where they implemented Party diplomacy with 'fraternal' familiarity. In the Soviet embassies in the Western countries they occupied positions of Party Secretary with the rank of councillor and minister (not on the ambassadorial level) or positions as chairmen of labour organizations or top administrative and management posts within the embassies.

In the central headquarters they were employed in the various functional subdivisions, to which they would be assigned in classical bureaucratic manner, that is by merely inflating the existing organizational structure by the creation of extra reserved positions. The main reserve to which reinforcements were sent was Party committees and personnel departments, where they felt confident and behaved despotically, raising all sorts of hurdles to the careers of young people and professional diplomats.

This digression into the Party's cadre policy in the Soviet MFA was essential in order for us to be clear of the fact that although the Soviet MFA ranks were 100 per cent filled with Party members with same colour Party cards, the real weight of these cards varied. The professional diplomats were constantly aware of this, so that a covert sense of belonging to a different 'caste' from that of the outsiders was always present. Leading Party members serving abroad have had this feeling in abundance since the first years of perestroika and, in particular, since 'deideologization' became the catchword. The CPSU headquarters on Staraya Ploshchad was quick to perceive the changing situation.

In mid-1990 the CPSU Central Committee took the decision to disband unified Party committees in diplomatic representations abroad. By the same decision the organizational structure was expanded to include 150 extra positions for the reassignment of ex-secretaries as embassy staff managers, while in large consulates new consul positions were introduced for the same purpose. The so-called 'Party call-up' into the Diplomatic Academy was abolished and replaced by a 'people's deputy call-up' to enable the same Party functionaries to assume the positions of ambassadors and consuls.

The perestroika years in the Soviet MFA were highlighted by a cadre reshuffling and the drafting of new operational guidelines. The position of economic minister was introduced by special decision. This position was occupied in 22 major embassies by former Party, state and administrative officials who had lost their previous jobs. They were assigned a weighty task, that is to devise strategies for commercial, economic and technological cooperation with the host countries. However, these people found it hard to accommodate to their new jobs and became simple commercial operators, often creating conflicts with embassy economic task forces and with trade representations. Though these facts were hardly a secret to the government, the last cabinet just prior to the August 1991 coup took the decision to establish such positions for another 25 countries.

All these positions were created despite the fact that a large number of diplomats had already been assigned a plethora of tasks bearing on economic matters. The Soviet embassy in the United States had the following positions: a counsellor for sea transportation and a counsellor for the fishing industry, a counsellor for agriculture and another one for land improvement, two counsellors for culture, a counsellor for information services and a counsellor responsible for a magazine with no readers, entitled *The Soviet Land*, and a counsellor responsible for the construction of a new embassy building – more than 20 counsellors in all. A similar solid pack of high-ranking diplomats doing next to nothing existed in other embassies too. (Nor did all these extra people produce any positive results by no means: for example the counsellor for agriculture in the Soviet embassy in London once complained that he was called upon every year by the Soviet Ministry of Agriculture to collect statistics on the output of broiler chicken.)

There were other more serious situations as well. In many embassies there were counsellors for liaisons with the Communist Parties of the host countries. In 1955 the State Committee for Cultural Relations was established and counsellors of culture were dispatched to several dozen countries. Their work initially duplicated that of the representatives of the Union of Soviet Societies for Friendship and Culture (SSFC), who usually held posts no higher than third or second secretaries. Naturally the SSFC could not tolerate such an affront and had its representatives promoted to the same rank. When the CPSU Central Committee established its Department of Information, several counsellors for information were sent to overseas embassies. They began to intrude into the business of the counsellors of culture and duplicated the jobs of press attachés and the counsellors in charge of the activities of the Press News Agency (APN). For example, in the Soviet Embassy to Mongolia there were 22 (*sic*!) Party or Komsomol functionaries on the roster of the diplomatic corps with the rank of counsellors, secretaries or consuls, with the sole responsibility of managing the affairs of the Soviet community residing there. This situation persisted until 1991. Basically the same situation occurred, if in different years, in the Soviet embassies in Cuba, Vietnam, the GDR, Poland, Angola, India, Egypt, Iraq, Algiers, Nigeria, Syria and in other countries.

Between 1955 and 1989 the number of Soviet MFA embassies and institutions abroad grew by 2.5 times, while the number of personnel increased 3.6 times. The first figure of course represents the real dynamics of the development of international relations and bilateral ties of the USSR in the post-war period; the second figure, however, merely reflects a game the Party and cadre bureaucracy played with the Foreign Ministry.

The budget figures are even more impressive: in 1971 foreign representations spent 31.5 million of foreign exchange roubles, but by 1989 their budget had more than tripled to 101.5 million roubles, which was the equivalent of US$175 million.

All these distortions demanded surgical methods to conform to the reorganization declared by the new management of the Russian MFA.[6] However, it was essential to retain the collective experience and individual skills of the diplomats. Administrative cuts in staff size had to be effected in a balanced manner. Experts are agreed that before any personnel reorganization takes place a new foreign policy strategy must be worked out and the deideologization of the perestroika period must be replaced by patriotic ideals.

The general spirit prevailing in the MFA's foreign representations made such an approach rational enough. It was a common opinion that for the Soviet Foreign Ministry, perestroika translated into a general shake up that continued to the very end. There was no denying that 'surgery' was needed to rid the Ministry of the evils of the earlier cadre policy, steeped in nepotism, favouritism and paternalism. However, that was not all, for staff, especially leading officials, began to be knocked about like billiard balls; the times were replete with uncalled-for reorganizations, abolitions and decisions to merge old departments or to break them up into smaller units to set up new departments. At the same time, the Ministry began allocating to itself new functions for which it was unsuited, as if it was determined to take on a heavier load than it could carry.

The psychological atmosphere in the Soviet MFA of this period was one of pessimism and a wait-and-see attitude. With the Union institutions in their death throes and the reforms limping along, people were uncertain of their own future. The result was growing apathy, fixations and indecision. In the central offices, with its large staff, it was relatively easy to allay distress, whereas in the embassies abroad it was hard going. When people are away from their homes, they acquire a sense of being involuntarily confined to a small group of individuals with its inherent disharmony and pernicious rumours. In such an environment, a general loss of spirit and increasing professional incompetence accompanied an indifference to state interests and a dereliction of duty. Cases of resignation multiplied. An acceleration of the reorganization was deemed essential to check these trends. The Russian MFA did not come up with a general foreign policy plan until 1993, of which, however, most experts were dismissive. However, this plan had a further braking effect on the creative potential of the diplomats. Although top-level

Russian MFA officials repeatedly declared that no professional would lose their job on the grounds of their former affiliation with the Union MFA, such cases multiplied, producing depression and discontent. Dismissals were not done in a direct manner; a pretext was invented in each case and experienced diplomats had to resign. The cadre drain was accompanied by uncertainty and instability in the conducting of foreign policy and by mounting public criticism. Whereas in 1988 only 40 diplomats resigned from their jobs in the Union MFA, the drain from the Russian MFA totalled 400 in 1992, rising to 750 in 2 years.

The real catalyst of this painful process was the shortage of funds resulting from the general economic crisis in Russia. The state cut the MFA budget dramatically. Only 60 per cent of the minimal outlay was allocated to the central headquarters and the foreign offices. Foreign representations received the same. Some expense lines were only 25 per cent covered and in the worst case 15 per cent. Some of the more distant embassies and consulates were closed, until their aggregate number was less than the UK or France had at the time.

Excessive budget deficits left the MFA with few options, but one of these was to raise funds from sources other than the state. Another was consular fees. However, they could not resolve the problem completely. According to 1994 statistics they covered approximately 10 per cent of the actual expenses of the MFA headquarters and 8 per cent of the expenses of the overseas institutions. This revenue was for the most part used to establish an all-Russian system of new passports, while the rest was allocated to support the MFA's foreign offices.

Every sixth member of the MFAs staff was in urgent need of living quarters. During the 3 years the Russian MFA had been in operation, not one square metre of living space was provided, nor was there any financing available for that purpose. Given the current trends in the real estate sector, a junior diplomat would have to work 70 years to earn enough money to buy a one-room apartment.

Pensions for retired diplomats were also meagre. Such well-known former ambassadors as Dobrynin or Troyanovsky, who had spent their entire careers in the diplomatic service, receive around 100 000 roubles per month, while a retired colonel received 350 000.

In every third Russian diplomatic office abroad the wages were fixed at 1975 levels. In 12 countries Russian ambassadors received less than $1000 monthly. Such a development, compounded by a changing mentality under the new market conditions, caused a deterioration in the social status of the diplomatic service. Cadre numbers declined by 1000 to a total of 3000. The diplomatic staff abroad was reduced from 9500 to 7500.[7] Those who left the

MFA were mostly young men with promising careers. At the same time the number of fresh recruits also fell inasmuch that most MGIMO graduates, who traditionally had made up the bulk of new recruits, preferred the business sector to the diplomatic corps. As reported by the mass media, in 1994 Kozyrev twice applied to the State Duma and the government for a considerable increase in wages for the MFA to bring them at least up to a level comparable to wages in either the Ministry of Defence or the Ministry of Economics. However, both the parliament and the government turned a deaf ear to Kozyrev's appeal.

The MFA was also restructured. Adopted before the war and carried into later years, the MFA was organized on a territorial and functional principle as in most other countries. However, while the general principle remains intact, the two past decades and in particular the years since the start of perestroika have seen a visible change in favour of smaller structural units.

Until the middle or end of the 1950s, the Foreign Ministry's territorial units were four or six European divisions, the American division, the Near and Middle East division, three African divisions, and two Far East divisions (at one time there were three). The French colonies and overseas territories as well as the Spanish, Portuguese, Dutch and Belgian colonies were under the First European division together with the mother countries while the British colonies and dominions were under the Second European division together with Britain. The disintegration of the colonial system and changes in the global political configuration led to changes in the Foreign Ministry's territorial subdivisions. At the beginning of perestroika it included six European divisions, the American division, two Latin American divisions, three African divisions, the Near and Middle East divisions, two far Eastern divisions and the Southern and Southeast Asia divisions while the former British dominions remained under the British division.

With the start of perestroika and the appointment of a new minister, the Soviet Foreign Ministry embarked on an urgently needed radical reconstruction. However, the long-awaited changes were accompanied by a totally unwarranted abolishment of long-established structures. The reformers changed the face of the ministry and the diplomatic service in a short time.

New territorial subdivisions were created by merging old ones and regrouping regions. Some solutions were suggested by the logic of the developments themselves. For instance, Canada was transferred from the British sphere to the North American region, Australia to the Far East and Malta to Mediterranean Europe.

Some of the changes, however, were unaccountable even in terms of a 'new thinking'. Regions were formed on an ideological principle: Europe was placed under a new Directorate of the Socialist Countries of Europe and Asia. It was manifestly absurd to pool together German and Korean problems and separate Vietnam from the rest of Indochina, not to mention the fact that Switzerland, which has always gravitated towards the Franco-Italian region, was incorporated into the German sphere, the Maghreb found itself in the Arab East and so forth; while the break up of the socialist camp resulted in a revision of geopolitical concepts, restructuring went on until the Soviet Foreign Ministry ceased to exist.

As regards the Ministry's functional subdivisions, of these there are no more than ten; purely administrative departments are excluded. They include the secretariats, policy planning and analysis, the press and information section, the protocol and the consular service, treaty law, history and archives, as well as subdivisions concerned with numerous general and global problems, including the UN, disarmament and regional conflicts.

Expansion of the Foreign Ministry and its function in fact began as far back as the 1960s. First the decision was made to establish the Directorate for Foreign Policy Planning, mentioned above and then the Ministry was given part of the liquidated Committee for Cultural Relations with Foreign Countries under the USSR Council of Ministers (it retained the same name but had considerably reduced powers); next new divisions were formed, the Executive Secretariat of the Commission for UNESCO was transferred and the Information Department of the CPSU Central Committee (foreign political propaganda) was abolished. No changes whatever occurred over the next two decades but in 1985 at least 15 functional subdivisions were added, many of which are still there.

However, whereas the territorial subdivisions grew in number under the impact of external, objective developments (the birth of new states), the increased number of functional subdivisions may be regarded as a sign of hegemonistic aspirations that bred even more functions. Indeed, in its final stage, the Soviet Foreign Ministry included even the former Ministry of Foreign Trade plus other structures involving foreign economic ties.

It was in fact, owing to this trend that by the end of the Soviet period the USSR Foreign Ministry Board of Directors include not one single territorial subdivision head – there were only heads of directorates. This was also an evident reflection of the new foreign policy concept, which tended to focus more on general, global arenas to the sphere of bilateral relations.

Some of the functional subdivisions were established very late. For instance, as talks on various nuclear missile systems and chemical, bacteriological and conventional weapons were drawing to a close, a subdivision was set up for the problems of arms limitation and disarmament. At the same time, a subdivision for security and cooperation in Europe and a subdivision for humanitarian cooperation were added to the Ministry.

The first reform of the Russian MFA in 1992 did not exactly rectify the above-mentioned distortions and deficiencies, but instead enlarged a number of existing subdivisions. Some artificial structures such as the Foreign Economic Relations Committee were disbanded and new departments were established – for instance, several in charge of CIS affairs and another responsible for liaisons with parliament, political parties and public organizations. An elementary structural unit would become a department. However, it was not long before it was realized that such a step simple lengthened the hierarchical ladder: deputy director of department, head of directorate, deputy head of directorate and then finally head of desk, which meant that another rung had put in its appearance between leader and executor. A department director is in principle invested with the same functions and is as responsible as the former head of a division; the officials on the above list used to serve as a sector. The end of 1993 saw another reorganization intended to create a better balance between the territorial and functional departments. The basic structures are now as follows.

1. Regional Subdivisions. Department in Charge of CIS Affairs, First European Department, Second European Department, Third European Department, Fourth European Department, Department for Cooperation in Europe, Department for North America, Department for North America, Department for Latin America, Department for Middle East and North Africa, Department for Africa, First Asian Department, Second Asian Department, Third Asian Department and Fourth Asian Department.
2. Functional Subdivisions. Department for Liaison with the Members of the Federation, Parliament and Political and Public Organizations, Department for International Organizations, Department for Disarmament and Military Equipment, Department for International Humanitarian and Cultural Cooperation, Department for Information and the Press, Department for Economic Cooperation, Legal Department, Division for International Scientific and Technological Cooperation, Personnel Department, Consular Service Department, State Protocol Department, Department for History and Documentation,[8] Department of Foreign Policy Planning, Department of Translation, Judicial Department, Administrative Department, Department of Information, General Management Department, Financial Department, Construction and Foreign Property Department and Supplementary Resources Department.

The reorganization included an ill-planned reduction of the Analysis and Foreign Policy Planning Division. Such a measure can hardly be judged rational in the face of the systematic criticism of the MFA in the Russian mass media for its 'unreasoned, improvised and erratic' foreign policy.[9] The consequences were even worse: the MFA cooperation with the Russian academic community, which had bloomed under the patronage of Minister Shevardnadze, came almost to a halt. The Russian MFA is hardly to be blamed; there were simply no financial resources nor incentives of note for fruitful cooperation with the academic community.

In early 1995, the situation in the MFA came under the Russian president's scrutiny. As a result Yeltsin issued a number of decrees aimed at raising the social standards for diplomats, developing the MFA material and technological potential and strengthening the status of the MFA in general.[10]

The salaries of diplomats stationed in poor-climate countries and low-income countries were to be raised. For diplomats serving in embassies in politically and militarily unstable countries, bonuses were introduced. There was US$30 million allocated for the repair and reconstruction of MFA buildings abroad. Welfare measures for MFA personnel was to be provided by a special fund for social and material development, created from a 10 per cent levy on the MFA's non-budget income from the activities of the Consular Service and Diplomatic Corps Service Division (UPDK). However, many analysts noted the sad fact that Russian diplomats' salaries were not to be increased regardless of the positive intent of these decrees. The continued existence of the Russian diplomatic corps is therefore still under threat.

The major criticism was directed towards the decree that set down the status of the MFA and its role in foreign policy decision making. During its 4 years of existence, the Russian MFA was sharply criticized by many experts for its inability to coordinate foreign policy, a task given to the Ministry by a Presidential Decree of 8 November 1992, as well as for its administrative inefficiency.[11] It was pointed out that the MFA's deficiencies were due to the lack of a viable decision-making mechanism in the field of foreign policy in general. To rectify this problem, a proposal was made to establish an inter-ministerial body under the president and the MFA was to find its niche within that structure. It is no accident that in February 1995 the presidential address to the Russian Parliament mentioned 'better coordination of foreign policy' as a priority task. Later in his address to the Duma Yeltsin was more specific: 'effective conduct of foreign policy requires establishment of an effective mechanism for inter-ministerial coordination reporting to the President'. The experts considered that this statement expressed the failure of the MFA to constitute this mechanism. If their forecasts are right and a coordinating body is established under the presidential administration, then the MFA will be relieved of some of its powers.[12]

Kozyrev therefore considered that the new Presidential Decree had successfully halted the formation of an interministerial coordinating and supervising body with a weighty say in foreign policy within the presidential apparatus. According to some estimates, such a body had been created by the minister himself in accordance with the provisions of the MFA statutes. The evidence given by some analysts to support this opinion was the declared intention to re-establish a department for analysis and foreign policy planning. Moreover, a number of observers considered the Presidential Decree to represent a substantial broadening of the Foreign Minister's authority, the most considerable since the end of the Second World War. To the end of the strengthening of the powers of the 'president–minister' duo, the decree provides for an unprecedented expansion of the authority of the MFA and the Foreign Minister. According to the decree, the MFA shall 'determine the general foreign policy strategy of the Russian Federation', conduct 'Russian foreign policy', coordinate and supervise the activities of other federal institutions 'so as to ensure a uniform Russian foreign policy in relations with foreign states and organizations' and 'promulgate legal acts that shall be binding on other executive branches of the Federation'. There is no procedure for the appointment of the minister or his endorsement by the legislature; the minister and his deputies are appointed by the president. The minister is responsible for appointing department heads and other head officials. The minister also submits proposals for the appointment and dismissal of ambassadors, as well as of the heads of official state and government delegations. Since the power to appoint ambassadors and the heads of official delegations is invested in the president, no other approval is needed. Russian press observers noted that 'the return of the nomenklatura', against which Kozyrev had warned in past times, had been successfully completed.[13]

In light of the above discussion, it seems evident that the situation in the MFA and the status of the MFA within the system of foreign policy decision making is still quite ambivalent. A new wave of criticism started on 17–18 May 1995 by the Russian media is testimony to this effect. For example, the Moscow daily *Nezavisimaia Gazeta* published a lengthy article signed by Nina Petrova, which contained the following lines:

> ... We may disagree with the Communist ideology, but it is a fact that in the former USSR there was a smoothly working system of decision-making in that field. After collapse of the old paradigm nothing was created in its place. The lack of such, as the past year's experience amply demonstrates (that is, Russian deliberations on the issue of the Kuril islands, NATO expansionist plans, the Bosnian crisis, the CIS affair, Middle East conflict resolution) results in actions taken on impulse, which

then prove to be incoherent and sometimes mutually contradictory. That practice grossly discredits the President's foreign policy and is viewed as a dangerous symptom of an unpredictable post-Communist Russia.

It is high time to introduce at least some basic orderly procedures for submitting proposals and for decision-making in the sphere of foreign policy and national security, which are properly the domain of the MFA and other bodies. There should be a supervisory agency encharged with ensuring that foreign policy is conducted in strict conformity with presidential guidelines. Improvisations and home-made actions must be thoroughly prohibited. Russia's voice should sound credible and consistent to the world at large. It is high time to activate the presidential mechanism for foreign policy coordination, and the prerequisite for that is the establishment of a strong, special body reporting to the president, such as was declared in his address to the Chamber of the Federation.

Finally, the need to replace the present Russian Foreign Minister is growing more urgent. Personally he has become a patent liability to the President and the Government at home, in that he is one of the major obstacles to the consolidation of political forces on foreign policy issues.[14]

Quite recently, in the summer of 1995, Prime Minister Victor Chernomyrdin set up a special government commission headed by Sergei Shakhrai to examine Foreign Ministry activities for their effectiveness and to prepare recommendations for improving its performance. Soon after the commission began its work, its chairman was dismissed and his place was taken by the Vice-Prime Minister Vitali Ignatenko, who was responsible for government relations with the mass media. The commission finished its job in early autumn and submitted its assessment to the prime minister and the president. After almost a month of silence, with no reports in the press concerning the reaction of either the president or the prime minister to the commission's findings, it was reported in early October that the president had expressed his displeasure at the performance of the Foreign Ministry at a meeting with his advisors. In a TV interview on 15 October Andrei Kozyrev indicated that 'the criticism of presidential aides is not the criticism of the President himself' and implied that he felt sure of his invulnerable stature. Only 3 days later Boris Yeltsin announced his decision to dismiss his foreign minister during an interview with the Russian and foreign press. Kozyrev was blamed for ineptitude in coordinating foreign policy and maintaining a dialogue with other government bodies that also have a say in the formulation of foreign policy. However, the very next day, 20 October, the President said at the airport before leaving for France that because of his frequent travels abroad

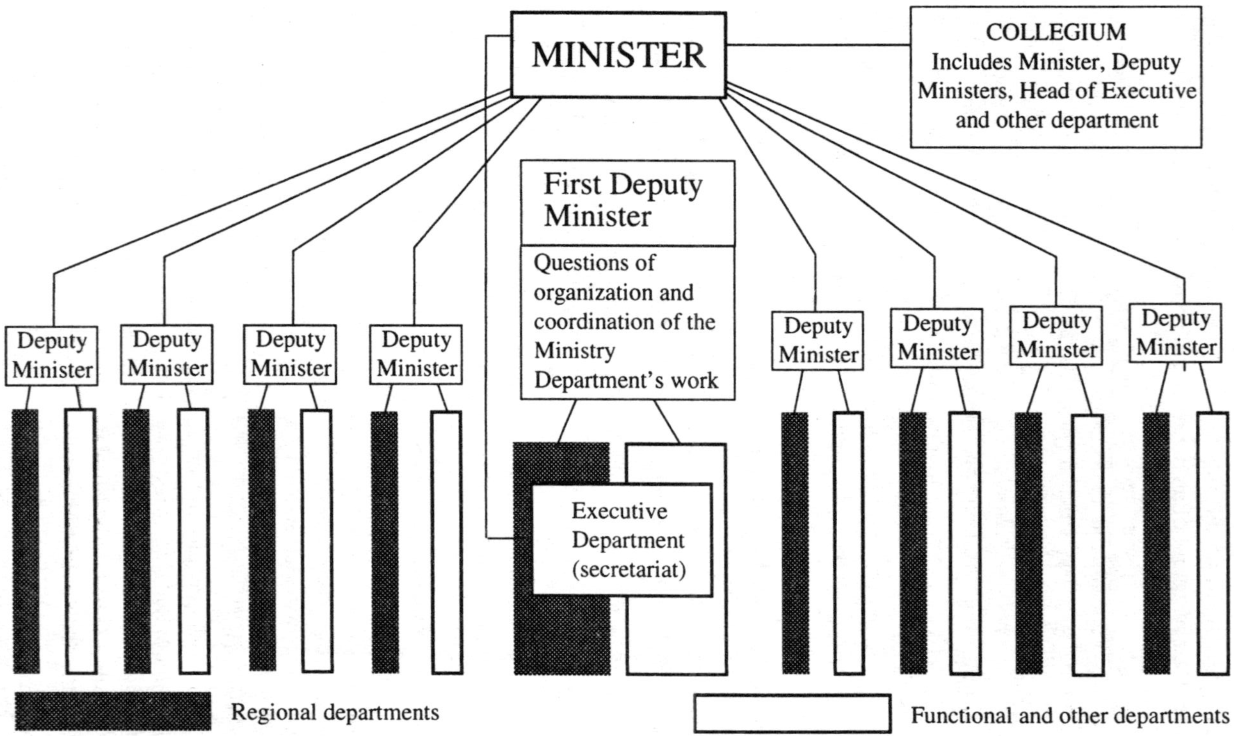

Figure 2.1 The Russian Foreign Ministry: Administrative Division

Andrei Kozyrev requires a good First Deputy to monitor the activities of the Foreign Ministry, watch over cadre policy and so on. The president's abrupt and unexplained correction of his assessment of his foreign minister's activities caused even greater confusion within the Ministry and occasioned a renewed blast of criticism from the press.[15]

A new sign of instability in the Russian MFA and of its head was the establishment of the President's Council on Foreign Policy, announced in late December 1995. Its task is to coordinate the various aspects of Russia's foreign policy. This, together with the fact that Mr Kozyrev was elected deputy to the State Duma and had to choose between that post and his ministerial post, not only was considered symptomatic of the weakness of the MFA, but also spurred rumours that the head figure in Russian diplomacy was about to retire. Speculation in the press was abruptly curtailed by the president's unexpected decree on 5 January 1996, announcing Kozyrev's retirement from his post as minister of foreign affairs. Three days later Evgenii Primakov was appointed to replace him by another presidential decree. Commentators are practically unanimous in their positive assessment of the two presidential decisions, regarded as a sign of a long-awaited consolidation of the Ministry and of foreign policy in general. The process of reform in the MFA still has a long way to go. Its performance can only be determined with reference to the overall process of stabilization of Russia's internal political, economic and social situation.

NOTES

1. A. de Tanguy, 'Vihod Rossii na mejdunarodnuiu arenu', *Mirovaia ekonomika i mejdunarodnyie otnosheniia*, No. 7 (1992), p. 67.
2. *Diplomaticheskii vestnik*, No. 1 (1992), p. 6.
3. *Diplomaticheskii vestnik*, No. 1 (1992), pp. 27–8.
4. *Diplomaticheskii vestnik*, No. 6 (1992), p. 10.
5. V. Kariagin, 'Diplomaticheskaia slujba: vchera, segodnia, zavtra', *Mejdunarodnaia jizn*, No. 10 (1994). *Diplomaticheskii vestnik*, No. 2–3 (1992), pp. 28–35.
6. *Diplomaticheskii vestnik*, No. 2/3 (1992), pp. 25–7.
7. *Diplomaticheskii vestnik*, No. 11/12 (1993), pp. 39–41. *Segodnia*, 25 November 1994.
8. *Diplomaticheskii vestnik*, No. 1/2 (1994), pp. 58–60.
9. A. Migranian, 'Vneshniaia politika Rossii: Katastroficheskie itogi trioh let'. 'Pora sdelat pauzu, pomeniat i politiku, i ministra', *Nezavisimaia gazeta*, 10 December 1994. S. Karaganov, 'Bez rulia i bez vetril', *Moskovskie novosti*, No. 66 (25 December 1994).

10. *Izvestiia*, 17 March 1995, p. 3.
11. *Diplomaticheskii vestnik*, No. 23/24 (1992), p. 59.
12. *Segodnia*, 12 February 1995.
13. *Segodnia*, 24 March 1995.
14. N. Petrova, 'Vneshniaia politika doljna stat prezidentskoi', *Nezavisimaia gazeta*, 17–18 May 1995.
15. M. Pavlova-Silvanskaia, 'Zaranee obiavlennaia otstavka', *Novoe vremia*, No. 43 (1995), pp. 8–9.

3 The Problem of Mongolia's National Security and its Guarantees

E. Boikova

Mongolia was the first Asian country of the 'world socialist system' to initiate democratization. This was in the late 1980s and by 1990, the process had become a full-scale peaceful democratic revolution.

Fundamental changes took place in all fields of social life in Mongolia – in the economy, in politics, in culture, in religion. One of the most striking effects of this process has been a fundamental change in Mongolian attitudes toward their national culture, traditions and customs.

After the democratic revolution of 1990, Mongolia was free to pursue an independent, pragmatic foreign policy, unencumbered by ideological influence. Before that time, the foreign policy of Mongolia, as well as that of the other countries of the socialist community, was tightly bound by the strictures of a 'coordinated foreign policy', first of all with the Soviet Union but also with its allies. Hence, Mongolia's foreign policy was oriented towards Europe despite the meagre possibilities of maintaining mutually beneficial bilateral relations with Western countries. Now, however, Mongolia is guided in its foreign policy by the criteria of effectiveness, equality and mutual advantage. Within a few years of the onset of democratic change Mongolia began to overcome its isolation. A prime task was to determine its new place and role in the world and to adjust its relations with Russia and China. Mongolia had to reduce its economic and political dependence on these two countries if it wished to participate more actively in worldwide cooperation.

The geopolitical factor plays an essential role in the political and socioeconomic development of any state. One can say that Mongolia's geographical position, 'sandwiched' between Russia and China, defines foreign policy priorities for it. In the early 1990s, Mongolia officially declared that it would cultivate its relations with its two neighbours on the principle of equality. Insofar as the geopolitical parameters of Russia and China were similar, Mongolia's approach to both of them proceeded along parallel lines. Its age-old problem, with Russia against China or with China against Russia, no longer exists. Rejecting the ideology of interalliance, Mongolia can now give priority to its own national interests in developing its relations with its two neighbouring countries. It is important that these relations must be balanced.

The reorientation of Mongolia's foreign policy has also cast the problem of national security in a new light. From the early 1920s down to 1990, the USSR had effectively assumed the role of ensuring Mongolia's external security – indeed, for all practical purposes it was its sole guarantor. For the better part of this century, Mongolia was under Soviet military and political influence. Soviet troops were stationed in Mongolia, the USSR sent weapons and military equipment and trained military specialists for the Mongolian Army and Soviet military advisers worked in the country.

Today Mongolia enjoys a relative political, social and interethnic stability. True, the different political parties and political forces each have their own views of where the country should be going and the internal political situation has been trying. However, now there are no serious internal conflicts (including ethnic) in Mongolia. Partial credit for this must be given to the idea of national revival, which brings together all the ethnic and social groups as well as the different political forces. It has become the foundation for the national unity of the Mongolians.

As for the problem of safeguarding national security, it has essentially two aspects: (1) internal – political and economic stability, maintaining a legal state, and the security of national culture, traditions and customs and (2) external – Mongolia's relations with Russia and China and with other countries and possible involvement in worldwide, regional and subregional conflicts.

In the light of the above, it is probably safe to say that no major local conflicts currently threaten Mongolia's security, although such a threat has not been removed completely, particularly on a subregional level. In 1994, a plan for the national security of Mongolia was approved by the Great State Khural. It states that national security consists of the following main components.

1. The security of Mongolia's existence.
2. The security of the social order and the state system.
3. The security of civil rights and freedoms.
4. Economic security.
5. Scientific and technological security.
6. The security of information.
7. The security of the Mongolian culture.
8. The security of the population and its gene pool.
9. Ecological security.[1]

The plan for national security is symbolic of Mongolia's real national independence, that is that Mongolia can henceforth choose its own priorities in cultivating its external contacts. All aspects of the plan show that Mongolian leaders see the problem of national security as a complex set of internal and external factors determining their country's development.

Factors affecting security are divided into internal and external in accordance with their origins and into immediate, temporary, long-term and permanent depending on their duration.

National security is ensured by social, political, organizational, economic, diplomatic and military factors, unilaterally or through the cultivation of international cooperation.

Mongolia provides for its national security by its own means as far as possible. It has declared that it will pursue a multibased policy, expanding its relations with other countries, particularly with influential ones. The foreign policy is manifested in the following ways.

1. The development of bilateral relations.
2. Participation in the solution of regional problems, in multilateral regional cooperation.
3. Cooperation with regional international organizations, including financial organizations.

Mongolia obviously does not have sufficient economic and military resources to meet its own security needs and safeguard its vital interests. To ensure its national security, Mongolia must rely exclusively on political, diplomatic and legal means, with additional support from its partners and from international, peaceful forces. Indeed, Mongolia does not have a large enough army to defend against any aggressor. The overall strength of the army is no more than 15 000.[2]

Mongolia has declared a policy of neutrality which will permit no foreign troops and arms, nuclear weapons and other kinds of weapons of mass destruction to enter upon or move over its territory.

Mongolia is currently drafting a law to make it a nuclear-free zone. The USA, Russia, France, Great Britain and China have officially recognized the nuclear-free status of Mongolia.

Let us now dwell in a bit more detail on Mongolia's contemporary bilateral relations with Russia and China. Mongolia's relations with its neighbours, which are based on mutual respect for each other's independence, sovereignty and territorial integrity and on the inviolability of state borders, play a key role in both its foreign policy and its internal democratic reforms.

In the early 1990s, its bilateral relations with Russia were practically dormant. They must now be restored, in some cases starting again from the bottom. Outwardly, it may have seemed that the decline in cooperative relations between the two countries was at Mongolia's initiative, taken for ideological reasons. However, the main factors in this development were the difficulties both countries were experiencing in implementing their economic and political reforms and the problems raised by the reorientation of Russian foreign policy towards the West. That is, the determining factor was the ideology of Russia's new political leaders.

After the disintegration of the USSR (which fundamentally altered Mongolia's international position), Russia was unable simply to succeed the Soviet Union in bilateral relations with Mongolia. Mongolia has been a sphere of national interest and influence since the end of the nineteenth century, first of tsarist Russia and then of the Soviet Union. The deployment of Soviet troops on the territory of Mongolia in the 1960s gave the USSR an ideal springboard for an invasion of China, if that should ever become a serious possibility.[3] However, Russia's interests in Mongolia have now changed. The primary aim of Russia's Eastern policy in the past was the development of relations with old as well as new, prospective partners – India, China, South Korea, Japan and the countries of Southeast Asia. The traditional partners, Mongolia and Vietnam, while remaining within Russia's sphere of national interests, occupied a less important position once the stereotypes of ideologized friendship no longer applied. The lowering of the level of confrontation in the world, including the northeastern Asian region and the deideologization of foreign relations have made Mongolia's importance to Russia as an ally less important in terms of the dictates of military strategy. However, Russia's orientation towards Western countries has since become more moderated, with more attention now being given to its own national interests; a more heedful eye to the East is evidence of that process.

In 1990, the country was the scene of a rather aggressive anti-Soviet campaign initiated by young Mongolian democrats (for the most part educated in the Soviet Union). They tried to arrive at an objective assessment – they thought – of the results of 70 years of development under the new historical conditions created by the revolution of 1921 and of Mongolian–Soviet cooperation during that period. Their conclusions were for the most part negative: the Soviet Union was blamed for most if not all the mistakes and errant courses in Mongolia's development. Some politicians even drew an analogy between the rule of the Chinese Tsing Empire in Mongolia before 1921 and the Soviet presence in the Mongolian People's Republic. For almost 3 years, the democratic Mongolian mass media worked at creating an image of the enemy in the person of the Soviet Union and then of Russia.

The Mongolian Government headed by D. Biambasuren, which came to power in 1990 and contained representatives of almost all the main political parties and movements, began actively to pursue a policy of 'self-reliance'; one practical result of this policy was the expulsion of all Soviet specialists, military consultants, builders and so on from Mongolia. Finally, in the mid-1990s the negative assessments and opinions began to recede, giving way to attempts at a more sensible approach to all issues of bilateral relations. We might comment in passing that it was rather unlikely that the new image of the Soviet Union/Russia as an enemy could take deep root in the consciousness of the Mongols, since for decades Mongolian and Soviet leaders had cultivated the sentiment of 'an inviolable Soviet–Mongolian friendship'.

Mongolia's aim in breaking relations with Russia was to free herself from political and ideological dependence on Russia, but the price of this was the loss of many of the advantages of the bilateral trade and economic ties. In the opinion of the Director of the Institute of Oriental and International Studies of the Mongolian Academy of Sciences, Ts. Batbayar, the Mongolian Government had let slip the chance to fill the void formed in Mongolia's foreign relations as a result of the disintegration of the Soviet Union by acting swiftly to restore full political and economic relations with the newly independent republics of the former USSR and in particular the Russian Federation; by early 1993 it was already late in the day.[4]

Nevertheless, Russia is still Mongolia's key economic and trade partner, although in 1994 Russian–Mongolian trade cooperation had decreased by 54 per cent compared with 1990.[5] Russia's share in Mongolia's total trade volume was 39.5 per cent in 1994.[6]

According to findings from sociologic surveys, a majority of Mongolians consider improvement and further growth of trade and economic relations with Russia to be necessary conditions for overcoming their country's economic difficulties.

By the end of 1992, Mongolian officials had realized as much as well, namely that without Russia economic development was likely to remain beyond the horizon. Although the new political forces were very determined to cultivate relations only with the economically developed Western and Asian states, sober-mindedness and an objective approach to this question prevailed. The fact of the matter is that Mongolia has no real choice; the country's geographical and geopolitical situation leaves no alternative.

The beginning of the normalization of Russian–Mongolian relations coincided with the final withdrawal of Soviet troops from Mongolia in 1992.[7] However, Mongolian scholar S. Bayar considers that 'the Soviet retreat from Mongolia can be viewed as a concession to China rather than respect for Mongolia's independence'.[8] He calls it 'one more move in the great game of Asia', but it is difficult to agree with this view.

In 1993, Russia and Mongolia signed a Treaty of Friendly Relations and Cooperation. This new treaty differs fundamentally from the earlier friendship treaty signed in 1966. That treaty gave priority to the interests of the socialist community rather than to national interests. The new treaty attends to the vital interests of the partners and is a legal document for an equitable and mutually beneficial cooperation that rules out any kind of interference in domestic affairs. Russia and Mongolia declared that they were ready to develop normal and stable relations while taking full advantage of their long and broad experience of cooperation and the positive traditions of neighbourliness. A very important clause of the new treaty commits both parties not to participate in any alliance directed against each other, nor to conclude any treaties or agreements with third countries that infringe upon the other's independence and sovereignty.[9] Russia pledges in turn to respect Mongolia's policy of not allowing foreign troops or nuclear and other weapons of mass destruction to be stationed on or to traverse its territory.

The problem of the repayment of Mongolia's debt to Russia, which is more than US$16 billion, heavily complicates the bilateral relations.[10] Mongolia insists that its debt to Russia is approximately US$10 billion; some Mongolian politicians and scholars even argue that Mongolia owes Russia nothing at all.[11] At Russian–Mongolian high-level negotiations the Russian delegation announced that Russia would not pressure Mongolia in this matter and would not allow it to influence Russian–Mongolian relations negatively.

Now that it is not dependent on Russia's political patronage, Mongolia is ready for reasonable military–technical cooperation. Such cooperation conforms with the interests of both countries and contemporary geopolitical relations in the subregion. In 1993, they signed an Agreement on Military–Technical Cooperation.

According to some Mongolian politicians, if Russia became the guarantor of Mongolian national security this would at the same time serve as a counterbalance to China and those South-East Asian countries hostile towards Mongolia. Even if it meant only political and legal and not military guarantees, the implementation of this idea would require devising a special political mechanism for cooperation in this area inasmuch as previous military cooperation had been limited to matters of defence directed towards China. However, neither the Russian nor the Mongolian Governments are ready to work out a system of unilateral guarantees for Mongolian national security. Russia is reluctant to play the role of guarantor. Moreover, Russia does not want to be accused of adopting 'the imperial syndrome' towards Mongolia. Before it can become a guarantor of the national security of any other country, Russia first needs political and economic stability. Besides, given all the conflicts, often military, taking place in the republics of the former

Soviet Union and in Russia in which Russian troops are involved Russia can ill afford to take up the problems of the national security of any other state. And to this it must frankly be added that Russia does not have the necessary political experience in peaceful conflict resolution.

The words of Russia's Deputy Defence Minister A. Kokoshin are to the point: 'We have one foot in Asia, the other in Europe; our face however is turned more to Europe'.[12]

Nevertheless, Russia and Mongolia have achieved some bilateral cooperation in problems of national security. In 1995, the representatives of the National Security Councils of the two countries signed a Memorandum on Bilateral Cooperation in the Sphere of National Security. This cooperation focuses primarily on such issues as the consolidation of regional and international security, the non-nuclear status of Mongolia, its economic security and a joint struggle against weapon and drug smuggling.[13] Thus, even if Russia did become a guarantor of Mongolia's national security, this could not occur earlier than 5–10 years.

Mongolian–Chinese relations have improved since the end of the 1980s, thanks to a joint effort. High-level bilateral contacts have been established in practically all spheres – political, economic, trade, technical and cultural. A number of treaties and agreements providing a legal framework for bilateral cooperation were signed between Mongolia and China. China is Mongolia's second most important trading partner (more than 24 per cent of the total volume in 1994).

Mongolian officials are looking forward to new positive turn and new prospects in Mongolian–Chinese relations. However, more and more, politicians have been voicing misgivings over Chinese intentions, which they fear are aimed at weakening Mongolia through the use of economic, demographic and propaganda measures.

Some political forces in Mongolia have doubts that relations with China will be of equal advantage to both. In 1994, Mongolia and China signed a Treaty of Friendly Relations and Cooperation. The Mongolian opposition perceived this treaty negatively. In their mind, it infringes considerably on Mongolia's rights from the point of view of international law and could morally damage the country. The treaty addresses, in particular, the sphere of international, humanitarian relations and contacts among peoples whereas the Mongols are in fact restricted in their contacts with the Mongol-speaking population in China. The treaty provides no mechanisms for resolving disputes, either through negotiations or by any other means.[14] The General Secretary of the Mongolian Democratic Party of Renascence, L. Purevdorj, feels that the Mongolian–Chinese treaty leaves the door open for China to adopt a high-handed approach to potential problems in bilateral relations.

Some politicians in Mongolia are not satisfied that the treaty is unconditional, in contrast to the Mongolian–Russian treaty, which was concluded 20 years ago.

Chinese commercial capital is now actively flowing into Mongolia. This could of course constitute a potential threat to Mongolia's economic security. China would obviously like to secure the Mongolian raw materials market for itself and to make Mongolia a market for low-quality Chinese goods. Indeed, China is pursuing a policy of calculated destruction of the Mongolian economy, a 'bloodless war' against Mongolia. The number of Chinese immigrants to Mongolia has greatly increased in recent years and their entry is now practically unregulated. Many Chinese have settled in the border areas of Mongolia. By official counts there are more than 90 000 Chinese in Mongolia, but unofficially there are probably twice as many. Mongolian politicians fear that Chinese immigration into their country, if allowed to proceed, could easily reduce the Mongols to a minority in their own country, which is exactly what happened in Inner Mongolia.

The official view is that Mongolian–Chinese relations are developing in an atmosphere of manifest trust and eagerness to expand economic bilateral cooperation. However, present realities have deeper historical roots which dampen these enthusiastic assessments somewhat. It is important to bear in mind that China has not abandoned its great power aspirations or its strategic policy of Sinization of small nations. Although Chinese leaders make regular pronouncements about friendly relations between their country and Mongolia, very many history textbooks, geographical maps and other documents have been published that treat Mongolia as a part of China. Mongolians of the older and middle-aged generations remember and feel certain that China has never lost its hope of annexing Mongolia. This has left deep traces in the national consciousness of the Mongols. Therefore, it is imperative that Mongol distrust of the Chinese and perceptions of China as a potential threat be allayed as quickly as possible. The Mongolians' traditional wariness towards China must necessarily influence the state of relations between these two countries.

For their part, Chinese leaders do not want Mongolian democratic reform to have destructive influences on multiethnic China and in particular not on Inner Mongolia, where they could provoke conflicts and reinforce separatist tendencies. However, at the same time China intentionally exaggerates the danger of pan-Mongolian ideas in Mongolia and their influence on the Mongol-speaking peoples. Since a normal development of Mongolian–Chinese relations should strengthen guarantees of Mongolia's national security, Mongolia is naturally interested in military cooperation with China. Contacts between Mongolia and China in the military sphere have remained minimal since the 1960s, owing to ideological and political differences. In 1991, the Mongolian Defence Minister visited China for the first time after a long hiatus.

Mongolia is apprehensive about China's nuclear tests close to the Mongolian border. China has conducted more than 40 nuclear tests at the Lop Nor test site, of which 23 were above ground. Unfortunately, China is generally dismissive of Mongolia's reaction to its nuclear tests.

A look at the Plan for Mongolian National Security will show that the above problems in Mongolian–Chinese relations have a direct bearing on at least four items in this document, specifically, those concerning external factors which could adversely affect Mongolia's long-term security: (1) the imposition of political, military, economic and ideological control over Mongolia, (2) destabilization of the Mongolian economy, (3) attempts to organize or organizing *coup d'etats* or the use of Mongolia as a bridgehead for policies and activities directed against other countries and (4) altering international borders, illegal border crossings and border violations and massive inflows of migrants from a neighbouring state.

China enjoys the same important status as Russia in Mongolia's official foreign policy doctrine. However, there is one major difference: Russia has never threatened Mongolian statehood, while historically China represents the threat of annexation for Mongolia. Obviously, this introduces serious complications in bilateral relations. Mongolia would certainly never regard China as a guarantor of its national security. It is not surprising for this reason that Mongolian foreign policy should lean towards Russia.

The normalization of Russian–Chinese relations is having a positive influence on the political atmosphere in the region. The stabilization of relations between the two nuclear powers is very important for Mongolia. In the 1950–1960s, Mongolia had reaped considerable benefits from mutual cooperation with its two neighbours and normal Russian–Chinese relations could provide new opportunities for Mongolia. Mongolia has a strong interest in successful Russian–Chinese cooperation in all fields and is eager to join any efforts aimed at maintaining the stability in the Central Asian region. However, the normalization of bilateral relations between Russia and China cannot be an absolute guarantee of Mongolia's national security.

In the early 1990s, Mongolia expanded its relations with the economically developed countries, particularly in the Asia–Pacific region, with a view to attracting foreign capital to bolster its economy. The official Mongolian view is that economic contacts must become one of the pillars of the country's foreign relations. The diversification of Mongolia's external economic ties was a priority as the country grew more independent. Having declared an open economic policy, Mongolia must now guarantee foreign business investments in the national economy. The Law on Foreign Investments has been in force in Mongolia since 1 July 1993. It precipitated a foreign capital flow in the Mongolian economy. The volume of foreign investment in the Mongolian economy quadrupled in 1994, compared with 1993.[15]

Mongolia has good contacts in a variety of spheres with Japan, the USA, South Korea, Hong Kong, Germany, UK and other European and Asian countries. Japan continues to nurture a major interest in Mongolia. After the Second World War when the Soviet influence spread into East Asia, Japanese foreign policy emphasized economic rather than military expansion. Mongolia is traditionally of great importance to Japan. Now Japan, like the USA and China, is eager to fill the vacuum that was left by Russia's departure. In 1990, Japan supported the political forces for renewal in Mongolia. Japanese capital has become more active in Mongolia as it has in other Asian countries and Japan is interested in investment cooperation with Mongolia. By the mid-1990s, Japan had become one of Mongolia's biggest trading partners and investors.

Mongolian officials are pursuing a policy of broader economic cooperation with Japan since they hope that it will help strengthen Mongolia. However, although they deny that encouraging Japanese capital expansion could be unsafe for Mongolia, the reality is that this expansion could have grave political as well as economic consequences.

It is particularly noteworthy that Japan has been contracted to develop a modern communication infrastructure in Mongolia. The Russian expert on Mongolia, G. Yaskina, thinks that Japan intends to exploit this infrastructure to further its strategic plans to meet its internal needs for raw materials at the expense of mainland countries.[16]

According to the Mongolian intelligentsia, the Japanese are using cultural aid to Mongolia to conduct pro-Japanese propaganda. Some politicians in Mongolia see Japan as a possible threat to the national security since Mongolia is still part of the Japanese geopolitical strategy in Asia.

Mongolia is developing economic, political, military and cultural cooperation with the USA and Germany. Military cooperation is definitely a new phenomenon in Mongolia's contacts with these countries: it entails the training of Mongolian military specialists and cooperation in military–technical fields. Both countries are prepared to expand these contacts to ensure Mongolia's national security. However, the possibility of an American and German military presence in the subregion could complicate the situation in general as well as Chinese–American relations. China obviously has no interest in strengthening the role of the USA in this area. Mongolia and the USA are conducting bilateral consultations on the issue of Mongolian national security. The USA is pursuing an active investment policy in Mongolia.

The American and Japanese factors in Mongolian affairs are growing stronger. Mongolian politicians feel that their 'geopolitical dream' of having a third partner is becoming a reality. What is the reason for Mongolia's desire to have this third partner? The answer is clearly that besides the tangible economic advantages and the possibility of broader human contacts and so on, the availability of a third partner, politically, economically and militarily strong, could serve as a counterweight in balancing Mongolia's relations with its immediate neighbours. As S. Bayar notes, 'the presence of three relatively equal partners will enable Mongolia to build up independent relations with all three while avoiding the dominance of any of them'.

Some Mongolian politicians think that Mongolia has in fact acquired a strong third partner which is not a single country, but a combination of several countries, including the USA, Japan, South Korea, Germany and some other Western countries, as well as international economic and financial organizations, such as the World Bank, the International Monetary Fund, the Asian Development Bank and others. Obviously, such a 'collective partner', while being relevant more to economic than to political and military issues, can serve as a valuable support and encourage Mongolia to continue its pursuit of radical economic as well as political reforms.

Democratic changes in the system of Mongolian foreign relations and its course towards a market economy were met with sympathy by the world community. In 1990, the economically developed countries united in a donor movement to support democratic reforms in Mongolia. Initially the members of 'the donor club' were Japan (the chief coordinator), the USA, South Korea, Germany, UK, Denmark and Holland. Russia joined the donor movement later. The participants in this movement are also international financial and economic organizations: the World Bank, the International Monetary Fund and the Asian Development Bank. Mongolia's prime concern was to resolve the problem of its narrow dependence on the USSR and to distance itself from China. It thus intended to use donor aid not only for economic but also for political aims. The donor movement is growing steadily. In 1991, at the first meeting of the donor countries, there were 14 participant countries and three international organizations. In 1994, 26 countries and six international financial organizations participated in the fourth meeting in Tokyo. In 1995, Mongolia will receive long-term preferential credits and a gratuitous aid of US$210.1 million (including US$40 million in different forms of gratuitous aid).[17]

Mongolia coordinates its economic and investment activity with the International Monetary Fund, World Bank and Asian Development Bank. The programme 'Stand By', aimed at stabilizing the Mongolian economy in coordination with the International Monetary Fund, was completed in 1992.

Since 1993, the Mongolian Government has implemented the Enhanced Structural Adjustment Facility programme in cooperation with the International Monetary Fund to transform the structure of the country's economy. Mongolia is engaged in a joint project for improving its economic structure, developing its infrastructure and so on. The United Nations Development Programme has worked out a special programme for Mongolia to the end of 1996. Mongolia is a participant in the Technical Assistance (of EU) for CIS programme of the European Community.

However, Mongolia's cooperation with the donor countries has its negative side. The large financial assistance makes Mongolia more dependent on them. Although the donor countries declare that their assistance is intended to help Mongolia overcome excessive dependence on other countries, Mongolia in fact continues to be dependent on its creditors. In 1992, Mongolia's foreign debt payments were more than US$100 million;[18] in 1994 it was US$120 million.[19]

The role of the donor movement in Mongolia's development is assessed differently by the different political forces in the country. There is no doubt that it has become a very important factor in the acceleration of Mongolia's economic development.

Mongolia actively cooperates with the European Parliament. In 1994, the European Parliament adopted a resolution 'On the Political Situation in Mongolia' in which it declared its intentions to develop bilateral relations with the Great State Khural of Mongolia. The European Parliament offered to conclude a partnership agreement which would help to not only strengthen democracy in Mongolia but also promote the stabilization of the region.

As mentioned above, no force in the world presently threatens Mongolia, but there are some potential hot spots of tension in Asia and in Northeast Asia in particular which could complicate the situation. As no mechanisms as yet exist for guaranteeing regional security in Asia, Mongolia has to define on its own the conditions necessary for ensuring its national security and decide what partners should serve as its guarantors.

Mongolia's plan of national security states that the main guarantors of national security are the people of Mongolia and the Mongolian State. International guarantees – political, legal and moral–psychological – require a combination of unilateral, bilateral and multilateral measures. According to the plan, military and political security can be ensured through a collective security system.

The settlement of international conflicts requires the participation of the world community. A unilateral guarantee by any one country of the national security of another is not adequate to ensure the successful settlement of internal conflicts or conflicts between states.

Mongolia pursues a deliberate policy of drawing an increasing number of interested countries into economic cooperation with it; the interests of these countries in Mongolia then is more long-term and in this way Mongolia also increases the number of potential guarantors of its national security.

The world community is interested in an economically strong, stabilized and predictable Mongolia. Mongolia for its part would like to create a triangle of potential guarantors including first of all Russia, the USA, Japan, Germany and South Korea. Mongolia thinks that the collective efforts of interested countries could be the most effective. However, these countries are not yet ready for such a project. Those international organizations with which Mongolia cooperates extensively could also become the guarantors of its national security. The world community is interested in continuing to support the process of political, economic, social, cultural and military change in Mongolia. It does not want Mongolia to cause or be party to any conflict in Asia. The world community wants an independent, democratic Mongolia as a factor in the stability of the Asian region.

NOTES

1. *The Mongolian Journal of International Affairs*, Ulaan Baatar, no. 2 (1995), pp. 79–80.
2. Since 1990 Mongolian armed forces have been cut by 19 000 troops of the estimated 33 000 strong armed forces, *Ug*, 16 January 1994.
3. S. Bayar, 'Mongolia's National Security Challenges', *The Mongolian Journal of International Affairs*, Ulaan Baatar, no. 2 (1995), p. 6.
4. *The Mongol Messenger*, special issue, January 1993.
5. *Zasgjin gazryn medee*, 27 March 1994.
6. *Mongolia News*, 12 December 1994.
7. The USSR began the withdrawal of its military forces from Mongolia in 1987 (65 000 troops and 90 combat aircraft).
8. S. Bayar, op. cit. p. 6.
9. *Diplomaticheskii vestnik*, Moscow, nos 3–4 (February 1993), p. 16.
10. *Ardyn erch*, 15 March 1993.
11. *The Mongolian Journal of International Affairs*, Ulaan Baatar, no. 2 (1995), p. 49.
12. *Mezhdunarodnaya zhizn*, Moscow, no. 2 (1995), p. 62.
13. *The Mongolian Messenger*, 5 June 1995.
14. *Il tovchoo*, 19 February 1994.
15. *Press Bulletin of the Embassy of Mongolia in Russia* (March 1995), p. 4.
16. G. Yaskina, *Mongolia: the Change of the Models of Development* (in Russian) (Moscow, 1994), p. 302.
17. *Ardyn erch*, 14 December 1994.
18. *Atlas of the TASS*, no. 42, 19 October 1992.
19. *Ardyn erch*, 9 January 1995.

4 Turkmenistan's Place in Central Asia and the World

R. Freitag-Wirminghaus

The Caspian Sea region has become one of the most sensitive areas of the Commonwealth of Independent States (CIS) and of an enlarged Middle East. The vast resources of oil and natural gas have given a new relevance to the newly independent states of Kazakhstan, Azerbaijan and Turkmenistan in the domain of energy policy and geopolitics, both within the region as a whole and beyond. To put their natural resources at the service of developing and stabilizing their economies, these states have to find a way to enter the world market.

However, Turkmenistan's relevance derives not only from its ranking as a country with the fourth largest deposits of natural gas in the world. Equally important is its geostrategic location. Russian nationalists still consider the Iranian–Turkmen border to be a displaced Russian border, although Uzbekistan and Kazakhstan are situated between Russia and Turkmenistan. For Russia as well as for Uzbekistan, Turkmenistan is not only a buffer state against Iran, it also lies on Russia's route to the Persian Gulf. Like its pipelines, its transport and communication networks are linked up with Russia. For Iran and Turkey, as well as for India and Pakistan, Turkmenistan is a major transit country to the other Central Asian countries. Since the road and the railway line between Mashhad and Sarakhs on the Iranian–Turkmen border were completed in May 1996, they link the old Soviet network with the Middle East and the Indian subcontinent. This gives Turkmenistan a new importance as a gateway to Central Asia. However, the only reliable guarantee of Turkmenistan strengthening its status and building a stable economy is the permanent growth of its natural gas industry, enabling it to export gas in large quantities.

The plan for the gas and oil industry envisions the development of hitherto untapped deposits. This will mean extensive dependence on direct foreign investments. However, in addition to massive investments and modern technology Turkmenistan also needs highly qualified personnel. The backward infrastructure, both social and economic, raises doubts that resources can be exploited as soon and as quickly as contemplated.

TRADITIONAL STRUCTURES AND THE AUTOCRATIC POLITICAL SYSTEM

Turkmenistan appears to be the most stable country of the CIS. This is mainly because it largely preserved its traditional structures during the Soviet period. Tribal structures still dominate the life of the individual and the community. Intertribal loyalty and family control over the young generation (50 per cent under 16 years of age)[1] are together the most important factor of social life. There is also loyalty – to a lesser degree, but growing – to the collective as defined territorially, that is the Turkmen nation, which is a legacy of Soviet nation building. However, loyalties to the tribe or local community are usually stronger. Turkmenistan cannot be called a modern nation.

Disparate group loyalties must be balanced against one another in the process of building a national state in Turkmenistan. Hence, administrative boundaries tend to follow tribal and clan lines. Extreme nationalism is the exception and, in contrast to the other republics, interethnic relations are relatively stable. The population is 72 per cent Turkmen, 9.5 per cent Russian, 9 per cent Uzbek and 2.5 per cent Kazakh.[2] Although influential posts in the presidential apparatus are held by russified officials from the old nomenklatura and even by Russians, a Turkmenization of public life is taking place. Ethnicity is becoming an increasingly important factor in hiring or renting apartments. The Turkmen language, which will convert to the Latin alphabet in 1997, became the official language in 1990. However, no mass emigration of the Russian population has taken place. The government is trying to prevent such an exodus and to this end has reached an agreement with Russia on dual citizenship and has passed legislation prohibiting the export of private capital. However, there is a discernible drain of the Russian population. Official statistics, which claim a rise in the Russian population in Turkmenistan, have presumably been deliberately manipulated to present an image of a state free of conflicts. In 1991 25 per cent of the urban population were Russians, most of them in qualified positions. In addition, 32 per cent of the skilled workers and specialists were Russians; technical and scientific progress therefore depends mostly on them. However, it is just these specialists who are departing.[3] Emigration has already produced a lack of qualified workers and specialists in the economy.

Urbanization took place largely between the 1920s and the 1960s when the urban population grew from 14 to 48 per cent. Later, however, it subsided again and the proportion of industrial workers on the whole declined. The proportion of industrial workers of ethnic Turkmen origin was only 18 per cent in 1979 and has decreased further since then.[4] This is a manifest sign that the society at large has not yet experienced a reorientation from a rural to an urban way of life. The result is a conservative society clinging to tribal structures and values and very little inclination to understand the necessity of reforms.

Such conditions are obviously favourable to the further consolidation of existing power structures. However, the price of solid political structures is an inadequate sensitivity to the urgency of implementing the reforms needed for economic development. The lack of qualified technical élites means that one of the crucial preconditions for a stable and prospering economy is missing.

The present authoritarian regime in a sense reflects the tribal and localist mentality of the society at large. The various elections, held in traditional Communist style, with the most recent one confirming President Niyazov's reign with 99 per cent of the votes, perhaps overstate the case. Nevertheless, Niyazov, the former First Secretary of Turkmenistan's Communist Party, does seem to enjoy full backing from almost the entire population. Calling himself Turkmenbashi, 'Leader of the Turkmen', he has the strongest support in the country, all ethnic and tribal differences notwithstanding. He has gained a reputation as a protector of the traditional values of Turkmen society and its political culture. An extreme overlapping of traditional tribal and clan structures with Soviet-style political behaviour typifies the present political system of Turkmenistan. Identification with Turkmenbashi is a constitutive element of society. The excesses of the personality cult surrounding Turkmenbashi penetrates all spheres of life and at times seems a Stalinist caricature to Western eyes. However, for the rural population Niyazov is the khan standing above all particular clan interests and protecting the people from the abuses of bureaucratic tyranny. Yet communist elements seem to predominate over the traditional elements, considering that a khan was traditionally elected by a meeting of the council of elders in a free election and, moreover, for a limited time.

Power struggles are rife among the political class in the form of covert rivalry between different clans and tribes, but these have been cleverly exploited by Turkmenbashi to consolidate his position. To deter a threat to his position by competing clans, Niyazov has surrounded himself with loyal russified functionaries; on the other hand, representatives of the Turkmen élite with their tribal connections could be dangerous and are regularly replaced. However, the Teke tribe, to which Niyazov belongs, has more influence in the state apparatus than any other.

Turkmenistan was the first among the Central Asian states to receive a new constitution. It defines the form of government as a presidential republic. Only the president has the right to appoint and remove his local representatives, the hakims. The revival of the councils of elders on different levels signifies less a return to traditional values than a way to employ officials of the former nomenklatura. A parliament (madshlis) of 50 members serves as a legislative body. The People's Council (khalk maslahaty), Turkmenistan's supreme representative and legislative body, has only the power to legitimate the presidential orders. It consists of the members of parliament, the cabinet, the head of the supreme court and the provincial governors. The president possesses virtually unlimited power. He governs the country alone through his decrees and instructions. He heeds the opinions and wishes of the tribes, roughly 100 or so, among which are seven powerful clans, from whence originates the myth of his being an integrating figure. By the device of a plebiscite, in which he won 99.9 per cent approval, he was able to obtain constitutional guarantees and legalization of his position to the year 2004. According to its constitution, Turkmenistan is a democratic and secular constitutional state, but in reality it is a presidential autocracy which uses the constitutional idea of national unity to suppress opposition.

Niyazov was also able to integrate Islam into the image of Turkmen cultural identity and to gain the support of the Turkmen clergy, thus creating a curious blend of resurgent Islam and a secular dictatorship with its personality cult. An addendum to prayers runs 'All powerful Allah, preserve independent Turkmenistan, vouchsafe success to our beloved homeland and honoured President Saparmurat Turkmenbashi.'[5] One hundred and eighty mosques have been built, but the state still maintains strict control over the Islamic hierarchy. To underscore this point, the head of the Russian Orthodox Church in Turkmenistan was appointed deputy of the chairman of the Committee for Religious Affairs. Officially Turkmen Islam is portrayed as being unsuited by nature for militancy. The absence of a strong Islamist movement combined with the weakness of the national–democratic opposition is of course the best precondition for keeping intertribal disputes in rein.

The formation of political parties is not allowed in Turkmenistan. Niyazov's own Democratic Party of Turkmenistan, the successor of the Communist Party, is of no real significance. After Niyazov suspended the nationalist opposition, such as the Popular Front Agzybirlik, even as he appropriated the views of their nationalistic programmes, most of the critics of the regime emigrated to Moscow. Perhaps the most significant opposition group is 'Fonds Turkmenistan', a political–cultural organization founded in 1993 in Moscow by the former foreign minister Abdy Kuliyev. The democratic political opposition owes its weakness not only to oppression from the regime, but also to the fact that Turkmenbashi's sensitivity to tradition and his accommodation of national sentiments seems to be a more influential factor than the democratic demands put forward by the opposition. However, despite the profuse propaganda proclaiming Niyazov's popularity, there are signs of discontent among the population and if the economic situation continues to decline this discontent could grow. The first public demonstration against the government by some hundred people on 12 July 1995, in Ashkhabad demanding new elections of the president and the parliament, caught the authorities by surprise.[6]

To justify its aversion to democratic structures, the leadership states the case of Turkmenistan's historical and social evolution, saying that political parties would only be established along ethnic lines and thus be divisive. Turkmenistan therefore was not ready for political pluralism; on the contrary the unity of the nation had absolute priority. Azerbaijan and Tajikistan are cited as discouraging cases in point to back up these arguments.

ECONOMIC CRISIS

The same argument has been used to apply the brake to economic reforms. Indeed, Turkmenistan does not possess the skilled manpower or the experience to run private enterprises responsibly. There are still no companies free of state control. The state is the Turkmen business partner in new joint ventures with foreign investors. Major reforms have been delayed and little progress has been made in the area of privatization. It was announced that more attention would be given to privatization in the agricultural sector. According to Western experts, current policy will not produce an economic structure based on free enterprise. What is needed is a reform programme providing for less state regulation and a reduction of state subsidies.[7] The leadership's hesitation might make sense for political reasons. However, the government's policy can only succeed as long as enough export profits can be earned. However, because the Turkmen economy is highly specialized (it is predominantly agricultural, with cotton accounting for 60 per cent of the total agricultural production) it makes Turkmenistan highly susceptible to external influences. Turkmenistan must import most of its food. Although more than half of the population lives in the countryside, the agricultural productivity is very low, with some hidden unemployment. In Soviet times Turkmenistan was merely a supplier of raw materials to the manufacturing industry in Russia. Today, therefore, an infrastructure for a manufacturing industry of its own is almost completely lacking.

Turkmenistan is totally dependent on the industrial production of the other states in the CIS. However, the central distribution system of former days has now effectively collapsed. Turkmenistan, with its specialized economy, is crucially dependent on having a well-organized foreign trade system. Yet so far there have been no contracts with European countries in the gas sector and the export of natural gas to Europe passes through Russia together with gas from other regions of the Russian Federation. The export sales are not high enough to finance and modernize the infrastructure and look as if they will stay that way for some time. Furthermore, most foreign trade is still based on bilateral agreements with other former Soviet republics. As there is an extreme lack of domestic capital, foreign investments are urgently needed to build an independent economic structure. However, foreign investors are often hesitant, because the necessary infrastructure is not provided and laws protecting foreign investments are repeatedly set aside by presidential orders. Because of these obstacles some foreign enterprises in the natural gas and oil industry have pulled back.

Nevertheless, potentially Turkmenistan ranks among the biggest suppliers of energy and fuels.[8] In early 1993 the government approved a programme to extract resources in undeveloped areas. According to estimates of the World Bank the programme will require investments of US$8 billion by the year 2000 for the gas industry alone.[9]

Estimates by other international financial organizations in 1992 indicated that the exploitation and export of oil and in particular gas reserves could raise the average per capita income to US$2500.[10] The advent of a new era of prosperity was proclaimed, a vision being painted of a 'Central Asian Kuwait', in a country that had been the poorest and the most backward in the Soviet Union next to Tajikistan. The government promptly abolished heating and electricity fees, but later had to reinstitute them partly when the propaganda wave came to an end in 1993. The slogan 'ten years of prosperity' was changed to 'ten years of stability'.

Expected profits, however unrealistic, from gas exports had apparently become a defining factor of both the domestic and foreign policy. However, Turkmenistan was soon forced to accept the bitter truth that even the biggest deposits are of no benefit if the present customers cannot pay and potential future customers are inaccessible. All the client countries are in debt to Turkmenistan.[11] If and when they pay it is by barter. The Ukraine, in particular, one of Turkmenistan's biggest customers, was severely in arrears, so that Turkmenistan was forced to withhold part of the contracted quantities of gas and to cut back its own production. The total extraction fell from 652.2 billion m^3 in 1993 to 35.6 billion m^3 in 1994.[12] Other factors contributing to the reduced production were Russia's blockade and Uzbekistan's closing of the pipeline when Turkmenistan refused to pay higher transit fees.

Dubious investments by the government such as the construction of a big new airport and a number of luxury hotels did further damage, resulting in a crisis in 1994 of indebtedness and an acute shortage of foreign exchange. The only secure source of foreign exchange was cotton, but it was mainly traded on a barter basis. The current crisis, aggravated by the fact that Turkmenistan had the lowest standard of living in the former Soviet Union, gives no grounds for optimism.[13]

Turkmenistan still has the highest child mortality rate and the lowest life expectancy. The desolate ecological situation only underscores the pessimistic forecasts. Permanent oversalting of agricultural areas from irrigation requires an increased use of artificial fertilizers, which in turn contaminates the drinking water. However, as cotton is an important source of foreign exchange, its cultivation will continue to be promoted.

NATURAL GAS AND RUSSIAN DOMINANCE

Under these circumstances the expansion of the gas extraction industry seems to be the only alternative if decline is to be arrested. However, this means dependence not only on foreign capital and technical assistance, but also on foreign and, in particular, Russian specialists. If Turkmenistan is to achieve the significance it theoretically merits by virtue of its wealth in natural resources, it must enter new relationships of dependence without abandoning the past.

Russia will continue to have a major influence on Turkmenistan's future. It is doubtful that Turkmenistan will be able to control its own resources and so uphold its nominal sovereignty with economic autonomy. The lion's share of production is being exported to Russia. The whole of the oil industry is intermeshed with its Russian counterpart. An economic reorientation, therefore, to the West or to the countries of the Middle East might not be without its risk for Russia. It could deprive Russia of raw materials and reduce her industrial potential. If that were to occur it would have repercussions throughout the entire CIS. The Turkmen leadership therefore tries to maintain a balance between emphasizing its independence and preserving and even expanding bilateral ties with Moscow. Although Turkmenistan has no common border with Russia, most of its bilateral agreements are concluded with her.

Pursuant to its foreign policy doctrine of the 'near abroad', Moscow now attaches more importance to Russian–Turkmen relations than in the period directly following the collapse of the Soviet Union. Since 1993 a new phase of cooperation in economic and military matters has been inaugurated, based on a treaty of friendship and cooperation signed in July 1992. Most important is military cooperation with Russia. The security treaty between the two countries, containing a subsidiary agreement for joint defence of the southern border, is emblematic of Turkmenistan's continuing dependence on Moscow in foreign and security policy. There are 2000 Russian officers in the Turkmen army and most of the officer corps is of Russian origin.[14] Turkmenistan must pay the entire cost of maintaining Russian armed forces on its territory, while Russia continues to maintain some strategic military bases. Although Ashkhabad's military doctrine stipulates that its military forces shall enter into no military alliances, Turkmenistan does have some unmistakable features of a Russian 'military protectorate'. In May 1995, when Russia concluded 23 bilateral trade and economic agreements to the year 2000, Boris Yeltsin underscored the fact that Turkmenistan was the first country with which Russia was to have a strategic partnership. Moscow needs Turkmenistan as a gateway to Pakistan and India. Hence, one of the agreements concerns a project to establish a transport route from St Petersburg–Moscow–Astrakhan Turkmenbashi (former Krasnovodsk) to the Turkmen-Iranian border from whence the way is open to Iran and the Indian subcontinent in 1996.[15]

Turkmenistan is definitely regarded as a rival by Moscow in the gas sector. A blockade of the pipeline is an extremely effective instrument for manipulating the competitive stakes. Moscow resorted to this measure in 1994, which resulted in a reduction of Turkmen gas exports.[16] As the only route is through Russia, Turkmenistan is pursuing a two-pronged strategy; on one hand, building an infrastructure for independent gas export and, on the other, seeking cooperation with Russia in this sector. The delivery of 6 billion cubic metres of gas to Russia was agreed in 1995 in exchange for military equipment. A new agreement was concluded with the powerful Russian gas concern Gazprom on the policy towards customers inside the CIS and on the transport of gas to the Ukraine and the Caucasus via Russia. An agreement on closer cooperation with Gazprom in November 1995 and on establishing a new joint Turkmen–Russian gas company called Turkmenrosgaz opens the way to new joint projects in the eastern regions of Turkmenistan and on the Caspian shelf.[17] Turkmenrosgaz will have 100 per cent control of Turkmen gas deliveries to markets in the CIS. Under the agreement, Turkmenistan will sell gas destined for the other CIS countries at its border with Uzbekistan, while Russia will ensure its delivery to the Ukraine and the Transcaucasian countries.

A new payments procedure with the Ukraine was also agreed. Turkmenistan can now even increase its gas exports to the Ukraine. After 1996, Ukrainian companies, not the government, will be responsible for paying. This new policy reflects the Turkmen Government's realization that the CIS countries will remain its main customers for some time to come yet.

New ways were also found to gain new partners through trilateral agreements. An agreement on economic cooperation signed between Turkmenistan, Ukraine and Iran in September 1995 coordinates investment and trade on a barter basis. Turkmenistan supplies gas to the Ukraine, the Ukraine supplies Iran with rails for its railroads and Iran will build roads in Turkmenistan.[18]

Some energy experts believe that by continuing to supply oil and gas to debtor countries, Ashkhabad is not only bent on overtaking Russia in terms of both the scale of its gas exports and the size of the debt owed to it by the importing countries, but also on obtaining direct access to eastern and western Europe via leased seaports, many of which are linked by oil and gas pipelines to Turkmenistan.[19] Thus, Ashkhabad has agreed to lease several moorings at Ukrainian ports from Kiev and is intending to do the same with Georgia, thus gaining access to the Black Sea. As these countries are trying hard to diminish their independence from Russia, Ashkhabad may have set its sights on dominating the CIS gas market, partly in competition and partly in cooperation with Russia, which itself owes Turkmenistan money for gas supplies.

Through cooperation in the gas sector Russia hopes to gain a share in the planned pipeline to the west. Another plan is to participate in the construction of a pipeline to Pakistan and to reach East Asian markets via Turkmenistan. Such agreements are indeed useful for Turkmenistan, but the concessions will be in Russia's favour.[20] Russia cannot prevent the strengthening of Turkmenistan's ties with its southern neighbours, so it tries to use them for its own purposes. Russia has access to the Persian Gulf and the Indian Ocean through its infrastructural connection with Iran.

THE CONCEPT OF 'NEUTRALITY'

Turkmenistan's conflicting situation is reflected in President Niyazov's policy. On the one hand, the desire to preserve independence, which came to Turkmenistan almost as a windfall and to reap its advantages is enormous. On the other hand, there has been a growing realization of its dependence on Russia and to a lesser degree on the other CIS countries. As Turkmenistan is not self-sufficient in food, in 1995 it tried to renegotiate agreements with the countries of the Transcaucasus and the Ukraine. Pursuant to one agreement, the Ukraine will now pay for its gas imports partly with food deliveries.

In this regard, Turkmen foreign policy is regionally orientated, which clearly contrasts with the course taken by the other Central Asian republics. Of all Central Asian states, Turkmenistan maintains the most intensive and least strained relations with Russia and, at the same time, the most distanced relation to the CIS. From the very first day of independence, Turkmenistan adopted a cautious position towards the newly emerging CIS. It was the only Central

Asian country not to sign the CIS charter at the CIS summit in Minsk in January 1993. While declaring his full accord with CIS membership, Niyazov emphasized that no single structure of a supragovernmental nature that may infringe on his country's legitimate interests could be accepted. On the occasion of the signing of a contract on gas deliveries with the Ukraine in Kiev in early 1995, Niyazov once again underscored his reluctance to accept a stronger integration into the CIS. According to him, the CIS should be merely a consultative body, while concrete agreements should be bilateral. Addressing Russia he explained 'All attempts to form supra-national pacts clearly pursue selfish aims, the outcome of which will be a loss of independence.'[21] Turkmenistan did not sign the Treaty of Collective Security and, together with Azerbaijan, opposed the collective protection of the CIS borders, but, unlike Azerbaijan, it did sign a treaty with Russia concerning the protection of its border by both Turkmen and Russian border troops. It has also not been party to most of the CIS agreements in the economic and social spheres. For Niyazov, the CIS is considered a Russian attempt to regain control over Central Asia, whereas its purpose should have been to divide up the former USSR among its successors in a civilized way.

Turkmenistan's foreign policy, therefore, is to prefer bilateral to multilateral relations and to resist submission to a transnational political body or power. This position found its most emblematic expression in Turkmenistan's joining the non-aligned movement in October 1995.[22] Turkmenistan is now officially recognized as a neutral state and as long as it holds this status Turkmenistan may not enter into any CIS military pact.

Aside from the desire for independence, which Turkmenistan shares to some degree with the other republics, there are some peculiarities which account for Turkmenistan's special position.

As a small, marginal and underdeveloped republic inside the USSR, there was a consciousness of being severely exploited and prevented from making full use of its own resources. Its situation as the most southern republic, in direct proximity to Iran, endows it with the best geographical conditions of all the Central Asian republics for a reorientation towards the south. The expected profits from the export of gas strengthened the Turkmen leader's belief in his new foreign policy. Whether his idea will succeed or whether economic and geopolitical realities will necessitate greater integration into CIS structures, depends on the infrastructural link up of Turkmenistan with its southern neighbours.

The Economic Cooperation Organization (ECO) could well play a positive role. This organization, founded in the 1960s by Turkey, Iran and Pakistan, was given a new lease on life when the Central Asian republics joined in 1992 with the aim of coordinating their economic policies and creating the requisite infrastructure. However, this appears to be principally a matter of interest as regards mutual relations between Turkmenistan and Iran. Indeed, just as in the CIS the dominant trend is towards bilateral relations. Whereas in theory the ECO could become one of the biggest economic unions in the world, the reality is that it is merely a sounding board for declarations and intentions. Still, Russia seems to fear the potential of this union and the effect it could have on Russia's own industrial potential and transportation network. In 1993 it suddenly demanded that the Central Asian states make a clear choice between membership in the CIS and the ECO.

As Turkmenistan, in principle, opposes any centrally administered suprastate structure, it, too, is sceptical about an economic and political association of the Central Asian states. President Nazarbayev's of Kazakhstan idea of a Euroasian union was also rejected. Again, bilateral agreements are being preferred, though a number of agreements on regional cooperation have been signed. Joining the Kazakh–Uzbek–Kyrgyz partnership to establish a 'Central Asian Union' is not in Turkmenistan's interest, nor is Niyazov eager to join the Interstate Council of the three Central Asian presidents. Quite apart from Turkmenistan's dislike of dominating central structures, there exists a mistrust towards Kazakhstan and in particular Uzbekistan, which is suspected of striving to achieve a certain hegemony in Central Asia. A potential point of discord is the shortage of water resources in the region. Turkmenistan is aggravating the tension by building a branch of the Karakum canal. Turkmen overtures towards Iran were strongly criticized by President Kerimov of Uzbekistan owing to his fear of Islamic infiltration.

Nevertheless, cooperation is a need in the region, if only to prevent a common ecological catastrophe. Turkmenistan, Kazakhstan and Uzbekistan are at least endeavouring to cooperate on the Aral Sea problem. However, generally, Niyazov's pragmatic approach, free of ideological and ethnical, pan-Turcic or Turkestani designs, should further strengthen Turkmen national identity.

RELATIONS WITH TURKEY AND IRAN

The period of 'panturkic romanticism' with regard to Central Asia and the idea of a union of all Turkic countries under Turkey's leadership, seems to be over for the time being. After the pan-Turkic euphoria provoked by the decline of the USSR, Turkey's relations with the Central Asian countries were characterized by a healthy pragmatism. This is partly the result of disillusionment with Turkey's economic capacity to fill the vacuum left by the demise of the Soviet Union. Many of Turkey's promises went unfulfilled and administrative obstacles to foreign investors often prevented successful relations.

The debate on the competition between opposing systems in Central Asia, between the secular 'Turkish' model and the Iranian theocratic model, turned out to be just a Western fiction. However, it is obvious that in this regard Turkmenistan has a greater affinity to Turkey. By the end of the year 1994 approximately 2300 Turkmen students were studying in schools and universities in Turkey.[23] Adopting the Latin alphabet will bring Turkmenistan closer to Turkey as well. As Turks and Turkmen can understand each other more easily than can Turks and the other Central Asians, receiving Turkish television will bring about a convergence of the two languages. Aside from this subjective, ethnic affinity, symbolized in the annual meeting of Turkic presidents at the 'Turkic summit', in the end the prospect of economic benefit should prevail on both sides. For Turkey, Turkmenistan is a country of transit on the way to Uzbekistan, Turkey's most important partner in Central Asia. Moreover, Turkmenistan was traditionally regarded essentially as a seller of natural gas. In a basic agreement concluded in October 1994, Turkey guaranteed to purchase natural gas over a period of 30 years.

Turkey is by far the biggest and most important provider of technical and financial support to Turkmenistan and in 1993 the total credits granted amounted to US$92 million.[24] Numerous Turkish companies have invested, although they are hampered by Turkmenistan's lack of foreign exchange.[25] By mid-1995 a quarter of all the registered foreign companies were Turkish, with all the other countries far behind in this regard.[26] Turkish investors are given preference and, unlike others, none has retreated. The Turkish International Cooperation Agency (TICA), which is responsible for assisting the Central Asian countries, is the biggest bilateral supplier of financial aid. It assists the establishment of joint ventures and, preferably, small and medium sized Turkish enterprises. It will help to finance the rebuilding of the road and railway network and the transition to the Latin alphabet.

The other important partner outside the CIS is Iran. Its importance stems from its common border of 1500 km with Turkmenistan. Iran is a bridge connecting the world market with the Central Asian states and is therefore very interested in creating a transport and communication network. For instance, the Tajan–Sarakhs–Mashhad railway is completed and connects Iran with all the Central Asian countries and gives Turkmenistan direct transit access to the Persian Gulf and to Turkey, thus enabling it to break out of its isolation.

In 1992 Tehran started a diplomatic and economic offensive by founding the Organization of Cooperation of Caspian States. Initially, it was regarded as an Islamic organization with the slogan 'The Caspian Sea must be Islamic'.

Today the Caspian Sea is at the centre of several conflicts of interest, mainly over oil deposits, but also due to its ecological crisis. These conflicts can only be resolved through cooperation between all the littoral states. Thus, Turkmenistan and Iran are bound to one another in a new potential area of crisis. Some of the projects Iran had suggested, such as the establishment of a joint economic zone, were rejected by President Niyazov because of the lack of capital or so as not to provoke Russia.

There is no alternative to strong cooperation with Iran. Iran is Turkmenistan's only link to Europe and relations have been cultivated in appreciation of this fact. Against Russia's wishes, most of the 1994 cotton harvest was sold to Iran, thus obviating the one-sided dependence on Russia that had been the sole customer for Turkmen cotton.[27]

PROBLEMS OF TURKMEN PIPELINE POLITICS

Turkmen–Iranian cooperation can give new impulses to the entire region. The agreement with Iran over the 4000 km long pipeline project to Europe was followed by several other statements of intent and declarations, such as the construction of gas and oil pipelines to Pakistan with Russian participation or the building of pipelines across China to the Japanese city of Nagasaki via Uzbekistan and Kyrgystan or Kazakhstan.[28]

Because of Turkmenistan's geographical location, which is the main obstacle to the realization of the vision of the Turkmen leadership, pipeline construction must indeed be a political priority. The idea of constructing a transcontinental pipeline to Europe via Iran and Turkey has been at the centre of attention from the very outset and the project was agreed upon by both these countries in 1992. Pursuant to the agreement, Turkey would receive 2 billion m^3 a year, from 1998 and Turkmenistan committed itself to deliver 15 billion m^3 from 2010 to 2028.[29] After funnelling off its share, Turkey is to ensure transport of the gas to European customers.

In addition to the agreement with Turkey, an accord with Iran from 1993 regulates the purchase of gas, with an ultimate target of up to 28 billion m^3.[30] After 25 years Iran, which is willing to provide a large portion of the financing, would assume full rights to the pipeline, which runs through 1450 km of its territory. Thus, the future has new dependencies in store for Turkmenistan. To speed up the process, in September 1995 Iran and Turkmenistan signed an agreement for transferring 8 billion m^3 of natural gas annually, for a period of 25 years, from 1997. Therefore a 200 km pipeline – 140 km in Turkmenistan and 60 km in Iran – will be constructed immediately over the next 2 years. As Turkmenistan is having great difficulty raising the capital for the main gas pipeline project, this could provide the necessary financial backing. Gas deliveries to Iran to repay Iran for the construction of the pipeline could start earlier than projected. Iran will bear 80 per cent of the cost for this first pipeline and will deliver fuel oil in exchange.[31] According to the Iranian oil minister Aghazadeh, the agreement was designed to 'speed up the process' of constructing the entire gasline to Europe. By exporting oil and gas via the Gulf, the originally planned 2500 km pipeline to Europe could partly be financed and Turkmenistan would be less dependent on US banks.[32]

Despite these agreements, financing for the project is far from certain. The main obstacle is the resistance of the US Government to a route running through Iran. This is causing new concerns and hesitation among international financing institutions. However, the realization of the project is absolutely dependent on large credits from state export credit institutions and international banks. The international consortium Turkmenistan Transcontinental Pipeline (TTP), founded jointly for this purpose by all the parties to the project (with Russia also included for political reasons) can provide only part of the needed capital. Another problem not yet resolved is financing the link to the existing Turkish–European system. The TTP plan envisions a pipeline extending only to a place just beyond the Iranian–Turkish border. With so many different interests at stake, the situation is confused and far removed from a solution. Even as ties between Turkmenistan and Iran are becoming closer, thus improving the conditions for the construction of a pipeline, the USA is imposing a comprehensive economic embargo on Iran and urging its allies to avoid doing business with Iran. On the other hand, Iran hopes to transport Turkmen and Iranian gas to Europe via Turkey (a short link is to be built to Turkey by 1998 for local use) as the first step in the entire pipeline.

Despite all the obstacles, the most important precondition being Turkey's guarantee to purchase, everything seemed to be settled by early 1995. However, the American embargo forced the consortium to look for other routes. Because of the confusion, the Turkish pipeline company Botash proposed building a pipeline without Iran, beneath the Caspian Sea and via the Transcaucasus to Turkey.[33] The main rationale motive behind this proposal was to couple this plan with another projected pipeline for pumping Azerbaijani and Kazakh oil to the Mediterranean across Turkey. The confusion was compounded when in August 1995 Niyazov – in the presence of the Turkish Prime Minister, Tansu Çiller – made clear that he would insist on the Iranian route, arguing that the Caucasus would not be stable for a long time. He proposed a secondary pipeline via Georgia to Turkey complementing the already existing Russian pipeline to Georgia on the condition that Turkey would use this gas only for its own energy needs. As Ankara had already reached an agreement with Moscow to purchase natural gas from Russia and plans to increase the amount in the future, it did not respond to Niyazov's offers.[34] Turkey's hopes, provoked by the demise of the USSR, of acquiring its natural gas mainly from its 'Turkic brotherland' seem to be far from being realized. This development, together with the formation of 'Turkmenrosgaz', indicates that Turkmenistan is not able to compete with Russia in selling gas to Europe, including Turkey. Russia's policy of trying to dominate the sale of gas and oil to Europe seems to be more successful in Turkmenistan than in Azerbaijan. Obviously, US policy towards Iran and US support for the government in Moscow weaken the position of both Turkey and the Central Asian countries – which is in the interests of both Russia and Iran. The fact that Tehran and Moscow are strategic allies in the region – Moscow basically has approved the construction of a pipeline through Iran on the condition that Russia is involved – makes it impossible for Ashkhabad to meet Turkey's expectations. Systematic cooperation with Iran in the oil and gas sector seems to be most logical way to go for all participants. The intention to set up a tripartite consortium, composed of the oil companies of Iran, Turkmenistan and Russia, is an extension of such a policy.[35]

As there is no sign that the present dilemma will soon be resolved, Turkmenistan has no choice but to favour the alternative of a southern pipeline. After Niyazov and Pakistan's Prime Minister, Benazir Bhutto, had agreed in March 1995 on a pipeline to Pakistan, on 21 October 1995 Niyazov signed an agreement in New York with the US oil company Unocal and the Saudi Arabian company Delta Oil on the construction of a 1300 km gas pipeline to Pakistan via Afghanistan.[36] However, whether this southern outlet for Turkmenistan's natural gas to the Indian Ocean has better chances of being materialized than the Iranian–Turkish route, remains an open question. Although Western banks and financial institutions are interested, the fact that there was no official Afghan representative present at the signing ceremony indicates a problem. Building a southern gasline gives Turkmenistan an opportunity to reach the Indian market. Ashkhabad plans to sell oil and gas to India, with whom it also signed cooperation agreements in September 1995.[37] However, the dilemma remains: there is no real alternative to the most logical and economic route across Iran.

The proposed Turkmen pipeline, which is sometimes referred to in the press as 'Turkmen pipedreams', is wholly in line with international competition for the energy resources in and around the Caspian Sea and is now referred to as the 'great game'. Russia and the West are the main players in this 'game' and Iran and Turkey are important second-string players. The Caspian region is now emerging as a new focal point and self-contained region on the geopolitical scene, whereas formerly it was seen mainly as dividing

Central Asia from the Caucasian countries. Turkmenistan is the link between the Caspian region and the other Central Asian countries. A new American–Russian conflict of interest is beginning to emerge in this region, the points of main contention being control of the oil resources and the policy towards Iran. At the same time Turkey and Russia are also competing for influence in the Transcaucasus and Central Asia and for an oil pipeline from Baku to the west. For their part, Russia and Iran have begun to draft the contours of a new strategic partnership, with far-reaching cooperation in the economic, nuclear and military fields. It would appear under these circumstances that Turkmenistan has no other choice but to try to please everybody and pre-eminently Russia and Iran. Although it needs Turkey, too, it is dependent on Russia and Iran for access to the world market. Friendly strategic relations between Iran and Russia should therefore be useful. The most serious obstacle is the US policy towards Iran.

The Turkmen preference of bilateral and trilateral agreements instead of regional alliances seems reasonable enough. However, sometimes trilateral agreements, like the trade and cooperation agreement between Turkmenistan, Iran and Armenia, can cause political problems – witness Armenia's and Iran's tortured relationships with Turkey and Azerbaijan. If Russia, Iran and Turkmenistan should begin to negotiate a trilateral agreement on the development of oil deposits on the Turkmen section of the Caspian shell, it will first be necessary to define what that section is. Turkmenistan is currently in the midst of a dispute over the legal status of the Caspian Sea. Unless this dispute is settled, there will be no exploitation of resources. If Turkmenistan supports Russia's and Iran's view that there should only be joint exploitation of the Caspian (with thus the legal status of a lake), it may be acting against its own interests, while at the same time annoying Turkey and the West. However, because of the need to defer to Russian and Iranian interests Turkmenistan cannot afford to support Azerbaijan's and Kazakhstan's view that the Caspian is a sea and should therefore be divided into national sectors of the different littoral states. So far the leadership has refrained from taking a clear position and instead has emphasized the necessity of cooperation among the littoral states.

Thus, despite all efforts to pursue an independent foreign policy and despite having gained nominal independence, Turkmenistan's dependency on outside forces continues. New relationships of dependency have emerged. Dependency on Russia exists as before, but dependency on Iran, Turkey and the West is new. Turkmenistan needs them all if it is to create a material basis for political sovereignty.

Understanding that political and economic independence would be very much imperiled by a deep and protracted economic crisis, Ashkhabad took steps in 1995 to modify its relations with its traditional natural gas customers within the CIS and to deepen its relations with neighbouring countries, primarily with Iran, while at the same time looking beyond Iran, regarding it as a bridge to India and Pakistan and the Indian Ocean. Efforts to open a gas pipeline and bring an infrastructure to the south and east, plus the projected pipeline to the west, are steps towards loosening Turkmenistan's dependence on Russia. Ashkhabad's balanced policy with regard to Russia and the other regional powers and its care not to neglect its economic relations with Russia, are evident in Moscow's and Ashkhabad's agreement on the joint control over the supply of Turkmen gas to markets in the CIS. The confusion over the pipeline routes shows that there are still a number of factors making the realization of Turkmen 'pipedreams' extremely uncertain. At the least it will take some years. The ultimate outcome is highly dependent on factors on which Ashkhabad has no influence, for example developments in Afghanistan and the Caucasus or the US attitude towards Iran.

The propagandist vision of a 'Central Asian Kuwait' has of course quietly gone its way and in its place Niyazov has come up with a new slogan, namely an 'Asian version of Switzerland or Austria', which he uses in referring to Turkmenistan's newly achieved neutral status and its preference for bilateral or trilateral agreements with its neighbours. Niyazov's claim of a special role for Turkmenistan as a neutral country is an illusion of independence. However, neutrality does not mean independence, particularly from Russia; it implies it is merely a goal to be achieved.

Whether Turkmenistan can one day achieve the status of a politically sovereign country and take advantage of its geopolitical situation to become an important regional centre situation, depends not only on the exploitation of its natural resources, but also on its internal ability to overcome its low level of social development. Its dependency on foreign specialists and its lack of an engaged intelligentsia are serious handicaps. Domestic stability is a precondition for Niyazov to get on with this process. Social stability imposed from the top and the absence of serious opposition is the typical image of a stable traditional society, but for the outside observer some uncertain factors remain. Tribal allegiance still prevails over any kind of Turkmen national identity. Once Niyazov's reign has come to an end one day, power struggles among the small political élite will inevitably arise and the current stability may be destroyed by the eruption of clan rivalries.

NOTES

1. *Wostok*, no. 4 (1995), p. 49. 'Turkmenistan', *Thema*, pp. 35–66.
2. *Wostok*, no. 4 (1995), p. 38.
3. According to *Wostok*, no. 4 (1995), p. 51, 54 per cent of the questioned Russians are willing to leave and 26 per cent are undecided.
4. A.G. Nedvetsky, 'Turkmenistan', in M. Mesbahi (ed.), *Central Asia and the Caucasus after the Soviet Union. Domestic and International Dynamics* (University Press, Florida, 1994), pp. 191–206.
5. *Central Asia Newsfile*, vol. 2, no. 10 (October 1994), p. 11.
6. *Moskowski novosti*, 23–30 July 1995. *Inside Central Asia, BBC Monitoring*, no. 81 (31 July–6 August 1995), p. 3.
7. See R.T. Hermann, 'Turkmenistan. Wirtschaftstrends zum Jahreswechsel 1994/95', *BfAI Länderreport* (February 1995), p. 4.
8. According to estimates, Turkmenistan has 15.5 trillion m^3 of gas reserves and 6.3 billion tons of oil reserves. *Wostok*, no. 4 (1995), p. 52.
9. Bahro, Gundula, 'Saparmurad Nijasov', p. 206 in *Orient*, vol. 2 (1995), Opladen, pp. 202–8.
10. In 1995 the monthly income was approximately US$10. *Wostok*, no. 4 (1995), p. 49.
11. In 1994, the outstanding debts amounted to US$1.6 billion. *Neue Zürcher Zeitung*, 21 January 1995.
12. In 1991 it had amounted to 85 billion. *Die Presse*, 21 March 1995. *Nachrichten für Aussenhandel*, 1 February 1995.
13. The gross domestic product dropped to 20 per cent and the consumer prices increased 1100 per cent. *Handelsblatt*, 7 June 1995. The national currency, the manat, suffered an extreme devaluation and the US dollar has become the country's real currency. Basic food had to be rationed and the minimum wage was fixed to 1000 manat in April 1995. *Wostok*, no. 6 (1995), p. 23. Abdy Kulijew, 'Zwischen Diktatur und Sowjetnostalgie', pp. 20–3. According to A. Kuliyev, this corresponds to the price of 4 kg of meat or potatoes.
14. *Economic and Scientific Central Asia Survey*, vol. I, no. 3 (March 1994), p. 39. Source: *RFL/RL*, 28 December 1993.
15. R. Götz and U. Halbach, 'Turkmenistan: Informationen über eine unbekannte Republik. Teil I: Landeskunde und politische Entwicklung', *Berichte des Bundesinstituts für ostwissenschaftliche und internationale Studien*, no. 42 (1995), p. 23. Source: *Turkmenskaja Iskra*, 26 May 1995.
16. Through blockade of the export routes by Russia Turkmenistan was forced to reduce its gas output in 1994 to 35.6 billion m^3, that is half of the 1993 output. (In 1991 it was 85 billion m^3.) *Die Presse*, 21 March 1995.
17. 'Inside Central Asia', *BBC Monitoring*, no. 96 (13–19 November 1995), p. 3. According to Interfax, 15 November 1995.
18. 'Summary of World Broadcast (SWB), ME/2407 MED/4, *BBC Monitoring* (13 December 1995). Source: *IRNA*, 10 September 1995.
19. 'Inside Central Asia', *BBC Monitoring*, no. 92 (16–22 October 1995), p. 2. According to *Rossiyskaya Gazeta*, 14 October 1995.
20. *Wostok*, no. 4 (1995), p. 53.
21. *Süddeutsche Zeitung*, 21 January 1995.

22. Following a resolution submitted by Turkey and other states, the UN General Assembly recognized Turkmenistan's neutrality on 12 December 1995. *BBC Monitoring. Inside Central Asia*, no. 100 (11–17 December 1995), p. 3.
23. *Nachrichten für Aussenhandel*, 30 December 1994.
24. *Economic and Scientific Central Asia Survey*, vol. 1, no. 9 (October 1994), p. 39. Source: *Asia*, 30 August 1994.
25. Until 1994, there were Turkish investments of US$650 million. Outstanding debts to Turkish firms were US$100 million by the end of 1994. R.T. Hermann, 'Turkmenistan. Wirtschaftstrends zum Jahreswechsel 1994/95', *BfAI Länderreport* (February 1995), p. 3.
26. According to the Ministry of Foreign Economic Relations, out of 221 foreign companies, 54 were from Turkey, followed by Iran (27), Afghanistan and Russia (20), the USA (12) and Germany (10). *Eurasian File*, TICA, no. 45 (November 1995), p. 2.
27. In 1995 Turkmenistan exported its cotton to 22 countries. *Eurasian File*, TICA, no. 40 (September 1995/1), p. 1.
28. *Middle East Economic Survey* (MEES), vol. 38, no. 4 (23 October 1995), p. A7.
29. *Nachrichten für Aussenhandel*, 22 February 1995.
30. *Middle East Times*, 4–10 September 1995.
31. SWB, ME/2401 MED/2, 6 September 1995. Source: *ITAR-TASS*, 4 September 1995. *Middle East Economic Digest* (MEED) (15 September 1995), p. 18.
32. The Turkmen gas will flow into the existing pipeline running from Sarakhs to Rasht, where it joins the trunkline from the south. *MEED* (15 September 1995), p. 18. Importing gas from Turkmenistan would free gas that is currently shipped to northern Iran from the south for export. *MEES*, vol 38, no. 4 (23 October 1995), p. A7.
33. *Turkish Daily News*, 8 July 1995.
34. *Turkish Daily News* (18 October 1995), p. A2. R. Olson, 'Russia, Turkey and the Turkmenistan gas pipeline', *Middle East International* (22 September 1995), pp. 18–19.
35. This was discussed at a meeting between Turkmen Vice-President Ishanov and Iranian Oil Minister Aghazadeh. SWB, MEW/0415 WME/2, 19 December 1995. Source: *IRNA*, 10 December 1995.
36. Both companies are also members of the Azerbaijani oil consortium. Turkmenistan has guaranteed them 700 bn cu metres. *MEES*, vol. 39, no. 4 (23 October 1995), p. A5. *Financial Times* (23 October 1995), p. 5.
37. *Deutsche Welle Monitor-Dienst Osteuropa*, 22 September 1995. Source: PTI.

Part II
External Powers and Central Asia

5 Iran and Central Asia: Responding to Regional Change

A. Ehteshami

INTRODUCTION

The proclamation by the Upper Chamber of the USSR Supreme Soviet on 26 December 1991 that 'the Soviet Union no longer' existed may not have been an earth-shaking piece of news, yet its repercussions have been rippling through the post-Cold War order, changing and shaping the emergent new international system. Having not previously considered the unthinkable, few countries were prepared for the aftershocks of the implosion of the Soviet Union and its impact on the global system and on regional theatres – least of all Moscow's friends and allies. One such – recent – friend was Iran, whose leaders had been seeking closer economic and military ties with the Soviet superpower since 1988.

For Iran, whose own foreign policy was entering a period of reform in the late 1980s, the unravelling of the Soviet empire was an ambiguous event. On the one hand, the end of the Soviet Union and Russia's shortened reach relieved the threat of Soviet–Russian interference in Iran's internal affairs, thus presenting Tehran with unexpected opportunities in a region long closed to Iranian influence.[1] On the other hand, the disappearance of the Soviet Union was accompanied by a rising nationalist tide in the states of Central Asia and in Azerbaijan, whose post-Soviet élites' only effective tool for state building has been the resurrection of long-dormant ethnic identities. While Tehran has been in favour of the decolonization of Central Asia and the Caucasus, its leaders are apprehensive of the prospect of centrifugal forces, fed by ethnic and religious nationalisms, arising in Iran's new northern neighbours, many of whom have close 'cousins' in the Islamic Republic.[2] This, compounded by the international uncertainty that followed the collapse of the Soviet Union, may partly explain Iran's initial caution towards these republics – even though the Iranian Foreign Minister, Ali Akbar Velayati's, November 1991 trip to this region had paved the way at an earlier stage for easier Iranian access to the Muslim republics.[3] Furthermore, Iran was very reluctant to see its warm relations with Moscow marred by its being perceived as meddling in Russia's 'backyard'. The Iranian Foreign Minister himself remarked during his 1991 tour of the USSR that Iran's relations with the Muslim republics would be formulated within the framework of Tehran's relations with Moscow.[4]

This chapter intends to examine the basis upon which Iran developed its foreign policy towards the new states of the former Soviet Union and its overall approach and response to regional change. It will argue that the Islamic Republic's policy towards its northern neighbours took several years to mature, developing as it did in the course of major developments in its own political system after Ayatollah Khomeini's death in 1989. Iran's policy towards its 'new' neighbours can best be seen as a strategy of incremental engagement, in which policy has been guided by caution and underwritten by growing economic, geopolitical and geostrategic cooperation. However, to make sense of the pattern of regional relations that have followed upon the demise of the Soviet Union, and the policies of Azerbaijan and its Central Asian neighbours, it is necessary to look at the conditions under which the Central Asian republics emerged on the international scene as well as their own strategies for survival in a totally transformed environment.

CENTRAL ASIA: BETWEEN THE SECOND AND THE THIRD WORLDS

To further complicate relations between the new republics of Central Asia and their neighbours, unlike many of the Soviet Union's Warsaw Pact allies and European republics, which had managed to disengage themselves from the USSR by the time that the Union imploded, few practical measures had been adopted that would have enabled the Central Asian republics to chart for themselves a path separate from Moscow's. Unlike the Eastern European countries, who had found on the western side of the old Iron Curtain enthusiastic and rich friends with the resources to assist them in their conversion from Soviet Communism, the Central Asian republics have been blessed with no prosperous and industrially advanced neighbour or group of states which might have been able to bail them out of their immediate crisis or guide them in their period of transition.[5]

Born between the Second and Third Worlds, for these republics independence was at best a mixed blessing, for it seemed to be accompanied by the removal of the net that the Soviet Union had woven around them, which, for all its faults, had been an effective shield against the vagaries of the international system and the global economic division of labour. Now they found themselves exposed and vulnerable. In the words of the Kazakh President, Nursultan Nazarbayev, 'The North American continent is merging. You've got ... the European Union which is creating a common currency; it's coming towards a common government. In eastern Asia there is also such an organisation but we as yet are not with anybody.'[6]

For these reasons, as Olcott remarks, 'nationhood was reluctantly accepted'.[7] Now that the dust has begun to settle on the corpse of the Soviet Union, it is increasingly evident that the overwhelming sense of abandonment which followed the end of the Union has left a lasting impression on the leaders of the new Central Asian republics, manifesting itself in their international economic and foreign policies.

Yet a number of the Muslim republics of the Commonwealth of Independent States (CIS) are grooming themselves as the twenty-first century's 'Kuwait', 'Switzerland', 'South Korea' and 'Taiwan'. In so doing they are pointedly charting a particular path for their economic future and their future aspirations. However, they also seem to be identifying, with much support from international agencies such as the International Monetary Fund, the very nature, tempo and direction of change in their economies and social institutions – a commendable path as far as the world economy and the peoples of specific republics are concerned. But, as we know from the post-War experience of the Third World in general, for every Korea, Kuwait or Taiwan there exists several 'Bangladeshes', 'Sudans' and 'Chads', whose experience of development has, for several reasons, been on the whole negative. Economic prosperity in some of the CIS states, therefore, should not be viewed as a long-term solution to the economic problems of the region as a whole. As Apostolou notes, if the serious problems of the Central Asian republics (ranging from the absence of adequate administrative institutions to a growing dependence on one or two export items, such as hydrocarbons) are not resolved in the near future, 'then the very viability of these countries will be in question'.[8]

Thus, economically speaking, the prosperity of some of the Central Asian and Caucasian republics could encourage the birth of a multitiered economic sphere in Asia's heartland. Such a development, far from creating the conditions for the general economic development of the region, may in fact act as a fuse for lighting future political and military fires among the Central Asian republics themselves. Such a situation, of course, if it were to occur, will not be too dissimilar to the current Arab system and the relations between rich and poor Arab states, where the elaborate efforts of the haves to keep the Arab have-nots from access to the 'honey pot' is increasingly becoming its defining feature.[9] As Table 5.1 shows, the Arab world has, largely thanks to oil wealth, become a highly polarized region economically – a situation that is at variance with the current position in Central Asia.

TABLE 5.1 *Classification of economies by income, mid-1990s*

Income group	Middle East	North Africa	Muslim CIS
Low income	Yemen	Egypt Sudan	
Lower middle income	Iran Iraq Jordan Lebanon Syria Turkey	Algeria Morocco Tunisia	Azerbaijan Kazakhstan Kyrgyzstan Tajikistan Turkmenistan Uzbekistan
Upper middle income	Bahrain Oman Saudi Arabia	Libya	
High income	Israel Kuwait Qatar UAE		

SOURCE *World Development Report* (Oxford: Oxford University Press, various years).

The depth of future problems arising from economic stratification of Central Asia and the Caucasus is evident from the data contained in Table 5.2: of the eight states of Central Asia and Transcaucasus only four have the basic ingredients for penetrating the global hydrocarbons market, of which only two, Azerbaijan and Kazakhstan (with nearly 25 million of the eight countries' total population of around 70 million), will be able to pump oil and natural gas in reasonably profitable quantities. As international investors have so far only been interested in the hydrocarbon resources of the region the non-hydrocarbons economies are unlikely to develop at the same pace and, when the oil runs out in the region, all the Central Asian and Caucasian republics could again find themselves on the margins of the stratified international economic system, unless, of course, new opportunities for foreign investment and exports present themselves.[10]

However, largely motivated by self-interest, regional players, such as Iran, have already embarked upon a strategy of engaging the new republics in new regional ventures. Turkey and Iran, as well as Pakistan, China, India, Saudi Arabia and South Korea, have all been very keen to help in moulding the clay. Some countries though, particularly Iran and Turkey, have seen fit to reserve for themselves a much greater role in this endeavour than the rest of the pack; relying on historical, religious or cultural relics, they have liked being seen as mentors to Azerbaijan and the Muslim republics of Central Asia. Their overtures towards these states, thus, have also included – at times rather unwelcome – advice on a particular model of development these new republics ought to follow and on, say, the appropriate balance between Islam and political power in their evolving political systems.[11]

TABLE 5.2 *Oil production outlook of the Muslim republics of the CIS ('000b/d) Thousands of barrels per day*

	Azerbaijan	*Kazakhstan*	*Turkmenistan*	*Uzbekistan*	*Total*
1995	195	380	85	145	805
2000	400–500	800–900	150–200	200–250	1550–1850
2005	850–950	1200–1300	200–300	250–300	2500–2850
2010	1000–1200	1400–1600	300–500	300–350	3000–3650

SOURCE N. Guerer and F. Birol, 'Assessing the Future Oil Export Potential in Transcaucasia and Central Asia', *OPEC Bulletin*, September 1995.
Note. The total OPEC output for 2010 is estimated to be around 39.4 million barrels per day.

This process, however, has not been a unidirectional one. As will be seen, Iran's policies towards Central Asia and the Caucasus have taken place within its own changing domestic environment and agendas and Tehran's recognition – once its war with Iraq ended in 1988 and further reinforced by the end of the Cold War in 1990 – that it must redefine its strategies towards the region if it is to prosper economically and to retain its influence in West Asia's post-Soviet Union theatre.

IRAN REDEFINES ITS REGIONAL CONCERNS

For several (domestic, regional and international) reasons, Iranian foreign policy has undergone noticeable transformations since the late 1980s.[12] On the domestic front, the passing of Ayatollah Khomeini in June 1989 and the subsequent reform of the 1979 constitution has allowed for the emergence of a pragmatist executive leadership around a powerful 'President–Fagih' (Rafsanjani–Khomenei) axis. The emergence of an authoritative and effective 'presidential centre' at the heart of power has enabled the executive leadership to adjust (and to a large degree control) Iran's foreign policy agenda and domestic policies and priorities in accordance with the country's 'national interest' – a concept whose return to centre stage has in turn strengthened the pragmatist line, resulting in policies and strategies that are both more responsive and sensitive to the region's geopolitical realities. At the foreign policy level, this has manifested itself in a de-emphasis on ideological differences with other countries and a redoubling of efforts to find common ground for cooperation, particularly in the economic realm and, as Iranian officials themselves like to argue, for 'dialogue' between states and between competing political forces in the region.[13]

Secondly, Iran's economic difficulties, worsened by the weak oil market and Iran's continuing dependence on oil revenues, have encouraged the government to seek improvements in and modernization of its industrial base by attempting to liberalize the economy and reduce the state's control of economic activity.[14] It is apparent that Tehran has recognized that a precondition for the success of such a strategy is moderation in its foreign relations and a closer integration into the international economic system. Economic prosperity, moreover, has increasingly been seen as a necessary ingredient of the national security of the Islamic Republic.[15]

Regionally, the collapse of the Soviet Union and the demise of Iraq as Iran's most intransigent regional competitor has forced a reassessment of Iran's regional role. As already mentioned, the collapse of the Soviet Union and the Kuwait crisis have brought in their wake a number of challenges and opportunities for Tehran. Of the multitude of challenges facing Tehran, four in particular are worthy of a mention: (1) Iran's continuing regional and international isolation, magnified by the American strategy of 'dual containment' introduced by the Clinton Administration, (2) its continuing economic difficulties, (3) problems associated with its national security and (4) uncertainties about its role arising from regional changes and instabilities.

Iran's more immediate regional concerns, with implications for Iranian security, are largely products of the collapse of the Soviet Union. For instance, Iran needs to stem the tide of refugees (who numbered around 4 million in the mid-1990s) from neighbouring countries, in order to reduce the drain on its overstretched job market and financial resources.[16] Next, Iran has been anxious to prevent the outbreak (or contain the fallout) of armed conflict amongst its neighbours (hence its mediating role in Afghanistan, Iraqi Kurdistan, Nagorno–Karabak, and Tajikistan), first as a means of checking cross-border tensions in the area and, second, in order to reduce the chances of social disintegration.[17] The need to reverse the process of economic decline in Soviet successor states is a product of similar concerns: economic recovery will help these polities to rebuild themselves as well as to make a modest contribution towards Iran's own economic recovery. Finally, there is a growing recognition in Iran of the necessity of countering the degradation of the environment and the destabilizing effects of such degradation on its own territory as well as on its neighbours' social fabric. Iran also recognizes that it alone does not possess sufficient resources to deal with all of these problems; in order to make progress on these national priorities, therefore, it has had to look for new ways of regional cooperation and international support.

The irony is that far from seeking to destabilize the Muslim CIS countries, Iran's regional concerns have increasingly mirrored those of the Western countries. Yet the US, for other political and geopolitical considerations, has been keen to limit Tehran's role in the economic and cultural renewal of these republics.[18] In sum, Tehran's policy towards the CIS can be classified as one of incremental engagement, in which Iran seeks to minimize threats to its own security by promoting stability in neighbouring regions and by deepening economic exchanges.[19] This said, on the other hand, the pace of the Arab–Israeli peace process, the US military presence in the Persian Gulf region[20] and its policy of 'dual containment' and Tehran's continuing difficulties with some of its Gulf Arab neighbours have added to the sense of Iranian regional isolation, thus complicating the country's strategy towards its Arab and non-Arab neighbours[21] and, ironically, helped to push its attention northwards.

Traditionally, Tehran's foreign arena complications have tended to have a noticeable impact on the domestic balance of power, where critics from the power élites' various factions have developed a taste for challenging the government's policies. The two Rafsanjani administrations have not been immune from such forces and at critical junctures have had to adjust their policies to take account of criticisms from both the conservative–traditionalist and the radical–populist factions. As Chubin explains 'The system with several centers of power reflects not broad consensus but querulous diversity; policy results from competition and trade-offs, generating inconsistency and contradictions. If the price of getting one policy adopted is the acceptance of another group's pet scheme, the lines of various policies will diverge.'[22] Naturally, the consequences of this on the administration's overall economic and foreign policies have not been inconsiderable, causing it to risk losing its way on both fronts as it has had to make unwanted detours.

Internationally too, Iran's position is undergoing some changes. Iran is, in my view, finding itself increasingly moving towards the Euro-Asia orbit – even though it continues to function within the US-dominated system and promote closer economic ties with the rest of the Third World. In practice, in the nascent post-Cold War international system, this means deeper Iranian economic (and wherever permissible also political) interactions with the European Union states, Russia, China, India and Japan and further distance from the USA. While this trend may be good news as far as Iran's overall role in the international system is concerned, it does mean that the more structural the US–Gulf Co-operation Council axis becomes, the further east the Arab–Israeli peace process spreads and the closer Washington draws itself towards the Asian CIS republics, perhaps the less likely it will be that Iran and its Gulf Arab and Central Asian neighbours will travel within the same regional and international framework, making interaction between Iran and its two neighbouring regions more difficult and less certain in the future.

IRAN AND CENTRAL ASIA

Before the fall of the USSR the Middle East region was Arab dominated with Iran on its cultural and political margins. Now non-Arab Iran has acquired greater freedom of action and manoeuvrability and has, by way of illustration, been offered the opportunity to create a new regional subsystem around the states of Central Asia, with Tehran at its centre – a 'culture zone' of its own. Alternatively, it could have tried to absorb into the traditional Middle East subsystem the non-Arab Muslim republics of the former Soviet Union, thus creating a 'greater Middle East' with Iran as its geographical linchpin. In fact, Iran's response to the disintegration of the USSR has been far more complex than the above would suggest, not least due to the fact that such options as outlined above could never have been considered in a vacuum and not without a precise grasp of the impact of such geostrategic changes on the regional balance of power and the balance of forces among the established Middle Eastern actors.[23]

As senior Iranian officials themselves acknowledge, the passing of the Cold War and the emergence of new states in place of the monolithic Soviet Union compelled Iran to develop a more 'region-intensive' dimension to its foreign policy.[24] Broadly speaking, this policy has been manifesting itself in a two-pronged strategy: the consolidation of relations through bilateral, trilateral or quadrilateral economic, cultural and political ties, on the one hand[25] and the development of relations through contacts in multilateral fora, on the other.[26] None of these developments, however, have been at the expense of downgrading the importance of the traditional Middle East region or the position of Iran's southern Gulf Arab neighbours in Tehran's thinking, with whom, after all, Iran still shares much more in terms of economic interests than with its new ECO partners.

Geopolitically speaking, since the 1940s Iran has acted as the resident gatekeeper of the strategically important Strait of Hormuz. In the past, from this role Iran was able to extract a near-hegemonic status in the Persian Gulf.

Iranian officials like to argue that within West Asia's post-Cold War geopolitical space, Iran's role has been enhanced, not least due to the collapse of the Soviet Union, allowing Iran to emerge as the main gateway to Central Asia and its vast natural resources. Underpinning this strengthened geopolitical standing is easier economic and political access to the heartland of Asia. In practical terms, this has acquired two interconnected aspects: first, the rush to construct new hydrocarbon pipelines out of Central Asia and Transcaucasus and, second, the need to establish new road and rail networks southwards. In both cases geography dictates that Iran can be a vital link, 'the bridge', in these proposed transportation chains and networks in and out of these former USSR territories.

In geoeconomic terms, of course, agreements between the Central Asian and Caspian Sea states (such as Kazakhstan and Azerbaijan) and their neighbours with relation to transit hydrocarbons pipelines and other transport routes can have lucrative rewards. In addition, the geoeconomic picture is being complicated by the considerable competition between the regional powers themselves and Western concerns – in particular the oil transnationals – for the exploitation of the region's hydrocarbon resources as well as for the outlets of these resources. For Iran, whose initial steps towards cooperation with its new northern neighbours can best be categorized as tentative (see Table 5.3), the geoeconomics and geopolitics have come to form the two faces of the same coin. Rightly or wrongly, Iran sees itself not only as the vital bridge between Asia's landlocked heartland and the rest of the world, but also a 'resident' partner to any economic agreements that may be reached between these republics and Western commercial interests. In this complex strategy and thanks to undisguised warnings by Russia and the ruling élites of the Muslim republics themselves, the export of its Islamic revolution or any close and transparent allegiance with the Islamist movements of Central Asia has been constrained to take a back seat, to the dismay of the Tajiks, Azeri and other dissidents.

Given these possibilities and the potential opening up of the region to Iran, one has to account for Iran's initially timid approach towards the Caucasian and Central Asian republics. Foremostly, Iran was concerned not only with the impact of new regional players on its own security, but also with the consequences of its own diplomatic initiatives in Central Asia and the Caucasus on its good relations with Russia and, to a lesser degree, Turkey.[27] Secondly, owing to the post-1945 dynamics of the Middle East, Iran's entire regional policy had thus far had an Arab focus. So, the reorientation northwards of Tehran's diplomatic machinery has taken some time to show results. In addition, by 1992 the first Rafsanjani administration had entered the final year of its elected mandate and, in anticipation of electioneering politics, was more cautious in launching major foreign policy initiatives before August's presidential elections. Hojjatoleslam Rafsanjani's re-election as president in 1993 allowed his second administration to pursue its regional policies with renewed vigour. One priority in the second period was expansion of the ties with the republics of the former Soviet Union.

TABLE 5.3 *Iranian exchanges with the Muslim republics of the former USSR, 1992–1994*

	1992	*1993*	*1994*
Azerbaijan			
A	-	4	2
B	1	3	3
Kazakhstan			
A	–	4	2
B	1	–	5
Kyrgyzstan			
A	–	2	–
B	–	1	–
Tajikistan			
A	–	–	–
B	–	–	1
Turkmenistan			
A	1	5	6
B	–	4	4
Uzbekistan			
A	1	3	2
B	1	–	–

SOURCE Compiled from Iranian and Central Asian official gazettes and news reports.
Note. 'A' indicates visits by Iranian officials and 'B' indicates visits by Central Asian officials to Iran.

By early 1993, two other developments had enabled Iran to deepen its engagement with its northern neighbours. First, with the ECO emerging as an important regional body, Iran was able to use this vehicle for advancing its own interests in this region and, moreover, to use the organization to minimize tensions arising in its relations with Turkey over their independent involvement in this region. Second, despite some uncertainty and considerable US pressure, Moscow reaffirmed its earlier (military, civilian nuclear and trade) commitments to the Islamic Republic and showed signs of readiness to cooperate with Iran in Central Asian and the Caucasus. While not exactly an alliance between Tehran and Moscow, a close relationship has been in evidence since, particularly after the Russian Foreign Minister, Andrei Kozyrev's March 1993 trip to Tehran, which has allowed for the emergence of joint Iranian and Russian positions on, to take one example, the legal status of the Caspian Sea and for a convergence of views over the ending of the Tajiki civil war and the political crisis in post-Najibullah Afghanistan for others.

Iran's new initiative in upgrading its relations with the Central Asian republics was marked by its October 1993 diplomatic offensive. During this month, President Rafsanjani made his second trip to the region, heading a high-level delegation to four Central Asian republics (excluding Tajikistan) as well as to Azerbaijan and discussing with their élites bilateral cooperation and regional matters of interest. This trip was particularly significant for it seems to have laid down the basis for Iranian–Central Asian cooperation in the second half of the 1990s, as shown by the number of agreements reached between Iran and its northern neighbours – as many as 60 important agreements covering political, economic and cultural exchanges. It was also significant for another reason. Followed by the US Secretary of State's high-profile visit to Central Asia,[28] it highlighted US concerns about Tehran's drive to develop its existing foothold in Central Asia and the Transcaucasus outside of the West's orbit. The highly political nature of the US delegation's trip also illustrated the extent of American–Iranian rivalries in West Asia in general. In due course, this 'low-intensity' rivalry is likely to have a bearing on Iran's overall economic and political role in this region and on its potential to influence developments in the key countries among these republics.

CONCLUSION

Although one can find much evidence of political and economic activity in the territories of the former Soviet Union, the future of the region remains unclear, requiring another several decades – well into the twenty-first century in other words – before we can be reasonably sure of the position and role of the Central Asian republics in the emerging international system. Far from remaining independent players in the New World Order, the prospects of these states being reduced to peripheries of the powerful regional players cannot be ruled out. While from the early twentieth century Central Asia had fallen within the orbit of an overwhelmingly powerful Slavic (and European) power (Russia), in the course of the twenty-first century this region may well fall under the spell of several, non-European, regional powers – China, Iran, India and Turkey, to name the most prominent of the candidates – who could be co-existing as allies or be serious rivals in a new Asian subsystem. It is still impossible to speculate whether these powers will be able to count on support from other powers (like Japan, the USA, Korea, the European Union or Russia) in their struggle for domination of Asia's heartland – the crossroads between the prosperous Eurasian expanses – or whether they will seek to find unilateral (and highly destabilizing) survival tactics for the complexities of Asia's emerging balance of power equation. What is clear, however, is the fluid and unstable nature of interstate relations in post-Cold War West Asia.

For the moment, though, we can reflect on the fact that the end of the Cold War and the collapse of the USSR has already allowed the germination of unexpectedly friendly ties between several of Asia's future giants – Russia–Iran, Russia–China, India–Iran, Pakistan–China–Kazakhstan–Kyrgyzstan and even between Japan and China. Russia, the dominant Asian power, of course, could still manage to tear itself apart and shrink into a largely European power by the middle of the twenty-first century. If this were to happen, Siberia and much of its non-Slavic territories could either emerge as independent states or could as easily become satellites of Asia's rising powers, China, India, Iran and Turkey.

The geopolitical map of the region could change in other ways as well. By the middle of the next century, China, with its 1 billion and several hundred million people and the need to maintain a growth rate of around 10 per cent a year in order to be able to create 10 million new jobs a year for the entrants into its work-force, will be thirsty both for new territories and natural resources. Parts of Central Asia could fill the Chinese bill; much of this region is low in population, large in terms of territory (around 51 million people in 1995 and an area of 3 994 300 square kilometres) and very rich in primary inputs. China, therefore, may make a bid for some of the 'virgin' territories of Central Asia at the same time as expanding its presence in the Pacific.

Iran and Turkey too could witness vast improvements in their regional fortunes. In view of the post-Cold War instabilities caused by the Persian-speaking Asian states of Afghanistan and Tajikistan and Russia's inability to bring peace to these countries, Iran could capitalize on its natural advantages by offering to intervene in this region through carving out of Asia a more stable Persian-speaking 'zone of peoples'. It is not altogether inconceivable that in a post-dual containment environment, Tehran's strategy of threat containment could receive an approving nod from several Western countries, including perhaps the USA itself.

Likewise, Turkey could take advantage of the disintegration of Russia to develop a vast Turkic commonwealth of its own in the Caucasus and Central Asia. Whether Ankara's strategy will be reliant on Iran as an ally is hard to predict at present, but suffice it to say that dramatic domestic developments in Turkey itself (like the rise of its Islamist Refah Party),[29] will eventually feed into Turkish–Iranian relations and their policies towards the Muslim republics of the former Soviet Union. Judging by Turkey's current commitments towards the Turkic republics of the CIS (some $4.0 billion in investment by the mid-1990s, provision of training and job opportunities in Turkey, transmission of Turkish radio and television programmes, interstate joint ventures and so on), however, Turkey is well placed to carve for itself a new Turkic Asian constituency. Again, not only might the USA welcome such a move by its regional ally, but the European Union may take delight in it if it were to result in the postponement of Turkey's application to join the Union.

On another level, Iran and other oil-exporting Persian Gulf states as well should worry about the implications for their own future economic security of the new Transcaspian hydrocarbons exporters arriving on international markets. As Table 5.4 illustrates not a single OPEC country possesses the level of resources required to develop unilaterally its hydrocarbons deposits to meet the challenges (and expected surge in demand) of the twenty-first century, not even the formerly capital-surplus Gulf Arab sheikhdoms.

TABLE 5.4 *Main OPEC capacity expansion and estimated required investment*

OPEC member	*Sustainable capacity (mb/d) million barrels per day*		*Required investment ($billion)*	
	2010	*2020*	*2010*	*2020*
Indonesia	1.20	1.00	20	25
Iran	5.00	6.00	17	25
Iraq	6.00	7.00	13+	18+
Kuwait	3.50	4.00	8	12
Libya	2.20	2.10	14	18
Nigeria	2.75	2.50	15	20
Saudi Arabia	11.00	12.50	25	30
AU	3.50	4.00	10	13
Venezuela	3.30	3.50	23	31
OPEC Middle East share	29.50	32.90	77	105
Total OPEC	39.95	42.80	159	215

SOURCE ASP, 'The Financial Implications of Increasing Oil Output of Major Producing Regions', *Oil Market Trends*, vol. 45, no. 14 (2/9 October 1995).

This means that the main oil states are again likely to become almost totally dependent on the capital and technical resources of the same old 'imperial' Western oil transnational companies if they are to retain their shaky oligopoly of international oil markets and compete effectively with Azerbaijan and the other Central Asian hydrocarbons exporters of the twenty-first century. The irony here is that not only are the hydrocarbons exporters of the former Soviet Union already tapping the capital and technical pool of the same 'imperial' oil companies, in direct competition with the OPEC countries, but that some of the Middle East oil producers themselves, like Iran, Oman, Kuwait and Saudi Arabia, are assisting the Transcaspian states in the development of their hydrocarbons resources and their access to Western markets. The two regions, thus, could emerge as serious competitors on the oil markets of tomorrow, particularly if the nascent Russo–Kazakh axis does manage to construct a hydrocarbons consortium of its own in direct competition with OPEC.

Returning to the question of Iran's role in Central Asia and the Caucasus, it is remarkable how non-adversarial and non-adventurist the regime has been in its policies towards its much weaker and vulnerable northern neighbours. Despite several serious provocations, Tehran has continued to pursue its prudent policy of incremental engagement, in which, for the reasons stated, the search for joint venture agreements and cooperative relations has been the dominant trend. It is clear, therefore, that Iran has invested heavily in good relations with the Asian states of the CIS. But is it all worth it? In terms of geopolitical gains, undoubtedly it is true that Iran has benefited from the collapse of the Soviet Union, but in commercial terms a totally positive outcome would appear to be much less certain. For even if the Iranians, the government and private sector, were to strike successful commercial deals with these republics, the long-term viability of such deals and Iran's own ability to exploit them fully remain in doubt. As a Western diplomat has reported, 'Iran may be able to flog a few trucks up there, possibly some food and clothes. But the former Soviet Union is no pot of gold at the end of the rainbow to revive the Iranian economy.'[30] This view seems to indicate that after a short-lived diversion northwards, inevitably Iran is likely to retrain its sights southwards. Whether or not it does so will depend on its perceptions of its future role in the traditional Middle East subsystem, as well as on how it can participate in the 'new great game' – and win.

NOTES

1. We can see an example of this in the launching of a new shipping line by Iran between its Caspian Sea port of Bandar Anzali to the Russian Volga port of Astrakhan in May 1995, the first passenger ship to be making the journey in 100 years. See *Islamic Republic News Agency* report, 23 May 1995.

2. See V.F. Piacentini, 'Islam: Iranian Saudi Arabian Religious and Geopolitical Competition in Central Asia', in A. Ehteshami (ed.), *From Gulf to Central Asia: Players in the New Great Game* (Exeter: University of Exeter Press, 1994), pp. 25–46.
3. O.M. Smolansky, 'Turkish and Iranian Policies in Central Asia' in H. Malik (ed.), *Central Asia: its Strategic Importance and Future Prospects* (New York: St Martin's Press, 1994), pp. 283–310.
4. See Foreign and Commonwealth Office Background Brief, *Iran's Relations with the Southern Members of the Commonwealth of Independent States* (London: FCO, March 1992).
5. World Bank figures for 1994 show that the GNP per capita of the CIS Muslim states compares quite favourably with those of their southern neighbours. Turkmenistan's figure of $1700, Azerbaijan's $1670, Kyrgyzstan's $1551 and Uzbekistan's $1350 are not much smaller than the Turkish GNP per capita figure of $1820; Iran's figure of $2320 is smaller than Kazakhstan's ($2470). All the CIS Muslim countries have GNP per capita figures many times greater than those of Afghanistan ($250), Pakistan ($400) and India ($330). Only Saudi Arabia, Kuwait, Qatar and the UAE have GNP per capita figures much greater than those of the Muslim CIS countries.
6. *The Khaleej Times*, 9 June 1995.
7. M.B. Olcott, 'Central Asia's Catapult to Independence', *Foreign Affairs*, vol. 71, no. 3 (Summer 1992), pp. 108–30.
8. A.M. Apostolou, 'The Problems of Creating Economies in Central Asia' in A. Ehteshami (ed.), *From the Gulf to Central Asia: Players in the New Great Game* (Exeter: University of Exeter Press, 1994), p. 59.
9. For an excellent survey of the dynamics of the Arab system see P.C. Noble, 'The Arab System: Pressures, Constraints, and Opportunities' in B. Korany and A.E. Hillal Dessouki (eds), *The Foreign Policies of Arab States: the Challenge of Change* (Oxford: Westview Press, 1991), pp. 49–102.
10. C. Brown and Camilla Nilsson, *Economic Potentials and Investment Rationales in Central Asia Republics* (Jeddah: Economic Research and Information Department, Saudi Cairo Bank, 1994).
11. In this regard, the Azeris' decision in the referendum of 17 November 1995 to agree to the formal separation of the state and religion (and eliminating Islam as the country's official religion) came as a major blow to Iran, particularly as Azerbaijan is the CIS' only Shii-dominated republic, Iran's own sect of Islam. Another 'structural' problem for Iran is that the northern region's only Persian-speaking country is Tajikistan, which is culturally close to Iran but is an overwhelmingly Sunni country in terms of religious affiliations.
12. For further analysis see A. Ehteshami, *After Khomeini: the Iranian Second Republic* (London: Routledge, 1995); Hamid Zangeneh (ed.), *Islam, Iran, and World Stability* (New York: St Martin's Press, 1994).
13. See, for instance, President Rafsanjani's speech delivered at the December 1994 conference on the Persian Gulf region organized by the Foreign Ministry-affiliated Institute for Political and International Studies. *The Iranian Journal of International Affairs*, vol. VII, no. 3 (Fall 1995), pp. 697–700.
14. H. Hosseini, 'The Change of Economic and Industrial Policy in Iran: President Rafsanjani's Perestroika', and H. Akhavi-Pour, 'Privatization in Iran: Analysis of the Process and Methods' in H. Zangeneh (ed.), *Islam, Iran, and World*

Stability (New York: St Martin's Press, 1994), pp. 167–86 and pp. 187–99, respectively.

15. S. Shahabi and F. Farhi, 'Security Considerations and Iranian Foreign Policy', *Journal of Foreign Policy*, vol. IX, no. 1 (Spring 1995), pp. 39–55 (in Persian).
16. According to official sources refugees cost the Iranian Government around $2.5 million daily in 1995.
17. To underline the point about Iran's accommodationist policies in the north and its generally positive impact, one can draw attention to the results of an 1992 opinion poll in Armenia, in which Iran, with 55 per cent support, emerged as Armenia's second most popular 'desirable ally', followed by the US (35 per cent), Georgia (34 per cent), Turkey (29 per cent), China (13 per cent) and France (12 per cent). Russia was the polled Armenians' most popular ally, with 82 per cent. See BBC, *Summary of World Broadcasts*, SU/1573, 29 December 1992.
18. This tendency is amply illustrated by the US insistence in 1995 that Iran's already agreed upon stake of 5 per cent in Azerbaijan's International Oil Consortium (in which US companies have a 40 per cent stake) be withdrawn, which the Azerbaijani Government reluctantly accepted. The USA also insists, with Russian and Turkish approval, that none of the new oil pipelines under consideration be routed through Iranian territory.
19. With regard to Iraq, Iran has been pursuing a complex strategy of 'friendly neighbourliness', containment (through its support for UN resolutions on Iraq and by its regular contacts with Syria and Turkey) and indirect pressure (through maintaining its bridges with the Iraqi opposition).
20. A presence that was formalized with the creation of a new US fleet, the Fifth Fleet, in the Persian Gulf in 1995.
21. It should be noted, however, that since 1990 Tehran has been relatively successful in developing political or diplomatic relations with several of its Arab and non-Arab neighbours. Politically, Iran has good relations with Russia, the Central Asian and Caucasian republics, Turkey, Pakistan and India. Within the Arab world, Tehran has been able to develop political ties with Syria and Sudan and several Arab-based political movements. Diplomatically, Iran has been able to establish reasonably good relations with Saudi Arabia and its GCC partners, Jordan, Morocco, Tunisia, Egypt, Yemen and even its old enemy Iraq.
22. S. Chubin, *Iran's National Security Policy: Capabilities, Intentions and Impact* (Washington, DC: Carnegie Endowment for International Peace, 1994), p. 87.
23. For an overview of Iran's relations with and strategy towards the republics of Central Asia and the Caucasus see E. Herzig, *Iran and the Former Soviet South* (London: Royal Institute of International Affairs, 1995); M. Mohsenin, 'Iran's Relations with Central Asia', *Journal of Foreign Policy*, vol. IX, no. 1 (Spring 1995), pp. 164–84; E. Hooglund, 'Iran and Central Asia' in A. Ehteshami (ed.), *From the Gulf to Central Asia: Players in the New Great Game* (Exeter: University of Exeter Press, 1994), pp. 114–28; and, W. Scott Harrop, 'Iran's Steady Windows on Northwest Asia', *Middle East Insight*, vol. XI, no. 5 (July–August 1995), pp. 80–3.
24. This term has been introduced by the Iranian Deputy Foreign Minister, Abbas Maleki. See his article, 'Cooperation: a New Component of the Iranian Foreign Policy', *The Iranian Journal of International Affairs*, vol. V, no. 1 (Spring 1993), pp. 16–20.

25. For instance, Tehran has been very active in promoting trilateral ties with its neighbours, particularly where Iran is placed as the centre or the link in the chain: Iran–India–Turkmenistan, Iran–Bangladesh–Turkmenistan and Iran–Russia–Turkmenistan serve to illustrate the point. Iran has also agreed to help sell Turkmeni natural gas to Armenia and the Ukraine.
26. Such multilateral bodies as the ECO (which expanded its membership in 1992 to include all of the Muslim republics of the former Soviet Union and Afghanistan), the Organisation of Islamic Conference and the Caspian Sea Organisation have been particular targets of Iranian diplomacy. Furthermore, in January 1995 Iran went as far as reaching an agreement in principle with Kazakhstan, Russia, Turkey and Turkmenistan to transfer the natural gas output of the relevant countries to European markets via Iranian and Turkish territories.
27. M. Mesbahi, 'Iran's Emerging Partnership with Russia', *Middle East Insight*, vol. XI, no. 5 (July–August 1995), pp. 84–7; P. Robins, 'The Middle East and Central Asia', in P. Ferdinand (ed.), *The New States of Central Asia and Their Neighbours* (New York: Council on Foreign Regulations Press, 1995), pp. 55–74.
28. In an obvious gesture towards the most strategically placed of all Central Asian republics, namely Kazakhstan, Secretary Christopher agreed to increase the US bilateral aid package to this state by $85 million, to $140 million a year, as well as offering it $15 million per year towards the reclamation of the Aral Sea. See *New York Times*, 24 October 1993.
29. The anti-NATO and EU Refah Party, by capturing 21.4 per cent of the vote in Turkey's general elections in December 1995 and winning 158 of Turkey's 550 parliamentary seats, became the country's largest single parliamentary party. See 'Turkey: Guess Who Will Govern', *The Economist* (6 January 1996), pp. 33–4.
30. Quoted in *The Economist* (2 December 1995), p. 70.

6 Turkish Policy in Central Asia[1]

G.M. Winrow

INTRODUCTION

The main foreign policy objective of the current Turkish Government (like that of its predecessors) is to secure Turkey's full admission to the EU. This would result in the general acknowledgement of Turkey's European credentials. The refusal of officials in Ankara to recognize the Kurds in Turkey as a separate ethnic minority and the human rights violations committed by the Turkish security forces in their attempts to crush the terrorist (Partia Karkaren Kürdistan) Kurdistan Workers' Party, are seriously damaging the prospects of eventual Turkish admission to the EU. The Kurdish issue also has an important regional dimension. Thus, relations with neighbouring Iran, Iraq and Syria occupy a prominent position on Turkey's foreign policy agenda. Problems with Greece in the Aegean and with Russia in the Transcaucasus also occupy much of the attention of decision makers in Ankara. Difficulties in the relationship with Russia put an added emphasis on the importance of ties between Turkey and the US.

Hence, in spite of cultural, ethnic, historical, linguistic and religious links between Turkey and the four Turkic states in post-Soviet Central Asia[2] – that is Kazakhstan, the Kyrgyz Republic, Turkmenistan and Uzbekistan – relations between Turkey and these newly independent states by no means constitute a foreign policy priority for many officials in Ankara. Likewise, one should not assume that all of the Turkic states (including, here, Azerbaijan) perceive Turkey as their principal contact with the outside world. On the other hand, one should not underscore the significance of ties between Turkey and these states.

Many in Turkey had apparently hoped and believed that an active role in post-Soviet Central Asia would boost Turkey's international image and would enhance the prospects of Turkey's admission to the EU. This has yet to be realized, although the US administration is particularly appreciative of Turkish involvement in Central Asia believing that this has limited Iran's role in the region. Turkish officials are stressing the importance of Turkey as an intermediary between the West (the EU and the USA) and Central Asia.

The increasing rise of extreme nationalist sentiment in some quarters in Turkey, which is in part the product of the Kurdish problem and the Western reaction to Turkey's handling of the problem, will mean that officials in Ankara and other groups in Turkey will continue to stress the importance of ethnic bonds of solidarity with the Turkic states. Moreover, tensions between Turkey and Russia in the Transcaucasus are bound to have a spin-off effect on relations between the two in Central Asia, bearing in mind Moscow's concern for the fate of the 9 million or so Russians still living in post-Soviet Central Asia.

THE TRANSCAUCASUS–CENTRAL ASIA CONNECTION

Clearly, the decision makers in Ankara are confronted with specific problems in the Transcaucasus which are particular to that region. Fierce fighting in Nagorno–Karabak, which at times threatened to spill over into the Azerbaijani enclave of Nakhichevan, almost led to direct Turkish military intervention. Turkish officials have vehemently opposed Russian moves to break the Conventional Forces in Europe treaty limits on armoured vehicles and tanks in the northern Caucasus. They have also objected to Russian peacekeeping operations in Georgia and criticized Moscow's moves to resecure access to all former Soviet military bases in the Transcaucasus. Unlike Central Asia, the Transcaucasus is an area of vital security interest to Turkey.

However, the Transcaucasus is also strategically important for Turkey because it offers a direct access route – via the Caspian Sea – to Central Asia avoiding Russia and Iran. Stability in the Transcaucasus and improved relations with Armenia would facilitate contacts between Turkey and post-Soviet Central Asia. Bearing in mind the ideological differences between secular Turkey and the Islamic Republic of Iran and also taking into account Iran's own interests in Central Asia, Turkish officials are unwilling to remain dependent on land access to the region through Iranian territory. In the first 6 months of 1994 evidently some 3000 Turkish trucks used the road through Iran to Central Asia to transport commodities worth 300 billion TL (Turkish lira) (at the time 1$ = approximately 30 000 TL).[3] In spite of agreements concluded between Ankara and Tehran this land route is often blocked. The official opening of the Türkgözü border gate on the Turkish–Georgian frontier in August 1995 is likely to improve Turkey's access to Central Asia avoiding Iran.

The Transcaucasus–Central Asia connection is also assuming more importance for Turkey because of the increasing possibility that oil and gas from Kazakhstan, Turkmenistan and Uzbekistan could be transported to

Turkey and then to Western Europe and beyond after the building of new pipelines across the Transcaucasus. The Turkish economy would benefit from the royalty fees and transportation costs. Some of the piped oil and gas would likely be used by the Turkish consumer (the importance of this is discussed later). The construction of new pipelines across the Transcaucasus would make Turkmenistan and Kazakhstan in particular less dependent on Russia economically and politically. At present, the only pipeline routes from the former Soviet Central Asia pass through Russia. It appears that many officials in Moscow are opposed to the construction of alternative pipelines presumably because this would reduce Russian leverage over the Central Asians.

Currently three major export lines deliver oil from Kazakhstan to Russia. One of these lines from the Tengiz oil field runs around the Caspian Sea to the Russian Black Sea port of Novorossiisk via Grozny. Some Kazakh crude oil is able to be shipped to Baku across the Caspian Sea. As Turkmenistan's only major oil pipeline is used to receive Russian oil, for export purposes Turkmenistan is also currently dependent on shipping oil across the Caspian. The Caspian Pipeline Consortium – the members of which are Russia, Oman, Kazakhstan and the US oil company Chevron – is constructing a new oil pipeline from Tengiz to Novorossiisk which would bypass the unstable region around Grozny.[4]

Officials in Ankara are very much interested in piping some of the future oil exports of Kazakhstan and Turkmenistan across Turkish territory. There are plans to connect a Kazakh and Turkmen oil pipeline with a possible new pipeline linking Baku with the Turkish Mediterranean port of Ceyhan. There has been much discussion concerning the construction of a Baku–Ceyhan link after the agreement concluded in September 1994 between the Azerbaijani Government and an international oil consortium (including the Turkish Petroleum Corporation with an eventual 6.75 per cent stake) to explore and develop three offshore oil fields in the Caspian. New Kazakh and Turkmen oil pipelines could be laid under the Caspian Sea to be connected with the Baku–Ceyhan link at Baku or at another point on the link. The Baku–Ceyhan link could pass through Georgia or cross Armenia and Nakhichevan or Iran and Nakhichevan before entering Turkey. Turkish officials are exploring the possibility of transporting 25 million tons of oil per annum from Azerbaijan and another 20 million tons from Kazakhstan along these projected routes.

Some Kazakh oil may indeed be transported across Turkey in the future. The Caspian Pipeline Consortium has run into difficulties because of a dispute with Chevron over financing and share ownership. This has led the US administration to back publicly a pipeline route through Turkey as an additional route to the Tengiz–Novorossiisk option. Russian officials are likely to object to the construction of an oil pipeline under the Caspian Sea connecting Kazakhstan and the Transcaucasus. In mid-July 1995 there were reports that the Russian Foreign Ministry in diplomatic notes sent to Azerbaijan, Kazakhstan and Turkmenistan had threatened the safety of all Caspian Sea-related natural resource projects launched without its consent.[5] Sensitive to Russian concerns the Kazakhs are proceeding cautiously. Visiting Almaty in August 1995 Turkish Prime Minister Tansu Çiller was disappointed when she failed to secure definite commitments from President Nursultan Nazarbayev with regard to the construction of a Kazakhstan–Ceyhan oil pipeline. Instead, it was agreed to establish a consortium open to all interested states (that is, including Russia) which would consider the Ceyhan option and other possible routes.[6]

Before Turkey may transport and possibly consume Kazakh oil, an agreement will have to be reached on the route of a future Baku–Ceyhan pipeline. The American members of the international oil consortium will not be able to approve of a route through Iran. A line through Georgia could be sabotaged given the continued instability in that country. The Armenian option is only possible if the Nagorno–Karabak dispute is successfully resolved. Moscow is also lobbying for a possible Baku–Novorossiisk link, which would require the rebuilding and upgrading of an earlier constructed pipeline. In October 1995 the Azerbaijani Government and the international oil consortium agreed that 'early oil' extracted from the three offshore oil fields in the Caspian would be transported via the 'Russian route' (Baku–Novorossiisk) and also the 'Western route' (Baku–Soupsa, near Batum in Georgia). Oil from the Western route could then be shipped to Turkey where it could be refined and then consumed. This arrangement appears to increase the possibility that the eventual main pipeline for oil from Azerbaijan (and possibly from Kazakhstan) will run from Baku to Ceyhan along a path still to be determined.

At present, Turkmenistan's only gas pipeline for export to the West passes through Russian territory. In 1993 Moscow blocked Turkmen gas deliveries to Europe over a dispute on quota and tariff schedules. Eager to loosen their dependence on Moscow, Turkmen officials have concluded an agreement to transport Turkmen gas to Central Europe via Iran and Turkey. Surprisingly, Russian officials have not opposed this deal. Indeed, Russia is even represented on the steering committee which is working to realize this project. Perhaps, Moscow may be reasoning that the pipeline will never be built because of the high costs ($7 billion) and the possible difficulties of securing Western financial backing because of Iranian involvement. However, in a report released on 7 July 1995, the Turkish State Pipeline Company, BOTAŞ, proposed the construction of a Turkmen natural gas pipeline to

Europe along a route beneath the Caspian Sea and via the Transcaucasus and Turkey, thereby bypassing Iran.[7]

In August 1995 in Ashkhabad, Prime Minister Çiller held talks with the Turkmen President, Saparmurad Niyazov, on the future of the natural gas project. Turkish officials were evidently concerned that a proposed Turkmen–Iranian agreement to construct a natural gas pipeline to northern Iran could divert much of the Turkmen gas that could otherwise be delivered to and exported via Turkey. Indeed, 1 month after Çiller's visit, an Iranian–Turkmen deal along these lines was concluded. Niyazov had informed Çiller that the construction of a gas pipeline from Turkmenistan to Central Europe was no longer a priority, although in the near term he was prepared to allow the transport of Turkmen gas to Turkey via the upgrading of an existing pipeline running across Russia and Georgia.[8] Çiller's plans to convene a summit meeting in Turkey in autumn 1995 with the leaders of Uzbekistan, Turkmenistan, Georgia and Azerbaijan to discuss the possibility of constructing an Uzbekistan–Turkmenistan–Georgia–Turkey gas pipeline have not materialized. In talks in Tashkent in July 1995 Çiller and the Uzbek President, Islam Kerimov, had referred to the possibility of constructing such a gas pipeline.[9]

TURKISH INVOLVEMENT IN CENTRAL ASIA: AN OVERVIEW[10]

Turkish officials had showed little interest in the fate of the Turkic peoples in Soviet Central Asia until the final months before the disintegration of the Soviet Union. The Turkish Government was hence taken by surprise when the Soviet Union rapidly unravelled and the Turkic peoples there had independence literally thrust upon them. This lack of interest in developments in Soviet Central Asia is explained in part by the fact that, unlike parts of the Transcaucasus, Central Asia had never been part of the Ottoman Empire. Turkic tribes had originated from Central Asia and a number of these had migrated westwards in the Dark Age period. However, contacts between the Anatolian Turks and the Turkic peoples remaining in the region were cut in the mid-sixteenth century by the advance of Muscovy.

By the late nineteenth century some leading officials in the Ottoman Empire were attracted to the idea of Pan-Turkism. Many of the original Pan-Turkic thinkers were Crimean Turks who had recently fled to the Ottoman Empire to escape Russian persecution. Pan-Turkism has as its goal the establishment of some form of union of the Turkic peoples. This could entail a political union or empire or could take the shape of a looser cultural association or commonwealth. The original Pan-Turkic dream was effectively quashed with the death of Enver Pasha in 1922 who fell fighting with Basmachi rebels who were struggling to resist the imposition of communist rule in Central Asia.

In the following decades only fringe radical extremist groups in Turkey remained attracted to Pan-Turkism as Mustapha Kemal 'Atatürk' focused his attention on consolidating the Republic of Turkey based on a new Turkish nationalism. However, in his nation-building and state-building programmes Atatürk made use of the myths – based in part on reality – of the origins of the Anatolian Turks from Central Asia. The historians of the Atatürk era would embellish these myths with such notions that Central Asia was the cradle of Turkish civilization and, hence, reputedly, of all civilizations. Given the importance attached to these myths, it was perhaps surprising that Turkish officials paid so little attention to the developments in Communist Central Asia.

Turkey was the first state to recognize the independence of the Soviet Central Asian Turkic republics and the first to open embassies there. At the time there was a great euphoria in Turkey. This was whipped up by Turkish officials and the media. Western governments were also eager to promote the relevance for the Central Asians of the 'Turkish model' of a secular, democratic state based on a free market economy, in order to pre-empt the expansion of Iranian influence in Central Asia. The leaders of the newly independent Turkic states also played their part in stressing the importance of establishing ties with Turkey. For example, Kerimov, visiting Ankara in December 1991 at the time Turkey announced the official recognition of Uzbek independence, declared that he looked up to Turkey as an elder brother (*ağabey*). Kerimov noted that Uzbekistan and the other newly independent Central Asian states had much to learn from Turkey and added that Uzbekistan urgently needed economic, political and cultural assistance from Turkey.[11]

At the time the Central Asians, lacking experience in international politics and unsure of their future, were immensely grateful for Turkish offers of political and economic support. Stressing common ethnic links also helped the newly independent Turkic states in their search for an identity. However, in the euphoria, Turkish officials somewhat recklessly pledged to extend generous aid to the Central Asians. In reality, given the limitations of the Turkish economy, these promises could not be fulfilled.[12] Nevertheless, in the immediate aftermath of independence the Turkish Foreign Minister, Hikmet Çetin, toured Central Asia in February–March 1992 (including, interestingly, a visit to Farsi-speaking and largely non-Turkic Tajikistan) and the then Prime Minister, Süleyman Demirel, was welcomed in the region in April–May 1992.

This initial euphoria was shattered with the 'failure' of the first Turkic Summit held in Ankara in October 1992 – attended by the leaders of Turkey, Azerbaijan, Kazakhstan, the Kyrgyz Republic, Turkmenistan and Uzbekistan. In his opening remarks, the Turkish President, Turgut Özal, had announced that the twenty-first century would be the century of the Turks. He declared that a Turkic common market and a Turkic development and investment bank should be established and requested firm pledges from Kazakhstan, Turkmenistan and Uzbekistan to construct oil and gas pipelines from their territories to Europe via Turkey. However, the summit only concluded with the vaguely worded Ankara Declaration which was short on detail and specific commitments. The declaration talked about the possibility of cooperation in various fields, announced the formation of working groups to study various projects and spoke of the need to convene regular Turkic Summits in the future. It seems that by this time the Central Asian leaders, more sure of themselves having secured general international recognition and membership in various international organizations and by now aware of the relatively limited financial and technical support Turkey could offer, wished to maintain their freedom of manoeuvre and cultivate ties with other states interested in the region such as Iran. The Central Asians were also not prepared to antagonize Russia by committing themselves fully to exclusively Turkic bodies or formations.

In contrast, the much better planned second Turkic Summit, which assembled in Istanbul in October 1994, was a relative 'success'. The leaders praised what had become the regular meetings of ministers of culture and education, decided to hold similar gatherings of their foreign ministers and referred to the need to encourage interparliamentary cooperation. Unlike the first Turkic Summit, specific reference was also made to the Nagorno–Karabak dispute, with the leaders demanding that the Armenians should abide by all UN Security Council resolutions and, hence, withdraw from all territory occupied in Azerbaijan. It seems, though, that Nazarbayev was not prepared to upset Yerevan and Moscow by branding Armenia an aggressor. The leaders also declared that new oil and gas pipelines should be constructed using the most economic and shortest route and in this light they valued the work being done on the possibility of building lines to Europe and the Mediterranean via Turkey.

The third Turkic Summit held in Bishkek in August 1995 also made similar references to the Nagorno–Karabak dispute. The delegates appeared particularly careful not to antagonize Russia. Thus, in the Bishkek Declaration, the leaders pledged to boost bilateral and multilateral economic ties 'without prejudice to their international obligations' (that is Commonwealth of Independent States (CIS) obligations).[13] Oil and natural gas joint projects should be developed 'with all interested countries' (that is, including possibly Russia). The participants expressed their satisfaction at the initiation of parliamentary cooperation between their countries and underlined the importance of regular consultative meetings between foreign ministers or their plenipotentiaries. The declaration also expressed support for the efforts undertaken by Kazakhstan, the Kyrgyz Republic and Uzbekistan to set in motion and expand 'integration processes' in the region. In order to help finance joint projects and coordinate payments transactions these three Central Asian states had launched 1 month earlier the operation of the Central Asian Bank for Economic Cooperation and Development. The Bishkek Turkic Summit thus openly recognized and praised Central Asian initiatives to which Turkey was not a party.

Since late 1991 there has been heavy diplomatic traffic between Turkey and the newly independent Turkic states of Central Asia. Turkish businessmen are actively involved in the region, investing in various construction projects. Even with the constraints of the Turkish economy, the government in Ankara has still encouraged the allocation of credits to the Central Asians via the Turkish Eximbank to boost trade turnover and support construction work. Humanitarian aid has also been granted. Turkish officials have attempted to circumvent the problem of access to the region by developing telecommunications links and establishing airline connections. There is much cooperation in the cultural and educational fields. Turkish cultural centres and schools have been established in Central Asia and there are plans to open up universities in Kazakhstan, the Kyrgyz Republic and Turkmenistan. Since the 1992–1993 academic year students from the Central Asian Turkic states have been attending schools and universities in Turkey. In the 1994–1995 academic year 40 places in Turkish educational establishments were reserved for the first time for Tajik students. The Turkish television channel Avrasya is beamed to Central Asian homes with programmes broadcast in Anatolian Turkish with Turkish language subtitles.[14] Diplomats, police officers, security personnel, military cadets and religious officials from the region have all received training in Turkey.

TURKISH 'POLICIES' IN CENTRAL ASIA

No state is a monolithic entity. Foreign policy decision making to say nothing of its implementation is not left in the hands of one individual. In the making of the foreign policy of a relatively democratic state, inputs are bound to come from various government ministries, opposition political parties, interest groups, business lobbies and other agencies and public opinion. This may at times lead to contradictory policies and inconsistent behaviour by a particular state. However, overall, an outside observer is usually still able to perceive the general thrust of the foreign policy of a state towards another state or group of states. Ultimately, it is the Ministry of Foreign Affairs in close coordination with top executive officials which formulates guidelines and is in control of the day-to-day management of foreign policy. Thus, one is able to maintain that there is 'a' Turkish policy in Central Asia as the title of this paper suggests. However, there are indications that other groups, agencies and individuals are having an increasing influence on Turkish policy in Central Asia. The activities of these groups may run counter to the official line of the Turkish Ministry of Foreign Affairs (MFA). This could even complicate Turkey's relations with other states interested in Central Asia. Arguably, different 'Turkish policies' toward Central Asia are emerging. It is too early to assess how influential these other policies might turn out to be.

With reference to Turkish policy in Central Asia, the official line of the Turkish MFA remains predominant. However, the staff in the Ministry have had to acquire rapidly an expertise in a region which has been traditionally overlooked and disregarded by Turkish officials. A number of administrative arrangements have had to be made within the Ministry to accommodate for developments in post-Soviet Central Asia. This includes the appointment in 1995 of a minister of state responsible for the Turkic states. The Turkish MFA is eager to promote peace, stability and democracy in Central Asia.[15] It is willing to work together with other states with interests in the region to fulfil these objectives. Economic ties are encouraged. According to the Ministry, Turkey aims to facilitate the integration of the Central Asian Turkic states with the rest of the world by sponsoring and assisting them in their applications to join various international bodies. If necessary, Turkey will inform Western states of the specific problems the Central Asians might be encountering.

The Turkish MFA also intends to institutionalize further ties between Turkey and the newly independent Turkic states. This is meant to be an evolutionary process. The Turkic Summits are to be used as fora where problems of common concern may be addressed. The aim is not to establish a Turkic Union or a Turkic Commonwealth. A gradual institutionalization of ties is apparent when comparing the results of the first Turkic Summit with the following two summits. It appears that the Turkish MFA is attempting to stress the supposed political and economic relevance of the Turkish model for the Central Asians. However, the shortcomings of Turkish democracy and the weaknesses of the Turkish economy are well known. Turkish officials should be exceedingly careful not to come across as condescending when offering advice to their Central Asian counterparts.

The approach of Turkish businessmen towards the region would appear to complement the official line of the Turkish MFA. Peace and stability provide favourable conditions for further investment and the expansion of trade. Turkish entrepreneurs are probably less concerned about democratization in Central Asia. Sound commercial relationships may be developed with stable authoritarian regimes which are embarking on the path of economic reform. The commitment of the Turkish MFA to the principle of democracy should also at least be questioned given Turkey's swift abandonment of the Elchibey regime in the summer of 1993 when the democratically elected president of Azerbaijan was overthrown in what at first was a coup by a bunch of renegade military officers.[16]

Certain governmental officials, ministries, political parties, interest groups and academics in Turkey do have definite Pan-Turkic sympathies. They are attempting to influence Turkish policy in Central Asia. Their aims and objectives do not appear to correspond with the official line of the Turkish MFA. They seem to be in favour of the formation of what would amount to a Turkic cultural union or commonwealth. Even the then Prime Minister, Demirel, when touring the region in the spring of 1992, referred to the prospects of forming an 'association of independent Turkic states'.[17] The prominent Pan-Turkist, Alparslan Türkeş, the leader of the Nationalist Action Party, whom Demirel had surprisingly included in his entourage to visit Central Asia, has spoken of the need to establish a Turkic commonwealth or association which would have a high council of Turkic republics of presidents, prime ministers and foreign ministers that would meet several times a year under a rotating presidency.[18] Türkeş has become an increasingly influential figure in Turkish politics in recent years. The Çiller Government has come to rely on his party's support to avoid being outflanked by the rising nationalist–Islamicist opposition in Turkey embodied in the Refah Party.

Türkeş played a leading role in convening the first, second and third general assemblies of the Turkic States and Turkic Peoples' Friendship and Cooperation Group which assembled in Antalya in March 1993, in Izmir in October 1994 and in Ceşme in October 1995. Although the Turkish MFA did not organize these consultative meetings, various sessions were nevertheless attended and addressed by Presidents Özal and Demirel and Prime Minister Çiller. The general assemblies aim to develop cooperation in the fields of science, technology, education and culture. Most significantly, delegates to the general assemblies expressed their interest in realizing the proposal of Türkeş to establish a high council of Turkic republics. It should be noted that participants in the general assemblies were not only from the newly independent Turkic states but also included Turkic peoples living in various Russian republics such as Tatarstan, Bashkortostan and Yakutia. In particular the Izmir meeting, held immediately after the convening of the second Turkic Summit in Istanbul, alarmed Russian officials. The Turkish MFA is probably concerned that Moscow may not be able to differentiate clearly between the Turkic Summits and the basically Pan-Turkic general assemblies. This could result in Russia, fearful of Pan-Turkism, pressurizing Central Asian leaders not to attend future Turkic Summits. Officials in Ankara were probably thus relieved that the third general assembly was convened several weeks after the Bishkek Summit and that the assembly met in Turkey and not in the Kyrgyz Republic.

The Turkish Ministries of Education and Culture appear to share the Pan-Turkic sympathies of Türkeş and his supporters. Aiming to strengthen ties with the Turkic states, these ministries seem to be aspiring to place Turkey at the centre of what they perceive to be an emerging Turkic world or commonwealth. The Turkish Education Ministry has been heading a project with representatives from Azerbaijan and the Central Asian Turkic states to prepare standard history textbooks which were meant to be introduced in Turkey and throughout the region in the 1995–1996 academic year. Standard literary textbooks were also to be prepared.[19] In July 1995 the Turkish Education Minister, Nevzat Azay, on the occasion of the donation of 425 000 books to Azerbaijan, spoke of the importance of developing common history and literature textbooks, declaring 'We must protect the values we share through our history'.[20]

Progress has been made in introducing literary textbooks. However, the Turkish Education Ministry has failed to generate support to prepare common history textbooks. Each Turkic state prefers to write its own official history. A common 'Turkish line' on history has not been able to prevail over the different historical interpretations offered by Central Asian historians.[21] This is in spite of the fact that there are already a number of Turkish schools which have been established in Central Asia and Turkish teachers are working there. Teaching staff from the area have been trained in Turkey. There are also plans to launch an Open University programme for the region to be organized and broadcast from Turkey.

It appears that the Turkish Ministry of Culture is leading the work of the Turkic Cultures and Arts Joint Administration (TÜRKSOY). The members of TÜRKSOY in addition to Turkey are Azerbaijan, Kazakhstan, the Kyrgyz Republic, the Turkish Republic of Northern Cyprus, Turkmenistan, Tatarstan and Bashkortostan – note, the inclusion of the two Russian republics and the omission of Uzbekistan. Agencies in Turkey such as the Research Foundation of the Turkish World, the Turkish Cultural Research Association and the Turkish International Cooperation Agency (TICA) are supporting the activities of the Turkish Ministries of Education and Culture. In addition to its technical and training programmes, the TICA has helped to organize and sponsor 'Turkic meetings'/'Turkish-speaking meetings' of youth leaders, university rectors, news agencies and so on.

One may argue that there is a long-term strategy here to foster ties with the Turkic states and peoples in order to create in effect a Turkic commonwealth. As noted earlier, this is not the official line of the Turkish MFA. The inclusion of the Turkic peoples of the Russian Federation in this 'emerging Turkic world' is bound to alarm officials in Moscow. It is exceedingly unlikely that an actual Turkic commonwealth will indeed emerge in practice. As recently as 1989 and 1990 there was intra-Turkic violence in the Fergana Valley among the Meskhetian Turks and the Uzbeks and in Osh between the Kyrgyz and the Uzbeks. The proceedings and results of the three Turkic Summits clearly indicate that the current Central Asian leaders do not want to bind themselves exclusively to Turkey. Pan-Turkic political parties in the region such as Azat and Alash in Kazakhstan, Asaba in the Kyrgyz Republic and the Turkestan People's Movement in Uzbekistan are small, insignificant groupings, some of which are banned. Parties such as the illegal Alash also combine Pan-Turkic with radical Islamic views.[22]

Finally, another developing and separate 'Turkish policy' in Central Asia stems from the activities of unofficial Islamic Sufic orders (tariqats) based in Turkey which are now openly operating in post-Soviet Central Asia. The leader of the semi-illegal Nurcu sect in Turkey, Fethullah Gülen, who has close links with the Naqshbandiyya order, has been the subject of much publicity in Turkey in recent months. Gülen has personally established 150 religious schools in Central Asia and the Transcaucasus. Even the former Turkish Prime Minister, Bülent Ecevit, a stalwart of secularism, has praised the operation of these schools because in his opinion they would diminish the influence of Saudi Arabia and Iran in the region.[23] It would appear that at present the low-scale activities of unofficial Turkish Islamic groups in Central Asia does not pose a problem for the Turkish MFA. Gülen is not under the control of the religious Refah Party in Turkey. Of course, if Refah were to singlehandedly govern Turkey, the official line of the Turkish MFA would most probably be subject to considerable revision. In those circumstances, officials in Ankara would abandon their intentions of joining the EU and would focus more of their attention on the Middle East and Central Asia.

HOW IMPORTANT IS TURKISH INVOLVEMENT IN CENTRAL ASIA?

As noted earlier in this paper, although relations with post-Soviet Central Asia are important, they by no means constitute a priority in Turkish foreign policy, at least with regard to officials in the Turkish MFA. Nevertheless, in economic terms, the extent of Turkish involvement in post-Soviet Central Asia and its importance for the Central Asians should not be downplayed. By the end of 1994 the Turkish Government had allocated over $78 million of humanitarian aid to the five Central Asian states. Of the $666 million of credits the Turkish Eximbank had offered to these states, around $500 million had been opened. Of course, these figures scarcely match the size of loans and credits able to be offered by the Western states, Japan and the large international financial institutions. Turkey is, after all, a developing country itself, which has been suffering from a serious economic crisis since the start of 1994. The figures may thus be deceiving. For example, according to the recent statistics of the UN Economic Commission for Europe, of the total foreign investment commitments in Eastern Europe and the former Soviet Union in the last few years, the USA had committed $67 billion, followed by Turkey with a commitment of $15.2 billion. In reality, commitments are not always fulfilled. Thus, the short-term investment by Turkey in these states at the end of 1994 only totalled $24.5 million.[24]

Compared to the total amount of trade turnover, Turkish trade with the five post-Soviet Central Asian states is quite insubstantial. Turkish exports to the region in 1992, 1993 and between January and September 1994 (provisional figures for 1994) amounted to $83.9 million, $387.1 million and $310.8 million, respectively. These figures were 0.6, 2.5 and 2.5 per cent of total Turkish exports in these periods, respectively. The corresponding figures for Turkish imports from the region and its percentage of overall Turkish imports were $61.9 million (0.3 per cent), $162.8 million (0.6 per cent) and $133.4 million (0.8 per cent), respectively.[25] It appears that some Turkish companies, rather than trading, prefer to be involved in small to medium scale construction projects in Central Asia building hotels and textile and cement factories *inter alia*. These low figures are also in part due to problems in the distribution channels, banking services and the difficulty in transporting goods. Most importantly, the Central Asians lack the hard currency to buy Turkish products. They are dependent on either barter or trade credits.

The newly independent Central Asian states are still greatly dependent on trade with Russia and other former Soviet republics. However, Turkey appears to be a reasonably important source of goods for the four Turkic Central Asian states. According to the figures for 1993, excluding imports from the former Soviet Union, the imports from Turkey amounted to 22.5, 19, 16.7 and 16 per cent of imports made by Uzbekistan, Kazakhstan, Turkmenistan and the Kyrgyz Republic, respectively, whereas in 1993, only 5.8, 4.5, 3.5 and 3.4 per cent of exports (excluding exports to the former Soviet republics) from Turkmenistan, Uzbekistan, the Kyrgyz Republic, and Kazakhstan, respectively, were destined for Turkey. The corresponding figures for Tajikistan were appreciably lower.[26]

Currently, Turkey is mainly importing agricultural raw materials and food from Central Asia. Some iron, steel and non-ferrous metals from Kazakhstan are also imported. These products could easily be obtained from alternative sources. The trade turnover between Turkey and Central Asia could expand considerably if new oil and gas pipelines could be constructed across the Transcaucasus and through Turkey. Turkish consumers could make use of Kazakh and Turkmen oil and Turkmen and Uzbek gas. The hard currency the Central Asians could generate through the exports of oil and gas could be used to purchase more goods from Turkey and elsewhere.

In 1994 Turkey needed to import 22 million tons of oil. According to BOTAŞ estimates, by 2010 Turkey will have to import 40 million tons.[27] At present, much of Turkey's oil is transported from Russia. Iran is another important supplier. In 1995 Tehran exported 4.5 million tons of oil to Turkey. Officials in Ankara are looking for alternative suppliers. In the long term, therefore, Turkish consumers could make use of oil from Azerbaijan, Kazakhstan and even Turkmenistan if new pipelines were constructed across Turkey. Not all Central Asian oil would need to be shipped to other countries via Ceyhan.

As in the case of oil, Turkey is also not a major gas producer. Turkey currently imports 6 billion cubic metres of gas per annum from Russia and 2 billion cubic metres of liquified natural gas (LNG) from Algeria. Small amounts of LNG from Australia are also imported. Again according to BOTAŞ figures, by 2000 Turkey will need to import 20 billion cubic metres of gas annually and Turkish consumption will continue to rise thereafter. There are plans to import up to 10.5 billion cubic metres of gas each year from Russia and negotiations are ongoing with Qatar and Nigeria for supplies of LNG. In May 1995 an agreement in principle was struck between Ankara and Tehran whereby Turkey will receive gas from Iran over the next 23 years. The intention is to transfer annually at least 2 billion cubic metres of Iranian natural gas to Turkey.

Turkish officials are probably not keen to become too dependent on Russia and Iran for their energy supplies given that relations with these two states are not entirely smooth. Hence, Turkmenistan could be another important source of gas for the Turkish market. As early as 1 May 1992 Turkey and Turkmenistan had agreed to transport gas by a pipeline from Turkmenistan to Central Europe via Turkey. In October 1994 the heads of state of Turkey, Pakistan, Iran and Turkmenistan attended the symbolic inaugural opening of this projected gas pipeline. At the same time, a deal was also concluded whereby Turkmenistan agreed to deliver to Turkey 2 billion cubic metres of gas in 1998 rising to 15 billion by 2010.[28] However, as discussed earlier, first a gas pipeline to Turkey and then possibly on to Central Europe needs to be built.

Although Turkey is playing an important role in post-Soviet Central Asia, other states clearly are also actively involved in the region. Is there a new great game for influence as it were between Turkey, Russia, Iran and China? If so, this is not a zero-sum game. For instance, cooperation between Turkey, Iran and even Russia concerning the construction of gas pipelines has been previously noted. All states interested in the region are eager to promote stability there. This would facilitate the development of further economic ties and thereby in the long term help to strengthen the Central Asian economies. Poverty often leads to social and political discontent. Certainly, Russia, with around 9 million Russians still living in Central Asia, and Turkey and China is opposed to the spread of Islamic radicalism in the region from Afghanistan and parts of Tajikistan. Hoping to realize the construction of a whole network of oil and gas pipelines from Central Asia to the Persian Gulf, even the Iranian Government is counselling moderation and is not at least openly backing the extremist Islamic elements in the region.

In an interview in May 1995 the then Undersecretary in the Turkish MFA, Özdem Sanberk, noted that 'Instability in the Russian Federation means instability for Turkey as well. A chaotic Russia cannot be in Turkey's interests.'[29] Moscow's concern that Turkey may be helping to stoke up Pan-Turkic feelings not only in post-Soviet Central Asia but also within the Russian Federation has been noted earlier. One particular fear here is that Turkey could encourage the Turkic peoples in Tatarstan and Bashkortostan to attempt to divide Russia by seeking to link up their republics with the newly independent Turkic states of Central Asia.[30] However, fearful of the forces of Islamic radicalism, the current Central Asian leaders wish to remain under Russia's security umbrella. It is only in recent months that the Uzbek leadership, in an effort possibly to curry more favour with the West (but not specifically with Turkey), has resisted Moscow's attempts to deploy Russian troops on Uzbekistan's borders.

CONCLUSION

It appears that in the future Turkish involvement in Central Asia will be increasingly focused on developing further relations with Kazakhstan, Turkmenistan and Uzbekistan specifically because of the political and economic importance of these states. The Kyrgyz Republic will not be completely overlooked though. Prime Minister Çiller included Bishkek on her Central Asian tour in August 1995. Recently, agreements have been concluded to allow Turkey to develop a number of oil and gas fields in Kazakhstan. Kazakhstan's considerable energy reserves are clearly attracting Turkish officials. In June 1995 Nazarbaev requested from President Demirel a $100 million loan to be used on several agricultural projects. Nazarbayev promised to pay back the loan with agricultural products.[31] Two months later Çiller arrived in Almaty and announced that Turkey was ready to open a $300 million credit.[32]

Relations between Turkey and Uzbekistan are likely to improve following Çiller's successful visit to Tashkent in the summer of 1995. Turkey has promised to grant Uzbekistan a $100 million loan. Previously, the activities in Turkey of the Uzbek dissident Muhammed Salih, the leader of the banned Erk party, had caused friction in Turkish–Uzbek relations. The Uzbek ambassador had been recalled and many Uzbek students who had attended Turkish schools and universities were not allowed to return to Turkey to continue their studies. Apparently, Salih had been attempting to recruit Uzbek students studying in Turkey.[33] However, Salih is no longer in Turkey after having been granted asylum in Germany. Kerimov, though, has still not apparently renounced his ambition for Uzbekistan to form a new 'Turkestan' in Central Asia which would exclude Turkey. In an address to the Uzbek Parliament on 5 May 1995 Kerimov again appealed for the formation of a 'Turkestan' with the other newly independent Central Asian states (presumably under Uzbek leadership), in order to secure their independence and contain 'outside threats'.[34]

Turkish officials are also interested in cultivating ties with non-Turkic Tajikistan. In September 1995 President Demirel visited Dushanbe where he spoke of the need to develop a stable and peaceful 'Eurasia'. The Tajik President, Imamali Rakhmanov, urged Demirel to use his influence to bring about peace in Afghanistan. The Turkish President's trip to Tajikistan immediately followed by an official visit to Mongolia led the Turkish press to speculate wildly that Turkey was interested in the formation of a 'Eurasian' as opposed to a 'Turkic Union'.[35]

Barring a dramatic change in government, Turkish official policy toward post-Soviet Central Asia is not likely to change in the foreseeable future. The ultimate goal of the Turkish MFA and of the business community in general in Turkey remains membership of the EU. However, the Pan-Turkic hopes and aspirations of various groups and agencies in Turkey will not disappear. Indeed, Pan-Turkic sympathies would perhaps take a firmer hold if the situation in the Balkans continues to deteriorate and if the Kurdish problem in Turkey degenerates into a bloodbath. Under these circumstances, the rise of exclusive ethnic nationalism and xenophobia and the possible further strengthening of the much-talked of nationalist–Islamic synthesis in Turkey could eventually lead to an increase in support for Pan-Turkism. Continued exclusion from the EU could also play into the hands of the Pan-Turkic and Pan-Islamic lobbies.

NOTES

1. An earlier version of this paper was originally presented at the European Seminar on Central Asian Studies, Copenhagen, Denmark, August 1995.
2. This paper focuses on Turkey's relations with post-Soviet Central Asia. The author is of course aware that the term Central Asia may also apply to other states in the region such as Afghanistan, Mongolia, Iran, Pakistan and parts of China. The close contacts Turkish officials enjoy with the Uzbek warlord General Dostum, who remains in control of a large part of northern Afghanistan, should thus be borne in mind. However, it would be somewhat of an exaggeration to talk for instance of a straight Turkish (Uzbek)–Iranian (Tajik) competition for influence in Afghanistan given the highly complex and fragmented nature of Afghan politics.
3. *Sabah*, 2 July 1995 (in Turkish).
4. J.P. Dorian, I. Sheffield Rosi and S. Hartono Indriyanto, 'Central Asia's Oil and Gas Pipeline Network: Current and Future Flows', *East-West Center Working Papers*, Energy and Minerals Series, no. 9 (November 1994), pp. 10–15.
5. *Turkish Daily News* (*TDN*), 17 July 1995.
6. *Yeni Yüzyıl*, 16 August 1995 (in Turkish).
7. *TDN*, 8 July 1995.
8. *Hürriyet*, 19 August 1995 (in Turkish).
9. *TDN* and *Hürriyet*, 11 July 1995.
10. For a more detailed overview of Turkey's involvement in post-Soviet Central Asia, see, Gareth M. Winrow, *Turkey in Post-Soviet Central Asia* (London: The Royal Institute of International Affairs, Former Soviet South Project no. 1, 1995).
11. *Cumhuriyet*, 20 December 1991 (in Turkish).
12. For the argument that US officials were also in part to blame here by encouraging the Turks to believe that they would work together with Turkey to provide considerable financial assistance to the Central Asians, see, S. Sayari, 'Turkey, the Caucasus and Central Asia', in A. Banuazizi and M. Weiner (eds), *The New Geopolitics of Central Asia and its Borderlands* (Bloomington and Indianapolis: Indiana University Press, 1994), pp. 182–3.
13. The text of the Bishkek Declaration was obtained by the author from the Turkish Ministry of Foreign Affairs.
14. However, according to recent statistics, in Almaty very few Kazakhs actually watch Avrasya. See Michael Haney, 'Media use and Ethnicity in Almaty', *Central Asia Monitor*, no. 2 (1995), p. 16. According to various reports the

programmes are boring and are difficult to follow because Turkish, although closely related to Kazakh, Uzbek and so on, is still a separate language.

15. Information in this and the following paragraph was obtained from an interview with a prominent official in the Turkish MFA, Ankara, December 1994.
16. For further details see G.M. Winrow, 'Turkish Relations with the Newly Independent Republics of the Caucasus', *The Oxford International Review*, vol. 5, no. 1 (Winter 1993), pp. 45–8.
17. *TDN*, 4 May 1992.
18. Ibid., 11 June 1992.
19. *Cumhuriyet*, 13 December 1994.
20. *TDN*, 15 July 1995.
21. For an analysis of differing views Central Asian historians have of their histories, see, Büşra Ersanlı Behar, 'Bağımsızlık kimliği: Yeni Türk Cumhuriyetlerinde kultürel/siyasal dönüşüm', *Türkiye Günlüğü*, no. 31 (November–December 1994), pp. 108–9.
22. For an overview of Pan-Turkic parties and other political groups in Turkic Central Asia, see, Nihal İncioğlu, 'Yeni Türk Cumhuriyetlerinde Toplumsal Bölünmeler, Siyasi Güçler ve Yeni Siyasal Yapılanma', in Büşra Ersanlı Behar (ed), *Bağımsızlığın İlk Yìlları: Azerbaycan, Kazakistan, Kirgizistan, Özbekistan, Türkmenistan* (Ankara: T.C. Kültür Bakanlığı Milli Kütüphane Basımevi, 1994), pp. 105–42.
23. *TDN*, 6 July 1995.
24. *Economist Intelligence Unit Country Report: Central Asian Republics: Kazakhstan, Kyrgyz Republic, Tajikistan, Turkmenistan, Uzbekistan*, 2nd Quarter 1995 (London: EIU, 1995), pp. 17–18.
25. Figures from *DEIK (Foreign Economic Relations Board) Bulletin: the Turkish Economy by Figures, January 1995*, using information from the State Institute of Statistics (of Turkey).
26. These figures were calculated by the author using statistics from the State Institute of Statistics (of Turkey) and from the Economist Intelligence Unit, see note 24.
27. Information supplied by officials of BOTAŞ, the Turkish State Pipeline Company.
28. *Radio Free Europe/Radio Liberty Daily Report*, No. 206, 28 October 1994, by Vladimir Socor and Liz Fuller.
29. *TDN*, 31 May 1995.
30. A.G. Arbatov, 'Russian Foreign Policy Priorities for the 1990s', in T.P. Johnson and S. Miller (eds), *Russian Security after the Cold War* (Washington DC: Brassey's, 1994), pp. 26–7.
31. *TDN*, 14 June 1995.
32. Ibid., 16 August 1995.
33. A. Polat, 'Pursuing Dissidents in Exile: Illegal Activities of Central Asian Security Forces (Part I)', *Central Asia Monitor*, no. 2 (1995), p. 34.
34. *Open Media Research Institute (OMRI) Daily Report*, no. 89, part 1, 9 May 1995, piece by Lowell Bezanis.
35. See for instance *Yeni Yüzyıl*, 12 September 1995.

7 Afghanistan and Central Asia

A. Hyman

Afghanistan's importance to the republics of Central Asia comes from its geographic situation, as well as its close historical and cultural links to the rest of Central Asia. This basic fact is much more obvious since the USSR's disintegration and independence. In particular, since the opening of borders and greater freedom for foreign travel and trading from the republics of the former Soviet Union since 1991, the artificial insulation of subjects in one state is made far more difficult. Moreover, Afghanistan remains in many cultural respects a part of Central Asia.

Members of all five major nationalities of the former Soviet Central Asia are represented in the Afghan population. Three of the five Central Asian republics, Tajikistan, Uzbekistan and Turkmenistan, have borders with Afghanistan and it is their relations with the southern neighbour which will be concentrated upon here. Afghanistan's relations with Kazakhstan and Kyrgyzstan are rather undeveloped and look set to remain so, in part because the small Kyrgyz and Kazakh communities have all but vanished (in organized migrations to Turkey and Kazakhstan respectively) from Afghanistan since the civil war began in 1978.

The Tajiks, Uzbeks and Turkmen of Afghanistan are essentially of the same ethnic stock as the titular nationalities in the Central Asian republics to the north of the Amu Darya; indeed, many families of all three of these northern ethnic groups of Afghanistan migrated there from Fergana and other regions only as recently as the 1920s and 1930s, after the turmoil of the Russian Revolution and Civil War in the USSR. With their common cultural roots and a shared history, even now after generations of artificial isolation imposed under Soviet communist rule, even their languages differ little from their kinsmen in the ex-Soviet republics.

With Tajikistan there are strikingly close ethnic and cultural features. As two eminent Swiss ethnologists have written 'As far as populations are concerned, the north-east of Afghanistan and the south of Tajikistan can then be considered as one single and vast entity, which ethnic politics and socio-economic evolution have made evolve differently on either side of the frontier.'[1] The arbitrary nature of state borders between Afghanistan and its northern neighbours (as well as the Pashtun and Baluch borderlands in Pakistan) is, of course, due to Anglo-Russian rivalries in the last century and 'imperial engineering' or the creation of a buffer state between the two European empires in Asia. However, the rationale for the frontiers fixed between the ex-Soviet republics owes less to disinterested scientific (or pseudo-scientific) researches than to political decisions taken in the 1920s and after. Each one of them contains large minorities of other nationalities.

It is not only the USSR which has disintegrated. Political chaos inside Afghanistan has made it one of the broken-backed states of the Third World. The virtual disintegration of Afghanistan as a state has been a gradual process, in tandem with the growing weakness and disappearance of the state apparatus. This process actually began in the mid-1980s and became apparent several years before the collapse of the Najibullah Government in April 1992. Along with the loss of central control in most areas, it often took the form of a devolution of powers to war lords and local militia groups based on tribal or ethnic alliances or sectarian solidarity quite as much as party loyalties. This brought to local or regional prominence General Abdul Rashid Dostum in Mazar-e-Sharif and Ismail Khan in Herat, as well as many lesser figures in different provinces. Some of Afghanistan's minority communities, hitherto powerless, despised or discriminated (notably the Ismailis around Pul-e-Khumri and Hazaras in the central region of Hazarajat), have gained considerably in power and autonomy from the centre. This has gone on to alter the traditional internal balance of power established since the time of Abdur Rahman Khan, by which Pashtuns benefited at the expense of the other peoples of Afghanistan.[2]

While power and resources have devolved from Kabul to the provincial centres, much of Kabul itself has been destroyed. The 'government' under the interim president Burhanuddin Rabbani had few resources and was struggling against a formidable coalition of rival parties. The 'ministries' were hollow shells, more potential than actual centres of activity and whatever foreign development aid and humanitarian help went to Afghanistan, grossly inadequate as it was, usually bypassed this government.

A variety of threats to regional stability in Central Asia are perceived by analysts. One threat is claimed to be radical Islam or 'Muslim fundamentalism', sometimes used very questionably to describe the opposition parties of Tajikistan. Another threat which used to be asserted (and is linked to the first) was the inspiration among the Muslims of Central Asia from the much-vaunted Afghan 'victory of Islam' against communism and the USSR's military might. A third threat to stability comes from the grim state of the worsening unemployment. A further threat is identifiable in the upsurge of ethnic nationalism and rivalries in the region as a whole.

Significantly, in one recent study (by Maxim Shahshenkov, a Russian researcher based at the University of Oxford), a key political development is claimed to be the rise of the Tajik/Uzbek factor in Afghan politics.[3] This actually represents a strategic factor for all of Central Asia, one resulting from the reinforcement of existing ethnic identities. Shahshenkov goes on to claim it is likely to be through Afghanistan that the republics of Central Asia will be drawn into the politics of their Muslim neighbours. This might apply to the three republics with borders to Afghanistan (Tajikistan, Uzbekistan and Turkmenistan). Large numbers of their ethnic kinsmen are, of course, living across the border in Afghanistan.

The present scenario of anarchy inside Afghanistan along with indefinite prolongation of the Afghan civil war arguably carries with it serious geopolitical implications for the Central Asian region. The situation inside Afghanistan has clearly interacted with Tajikistan's civil war, enabling the Tajik opposition forces to fight on from the other side of the border. Afghanistan has often been blamed for training Tajik opposition forces and arming them since 1992, though these, as Muriel Atkin writes, 'are controversial subjects on which there is more propaganda than reliable information. Some of the least credible information comes from certain supporters of the old Soviet order who are biased against Islam and Muslims.'[4] Atkin goes on to state that such people are far from being dispassionate observers or analysts.

Tensions have been raised periodically by the killing of Russian border guards in action, as well as by bombing raids and the shelling of villages on the Afghan side of the border. A failure to reach peace could well result in one or more governments in Central Asia, anxious to get political stability, actively intervening on the side of political clients in Afghanistan. Support for ethnic kinsmen across the Amu Dayra borders could easily be translated into financial, logistical or military aid, as in the current case of Uzbekistan's links with General Dostum's Jonbesh, a regional administration which has attained full autonomy or independence of Kabul.

Such interventions from the north would arguably serve to counterbalance foreign influences and pressures from Pakistan, Iran and other regional states. Thus, it is natural enough if analysts speculate on the future emergence of a separatist movement of the Uzbeks of Afghanistan and conceivably also of Tajiks or Turkmen from northern Afghanistan, either wishing to form what would be effectively new mini-states or quite possibly to merge with the respective republics to the north. In such a case, there could well be backing for it from a Central Asian capital in the future, even if at present every government maintains that the existing state borders must be respected.

Under the simultaneous impact of independence for five Central Asian republics and the collapse of state power in Afghanistan, ethnic nationalism which has grown markedly among the various peoples or nationalities shared with Afghanistan could conceivably alter the state arrangements. Among the scenarios are federalism, some form of confederation or a looser form of connection between the three Central Asian republics and their respective ethnic kinsmen in regions across the Amu Darya in northern Afghanistan.

Thus for social scientists in the next decade, Afghanistan along with ex-Soviet Central Asia could well provide a fascinating real-life laboratory for testing the impact of the Soviet nationalities policy since Stalin. The map of Soviet Central Asia drawn in the 1920s, so often criticized for creating arbitrary or unjust borders along with artificial new nations and national republics, may not only endure but expand along essentially the same ethnic lines.

Other alternatives are there, though. Clearly, a pan-Turkic (or more properly, pan-Turkistani) dimension to changes in the Central Asian region exists alongside that of rival neighbour states and peoples. In terms of population and resources and probably also political ambitions, Uzbekistan far outweighs its smaller, weaker neighbours, not only Tajikistan, Kyrgyzstan and Turkmenistan but also Afghanistan. Some nationalists from the smaller republics do appear to fear that Russian power may eventually be replaced by a 'Greater Uzbekistan'.

As far as the Tajik and Persian-speaking communities are concerned, another scenario may be opening up. According to the Rand analyst Graham E. Fuller 'any breakaway of northern Afghanistan could lead to a consolidation of the Tajiks and create a continuous Persian-speaking belt from the borders of China to the Persian Gulf, a belt that would rival the Turkish belt to the north'.[5] Presumably in this vision Fuller is including with the Tajiks other Persian-speaking peoples of central and western Afghanistan, the Mongol–Turkic Hazaras and Aimaqs. Definitions of 'Tajik' vary greatly depending upon the perspective of the observer. Even so, there would never exist 'a continuous Persian-speaking belt' as such; rather there would be isolated pockets where various Persian dialects and languages continue to exist alongside Turkic languages.

Afghanistan was a fragile state even before the civil war began in 1978. Given the prospect of continuing political instability and, in many areas, the likelihood that semi-independent commanders or 'war lords' will contest for power with each other and an enfeebled, unstable central government, any realistic assessment must deal with the possibility of a disintegration of the country into its main ethnic and tribal components. The tensions between its diverse ethnic and tribal elements could be the catalyst for disintegration.

Such a scenario cannot be dismissed out of hand, given that the half of the country north of the Hindu Kush is now more than ever distinct from the south. This is a result of a steady process through the 1980s of many Pashtuns being forced out from the northern lands where they had been settled in a deliberate state policy.

As for the non-Pashtun nationalities of Afghanistan, most have gained substantial autonomy or independence from the centre during the war. Besides the Persian-speaking Hazaras and Aimaqs settled in the central region, it is the Uzbeks, Tajiks and Turkmen who now stand out as the masters in what used until this century to be called 'Afghan Turkestan', by analogy with Russian and Chinese Turkestan, that is an integral part of Central Asia.

With the new-found independence of Uzbekistan, Turkmenistan and Tajikistan, links are being forged on both sides of what used to be well-guarded, closed frontiers. For the future, the potential appeal of irredentist ideas cannot be discounted. Indeed, there has been keen interest in nationalist circles in Uzbekistan for what is thought of as the Uzbek cause in Afghanistan and calls have even been made for a confederation or the merger of Uzbek-dominated areas of Afghanistan with the republic.

Instability in Afghanistan as well as Tajikistan is clearly contributing to a more strident nationalistic mood which has to be reckoned with. The state borders set in the 1920s had never been questioned openly by the respective governments in post-Soviet Central Asia. In what must rank as a significant statement (coming from an official), a challenge to the *status quo* on state borders in Central Asia was made by Tajikistan's Interior Minister, Yaqubjan Salimov, who, in June 1995, called for a unification of all ethnic Tajiks, regardless of which state they currently lived in.

> I call on all those Tajiks, citizens of Tajikistan who have a drop of young blood and manliness, a little Tajik shame and honour: let us brothers unite together! Let us try to regain the land of the Tajiks, the land of the Samanids, in order to be able to hold our heads up high and say that we are Tajiks! ... There are six million (Tajiks) in the fraternal republic of the Islamic state of Afghanistan. But because we are not united, are not like-minded, (only) three million of us live in the state of the Tajiks, in the country in which we want to unite all Tajiks today.[6]

However rhetorical, this speech by an official of the government at the time (Salimov was for other reasons soon sent away to Ankara as ambassador) implicitly challenges the territorial integrity of both Uzbekistan and Afghanistan. All the governments of the region claim to support the *status quo* in state borders. However, in nationalist intellectual circles there is considerable interest in some form of federation or uniting with their ethnic kinsmen living across the borders or even changes to existing borders. This is particularly evident in the case of the Tajiks and Uzbeks. The formation of a 'Great Khorasan' state is publicly advocated by a group in Tajikistan calling itself the 'Great Ariana Society', while the idea of a 'Greater Uzbekistan' incorporating Uzbek-settled lands in other republics (or even the whole of 'Turkestan') attracts nationalists in Uzbekistan.

Extreme nationalist groups are by no means limited to the Turkic peoples or Muslims of Central Asia. The recent phenomenon of the Cossack revival spread rapidly in northern Kazakhstan, dominated as it is by Slav settlers. Calls for a revision of the borders by Cossack groups and Russian nationalists roused the counter Alash movement of Kazakh ultranationalists, voicing strident Kazakh demands. As yet, though, the impact of irredentist ideas is barely perceptible outside the intelligentsia of Central Asia. The ugly, violent, xenophobic side to ethnic nationalism in Central Asia was witnessed in 1990–1991, in a series of riots and virtual pogroms.

Gradually, from 1978 and in particular from 1980, after the Soviet military intervention, the PDPA (Peoples' Democratic Party, later Watan) Government in Afghanistan came to rely on Uzbekistan, Turkmenistan and Tajikistan as a key part of the Soviet backing for the regime supplying a wide range of goods in short supply. There was rapid expansion in political and economic links to bolster the Kabul regime, as in help with higher education and linked cultural initiatives. This was part of the 'internationalist duty' the Central Asian republics were obliged to perform as part of the Soviet strategy in Afghanistan.

Soviet development projects, notably for gas production and export, were to a large extent concentrated in the north of the country. Trade agreements concluded directly between the northern provinces of Afghanistan and the republics were often made on a bilateral basis, bypassing the central government in Kabul. A concentration on building roads, a railway, a river port and new bridge links across the Amu Darya was part of an infrastructural network bringing closer together the northern regions of Afghanistan and Central Asia.[7]

Like India, Afghanistan had maintained a consulate in Tashkent, upgraded in 1992 to embassy status. Cooperation with the Central Asian republics in many varied fields has begun and already in trade the links are considerable. Petrol is being bought from Turkmenistan and future help is promised from Ashkhabad in exploiting Afghanistan's own gas and oil reserves. Private traders from Afghanistan are most conspicuous in Tashkent, the biggest of the Central Asian cities and some have moved offices there from the ruined capital Kabul.

Independence for the republics to the north has served to increase pressures for greater autonomy from Kabul of northern Afghanistan's major nationalities, the Tajiks and Uzbeks and possibly Turkmen. The reality of irredentism as a potential force in the region cannot be ignored.

There is a considerable influence of the various neighbour states over the political struggle inside Afghanistan, in its present condition a broken-backed state with a greatly weakened centre. In the past Afghanistan had to reckon with four powerful direct neighbours: Pakistan to the south, Iran on the western border, the Soviet Union along the northern borders and China along a narrow, inaccessible strip across the Pamirs (the so-called Wakhan corridor). Now in place of the USSR (called the 'Great Northern Neighbour' in the PDPA vocabulary), Afghanistan has the three Central Asian republics to reckon with.

Cross-border contacts have flourished since 1992 between the Ismaili communities living in the Pamirs, in the province of Badakhshan in northeastern Afghanistan and Tajikistan's Gorno Badakhshan autonomous region, which actually declared its independence from Dushanbe in April 1992, with the start of the civil war. The appeal of ideas of independence for this small Pamiri community of Gorno Badakhshan has not faded, but practical difficulties of economic survival have intervened.

In the current greatly weakened state of Afghanistan, its government (like that of Tajikistan) seems fated to be more a passive spectator than an actor in the redesigning and expansion of regional cooperation, let alone any basic reorganization of the states. For Pakistan, any dismemberment or secession of the northern half of Afghanistan would inevitably present a serious challenge to its own stability, because the southern half of Afghanistan has a mainly Pashtun tribal population closely related to the Pashtuns (Pathans) of Pakistan's two provinces of North West Frontier and Baluchistan.

In such an eventuality, many observers would expect a revival of the 'Pukhtunistan' ideal of a merger of the Pashtun lands or a revived call for independence for the Pashtuns of Pakistan. Though politically quiescent (or even dead) since the late 1970s, the Pukhtunistan issue constitutes a latent irredentist cause at the disposal of radical leaderships in both countries and a latent source of conflict between the two countries.

With the liberalization of Soviet trade and frontier controls since gaining independence from Moscow, though, the Central Asian republics to the north have a potentially important role to play for mutual benefit. Turkmenistan, Uzbekistan and Tajikistan, which share a 1200 km border with Afghanistan, are neighbours of obvious importance for the future, even if Pakistan and Iran are certain to remain more significant for work, trade and other contacts. Relations with the two key neighbour states, Pakistan and Iran, where millions of Afghan refugees are still living, are bound to remain crucial and of more importance for any government of Afghanistan.

Some observers maintain that it is through Afghanistan that the newly-independent republics of Central Asia are likely to be drawn into the politics of their Muslim neighbours. The interaction and interdependence of events in Afghanistan and Central Asia seem to be growing. One way of measuring this may be the flow of weapons between militias or *mujahidin* groups in northern Afghanistan and the opposition parties in Tajikistan, as well as trading in narcotics. Another way is observing the flow of refugees, across both sides of the Amu Darya: of Tajiks into northern Afghanistan and of Afghans to Uzbekistan.

Tajikistan's civil war has led to great destruction and fear which generated a wave of refugees from the republic in 1992. Some 60 000 desperate Tajik refugees from Tajikistan's civil war crossed the Amu Darya river in 1992, seeking refuge in the areas around Kunduz and Maimana in Afghanistan. In the other direction, thousands of Afghan refugees have fled to the north, mostly from families of former civil servants, army officers and other employees of the PDPA regime. They are currently living in Central Asian cities (mainly now in Tashkent and other cities of Uzbekistan) or in Moscow.

The Afghan refugees in Central Asia are, of course, only a tiny fraction of the total number and unrepresentative in many respects by class and education. In spite of all the uncertainty and dangers, especially from mines, more than 1 million Afghan refugees returned to their villages from Pakistan and Iran from the summer of 1992 to restart a normal life.

In the peak month of July 1992, according to the UN High Commission for Refugees, 357 000 Afghan refugees left Pakistan. Around 1 million Afghan refugees living in Iran have been returned since 1992, many forcibly by the Iranian authorities, Herat and other western provinces. Most of the returnees have gone back to their villages and to farming. This must give legitimate grounds for hope that stability will grow steadily in the country, since the basis of Afghanistan's prosperity will remain its agriculture, like the other republics of Central Asia.

The highway south from Tashkent, the capital of Uzbekistan, to the Afghan border at Termez is not a long drive. Many convoys went down it from 1980, as part of the Soviet war effort. The long war in Afghanistan has left an undeniable impact on attitudes in Central Asia towards Afghanistan and the Afghan people. One aspect of the troubled Afghan inheritance is the place of the 'Afgantsy', the war veterans in civilian society. For the USSR the Afghan war ended in 1989, with withdrawal of the last Soviet units, but for the individual soldiers, self-identification with the Afghan war is often strong. Long ignored, the special needs of the returned soldiers who served in the Afghan war have become increasingly recognized by governments in the republics. The change was due not only to a greater frankness under glasnost, but efforts of activists among the veterans to get what they see as their rights.

In Uzbekistan, which supplied most of the soldiers from Central Asia who served in Afghanistan, there are two organizations set up on behalf of the 'Afgantsy'. They link some 20 000 war veterans, drawn from Uzbeks, Russians, Tajiks and other nationalities living in the republic. Helped by strong sympathy and backing from some influential figures in the ruling party, including some who themselves served in Afghanistan, the government of President Islam Karimov has granted the war veterans some special privileges. However, for quite a few of the 'Afgantsy', these privileges remain on paper. This is particularly true of those soldiers who returned injured or permanently crippled, who often get rather little practical help.[8]

Political independence for the Central Asian states has so far brought mostly formal changes in the military sphere. It is still the Russian military which dominates. The republics' non-CIS borders with Iran, Afghanistan and China are still effectively under Russian military control, guarded by forces obeying orders from Moscow. Steps towards the creation of small national armies have been taken only by Kazakhstan and Uzbekistan, the two major republics in terms of population. Both are building on a predominantly Russian officer corps. The bulk of Russian armed forces in the region are still based in Turkmenistan.

A regional security framework on the basis of Muslim states alone, which was being projected in Iran and Pakistan at the time of independence, is much less probable than a continued reliance on Russian military support and participation in Russian-dominated bilateral security arrangements. The key to future regional stability will certainly depend not only upon Russia but also upon Uzbekistan, Russia's ally and in most respects the key republic in the region.

The propositions that security interests in Central Asia are interconnected and that the region constitutes a specific security complex have been explored by numerous writers since 1991.[9] This interlinkage exists in spite of the great differences in size and power of the various republics. Indeed, as Mehdi Mozaffari argues, even 'Kazakhstan cannot afford to be, and indeed is not (essentially for fear of a *domino effect* and ensuing regional instability) indifferent to events in Tajikistan or Uzbekistan and vice versa'.[10]

The security linkage between Afghanistan and ex-Soviet Central Asia is very clear in the case of the ongoing civil war in Tajikistan, in which Russian–Uzbek forces since 1992 have been the main support for the bankrupt regime in Dushanbe. The role of Afghanistan in the various paramilitary groups active in Tajikistan is analysed by Susan Clark, who also spells out some of the dangerous security issues raised from the virtual collapse of the two neighbouring states of Afghanistan and Tajikistan.[11]

Afghanistan has a formal link with the Central Asian republics through its being accepted as a member of the expanded Economic Cooperation Organization, the regional grouping of Turkey, Iran, Pakistan and six mainly Muslim former Soviet republics. Afghanistan forms a potential 'landbridge' for bulk trade between the Central Asian republics and Pakistan, with its port Karachi or possibly another new port on the Arabian Sea.

The vital precondition for this would be, of course, an enduring peace settlement in Afghanistan or conclusive victory for one party or coalition. The ebb and flow of advances and retreats by Jamiat Islami and Taliban forces in northwestern Afghanistan in 1995 made such an outcome a remote prospect. Without it, though, neither the proposed highway and rail link across Afghanistan are likely to be completed or to have a big impact on the volume of trade passing from Central Asia to world markets. This new infrastructure and rerouting of existing trade routes will take considerably longer to develop than most observers anticipated.

The economic and infrastructural links forged mainly after 1978 between Afghanistan and the Central Asian republics, along with the USSR as a whole, were often interpreted in geopolitical terms as a Soviet strategy to realign and integrate northern Afghanistan's economy into that of the Central Asian republics. There is some justification for this judgement, yet from a historical perspective, though, these developments are part of an ancient pattern of trading and political links between Balkh, Kunduz and the rest of Central Asia, artificially interrupted by Soviet policy for half a century from the 1920s.

NOTES

1. P. Centlivres and M. Centlivres-Demont, 'Tadjikistan et Afghanistan' in M. R. Djalili and F. Grare, *Le Tajikistan à l'épreuve de l'indépendance* (Geneva: Institut des Hautes Etudes Internationales 1995), pp. 17–27.
2. For a new, comprehensive survey see further B. R. Rubin, *The Fragmentation of Afghanistan* (New Haven: Yale University Press, 1995). Another recent study is R. Bakhsh Rais, *War Without Winners. Afghanistan's uncertain transition after the Cold War* (Karachi: Oxford University Press, 1994).
3. M. Shahshenkov, *Security Issues of the ex-Soviet Central Asian Republics* (London: Brasseys/Centre for Defence Studies, 1992).

4. See Muriel Atkin, 'Tajikistan's Relations with Iran and Afghanistan' in A. Banuazizi and M. Weiner, *The New Geopolitics of Central Asia and its Borderlands* (London: I.B. Tauris, 1994), pp. 105–6.
5. G. Fuller, 'The New Geopolitical Order' in A. Banuazizi and M. Weiner, *The New Geopolitics of Central Asia and its Borderlands* (London: I.B. Tauris, 1994), p. 39.
6. Radio Tajikistan, 10 June 1995, quoted *Inside Central Asia*, 12–18 June 1995.
7. See further A. Hyman, *Afghanistan Under Soviet Domination, 1964-91* (London: Macmillan, 1992); and H. S. Bradsher, *Afghanistan and the Soviet Union* (Durham: Duke University Press, 1985).
8. A. Hyman, 'The view from Tashkent' in *Afghanistan Info* no. 33 (Neuchatel, April 1993), pp. 21–22.
9. M. Mesbahi, 'Russia and the Geopolitics of the Muslim South' in M. Mesbahi (ed.), *Central Asia and the Caucasus* (Gainesville, Florida, University of Florida, 1994); and H. Malik (ed.), *Central Asia. Its Strategic Importance and Future Prospects* (London: Macmillan, 1994).
10. M. Mozaffari, *The New Security Systems in Central Asia and Caucasus*, paper for the XVIth World Congress of the International Political Science Association, Berlin, August 1994.
11. S. Clark, 'The Central Asian States: Defining Security Priorities and Developing Military Forces', in M. Mandelbaum (ed.), *Central Asia and the World: Kazakhstan, Uzbekistan, Tajikistan, Kyrgyzstan and Turkmenstan*, NY: The Council on Foreign Relations, 1994 (New York, 1994), pp. 188–92. See also B. Rubin, 'Tajikistan: from Soviet Republic to Russian-Uzbek Protectorate', ibid.

8 Central Asia: the View from Beijing, Urumqi and Kashghar

M. Dillon

INTRODUCTION

Most research on contemporary Central Asia has concentrated on relations between the Commonwealth of Independent States (CIS) Central Asian states, their connections with Russia and on the post-Soviet political, social and economic systems that are emerging in the region. This is understandable given the political, cultural and linguistic ties that bound the states of the former USSR together and tended to separate them from the rest of Asia. However, the momentous political changes that have taken place in former Soviet Central Asia have been paralleled by unprecedented economic changes in their eastern neighbour, China, which is set to become one of the leading economies of the world if its political stability can be maintained. This could have profound implications for the economic future of Central Asia. The government of the People's Republic of China in Beijing, which is still nominally communist in spite of its policy of creating a dynamic market economy, has been watching post-Soviet political and religious developments in Central Asia with concern. At the same time it has swiftly concluded diplomatic and trade agreements with the governments of the newly independent states and participated in joint meetings to discuss key issues such as troop reduction, boundary agreements and border trade. This study is an attempt to examine the main issues in China's relations with the Central Asian region, with particular reference to Kazakhstan.[1]

Part of the Central Asian cultural region falls within the borders of the People's Republic of China. This area is known to the Chinese as the Xinjiang Uyghur Autonomous Region, but to many of its indigenous people and to Uyghur émigrés as Eastern Turkestan. In fact, Central Asian influences have also extended further east into China and Muslim communities with historical links to Central Asia have played an important part in the history of the Ningxia Hui Autonomous Region and the Gansu, Qinghai and Shaanxi provinces. The Xinjiang Uyghur Autonomous Region is on the northwestern border of China, stretches 2000 km east to west and 1650 km north to south, has an area of over 1 600 000 km^2 and is the largest administrative unit in the People's Republic of China. It has common borders with Mongolia, Afghanistan, Pakistan and India and with three Central Asian states, Kazakhstan, Kyrgyzstan and Tajikistan and is close to Uzbekistan and Turkmenistan. Its nearest neighbours within China are Gansu and Ningxia, both of which have significant Muslim communities, Tibet, which constitutes Beijing's main separatist predicament and Qinghai, which is part of old Tibet and has Tibetan Buddhist and Muslim communities.[2]

The population of Xinjiang is divided between the non-Han groups who are predominantly Muslims and who mainly speak Turkic languages and Han[3] Chinese who have migrated into the region in a series of waves of resettlement since the late eighteenth century. The Muslims are in the majority, but are divided linguistically and culturally. The largest group are Uyghurs, traditionally agriculturalists, craftsmen and traders, who are related to the other Turkic peoples in Xinjiang and the rest of Central Asia. The majority of Uyghurs live in Xinjiang which they regard as their homeland, although there are also émigré communities in Kazakhstan, Turkey and in western Europe, notably Germany. Some analysts have argued that Uyghur nationalism is a relatively recent phenomenon because Uyghurs in the past are believed to have identified primarily with the oasis towns in which they lived rather than with a generalized Uyghur nation. However, centuries of Chinese rule, which is resented by most Uyghurs, the historical example of separatist movements including Yakub Beg's administration in Kashghar in the 1860s and 1870s, Muslim rebellions in the 1930s and the establishment of the East Turkestan Republic in Ili in the 1940s and recent contact with fellow Turkic-speaking Muslims in Central Asia have stimulated the idea of a single Uyghur identity, particularly in the region known as Altıshahr (Six Cities) in Turkic languages or *Nanjiang* (Southern Xinjiang) in Chinese, which borders on Pakistan and Afghanistan and in which 80 per cent of the Xinjiang's Uyghurs live.

Other major non-Han ethnic groups in Xinjiang include the Kazakhs, Kyrgyz, Uzbeks and Tajiks, all with relatives in Central Asia and the Muslim Hui (known as Dungans in the former Soviet Union), whose language and culture is closer to that of the Han Chinese.[4] It should, however, be appreciated that Muslim communities are not confined to Xinjiang: they are found throughout China, particularly the Hui who live in every province.

In this paper, the cities Beijing, Urumqi and Kashghar are used to represent different perspectives, which correspond very roughly to those of the key groups in those cities. Beijing represents the official national government policy and that of the Chinese Communist Party from its eminence in the

Zhongnanhai complex (China's Kremlin) in central Beijing. Urumqi characterizes the perspective of the government of the Xinjiang Uyghur Autonomous Region, shared between the Han and Uyghur but dominated by the Han and resolute in its determination to develop a united and economically developed Xinjiang under Beijing's rule. Kashghar symbolizes the viewpoint of the non-Han in Xinjiang and particularly in southern Xinjiang, the Altıshahr, in which Kashghar is situated. It is also the position most sympathetic to separatism and therefore most feared and abhorred by Beijing. 'Splittism', the official locution for any questioning of the territorial integrity of China, is one of the most serious political offences of which anyone can be accused.

BEIJING, URUMQI AND THE CENTRAL ASIAN REPUBLICS

Beijing moved remarkably rapidly to establish diplomatic relations with the Central Asian republics as they gained their independence after the breakup of the Soviet Union in 1991. The Chinese Foreign Minister, Qian Qichen, interviewed in November 1992 after a visit to Uzbekistan, Kyrgyzstan, Kazakhstan and the Russian Federation, was optimistic about prospects for trade between China and Central Asia, but pointed out that 'since China had neither contact nor economic and trade cooperation with Central Asian republics in the past, there was no mutual understanding'. This lack of contact is evidence of the depth of the Sino-Soviet split which began in the late 1950s, became public in 1960 and brought China and the Soviet Union to the brink of war in 1969. Foreign Minister Qian emphasized China's current policy of maintaining 'good-neighbourly, equal and mutually beneficial cooperation between China and the CIS'.[5]

The administration in Urumqi were also enthusiastic about the benefits to China of the breakup of the Soviet Union. Song Hanliang, Secretary of the Xinjiang Autonomous Regional Communist Party, speaking at the National People's Congress in Beijing in March 1992, highlighted export opportunities.[6] The establishment of formal relations between Xinjiang and the individual CIS states became a high priority: Tomur Dawamat, then Chairman of the Autonomous Region Government visited Kazakhstan and Uzbekistan in November 1990 and after signing a trade agreement with China, the President of Kazakhstan, Nursultan Nazarbayev, predicted economic and political benefits from the developing rail network.[7] These predictions proved correct: by 1995, border trade between Xinjiang and its Central Asian neighbours, which had been almost non-existent before 1991, was worth something in the region of US$570 million.[8]

Border security meetings with a joint delegation from Kazakhstan, Kyrgyzstan, Russia and Tajikistan have discussed troop reductions,[9] as did President Yeltsin during his visit to China in December 1992. The Russians are playing their traditional role of senior partner and a joint Russian and Chinese memorandum has detailed planned troop reductions up to the year 2000.[10] Meetings on border issues continue and a document on the principles for the compilation of a topographical map of the border was signed, but discussions continued into 1993.[11] The first session of the working group on drafting border agreements between China, Russia, Kazakhstan, Kyrgyzstan and Tajikistan took place in Beijing on 15 April 1993. The discussions were mainly about the legal framework for delineating the western sector of the Russo-Chinese border.[12]

Political stability in Central Asia could lead to unprecedented economic development for China and the CIS and that is the Urumqi perspective, but this depends on the outcome of the civil war in Tajikistan and the political crisis in Uzbekistan. Some refugees fleeing the fighting in Tajikistan have moved into the Pamirs near to the Tajik regions of Xinjiang. In Uzbekistan, there is growing support for militant Islamic groups, particularly the rigid Saudi-backed Sunni Wahhabi sect which is funding the building of mosques and *madrasas* (Islamic schools), some of which may be providing military training. The Wahhabis are opposed both to Sufism, long established in Central Asia and China and to the Islamic Renaissance Party, which is linked to the Muslim Brotherhood.[13]

OPPOSITION TO CHINESE CONTROL: THE KASHGHAR PERSPECTIVE

Chinese control in Xinjiang is very tightly enforced so organized political opposition has of necessity been clandestine,[14] but Turkic people have continued to assert their ethnic identity through the open expression of their cultural distinctiveness. Chinese officials allow this to continue and regularly take part in these and other Muslim festivals, describing them as 'festivals of unity', while warning against separatist activities, 'carried out under the pretext of religion'.[15]

When intellectual or cultural assertions are seen as a threat, the response from Beijing has been swift and often harsh. A book by Turghun Almas, *The Uyghurs*, was attacked in summer 1991, because it portrayed the Uyghurs as a separate nation, distinct from the Han Chinese and tried to demonstrate that Xinjiang has not been an integral part of China since the Han dynasty and that the Uyghurs are culturally and ethnically related to other Turkic peoples. Two other books by the same author, *A Brief History of the Xiongnu* and *Ancient Uyghur Literature* were also attacked[16] because of similar pan-Turkic sentiments. Pan-Turkism is one of the great fears of the authorities in Beijing and Turghun Almas is reported to be under house arrest in Urumqi.[17]

Ethnic or nationalist agitation, whether motivated by political or religious issues is usually depicted by the Chinese authorities as riots, hooliganism or sabotage. The many examples include disturbances in Aksu in April 1980, a major riot during the lunar New Year in Kashghar the same year, protests against the use of Xinjiang as a base for nuclear testing on 12 November 1985 and demonstrations in June 1988 against the publication of a book, *The White House in the Distance*, which allegedly contained racial slurs against Kazakhs and Uyghurs and after racialist slogans had been found on a toilet door at Xinjiang University.[18] Protests in Qinghai, Gansu and Shaanxi in May 1989 against the alleged blasphemy of a book entitled *Sexual Customs* led to a riot, arrests and prison sentences.[19]

THE BAREN INCIDENT

Since the end of the Cultural Revolution in 1976, the most serious disturbances in Xinjiang for which there is corroborated evidence were in the town of Baren in Akto county in the Kizilsu Kyrgyz Autonomous Prefecture in southern Xinjiang in April 1990. A group of Kyrgyz men meeting at a mosque on 5 April led a mass protest against Chinese control and called for the formation of an independent East Turkestan state. To crush the protests, the authorities sent in Public Security Bureau (*gong'anju*) police officers, members of the Kashghar garrison of the People's Armed Police, which is a gendarmerie or carabinieri specially trained in riot control techniques, militia units and 1000 regular troops of the People's Liberation Army.

There were conflicting reports of the number of casualties, with the foreign press quoting over 60 dead. The Chinese media reported that young Uyghur militants had been receiving weapons and unarmed combat training in an Islamic Holy War Force financed by contributions (extorted, according to the Chinese authorities) from the local Muslim population. Some reports suggested that the rebels were supplied with arms by *mujahidin* units in Afghanistan and named the leader as Abu Kasim from Karghalik, a town south of Yarkand in the Altıshahr and, like the Kizilsu Kyrgyz region, close to the border with Afghanistan.[20]

There have been reports of subsequent disturbances in Akto, the Kizilsu Kyrgyz region, Kashghar and Khotan in the Altıshahr and also on the northwestern border. After the Baren rising the Chinese authorities produced many local Uyghur, Kazakh and Hui Muslims who condemned the rioting, but the issue of an independent East Turkestan Republic had been brought into the open for the first time since 1949.

GHULJA (ILI), APRIL 1995

Unconfirmed reports suggest that there was serious unrest in six towns in the Ghulja (Ili/Yining) region of northwestern Xinjiang between 22 and 24 April 1995. On 22 April, as many as 50 000 people were reported to have taken part in rallies and demonstrations against Chinese rule in the towns of Mongolkure (Zhaosu), Tekes, Künes (Xinyuan) Gongliu, Qapqal and Nilka which surround Ghulja and are close to the border with Kazakhstan. The climax of the agitation came on 24 April with strikes by as many as 100 000 workers, teachers and shopkeepers. Demonstrators handed in petitions to local authorities and called for the end of Chinese rule in the Ghulja region and, for some demonstrators, its incorporation into Kazakhstan. They carried banners with slogans which included 'Establish a Kazakh State', 'End Communist Rule in Xinjiang' and 'Long Live Uyghur Xinjiang'. More than 3000 residents of Zhaosu and Gongliu are said to have surrounded local government offices, driven lorries at police stations and stolen guns and police vehicles. The local government offices in Zhaosu are reported to have been completely stripped. Public Security Bureau police and People's Armed Police Units dispersed the crowd with armoured vehicles but were faced with return fire from light machine guns manufactured in the former Soviet Union. Military units from Ghulja and Bole were sent to the two towns to restore order. Zhaosu was placed under curfew on 25 April and over 80 people suspected of involvement in the disorder were arrested. As many as 220 people may have been killed or injured and over 8500 rounds of ammunition were fired.

In the town of Tekes on 25 April, more than 500 people, many of them armed, descended on the local government warehouse in as many as 40 vehicles and ransacked it. Supplies of grain, cooking oil and petrol laid aside for use in emergencies were looted. On their way back to town they encountered an army patrol and in a battle that lasted half an hour, 160 people, 32 of them troops, were killed or injured.

Nilka and Qapqal experienced equally serious disturbances. Demonstrations on 22 April were followed by a sit-in at the offices of the municipal government on 23 April and strikes on 24 April, during which water, electricity and gas supplies were cut off. Crowds surrounded the government offices on 25 April, breaking into them in the afternoon and into the Public Security base and People's Armed Police barracks in the evening. As many as 3000 demonstrators surrounded the local military base demanding Chinese withdrawal from Xinjiang and the establishment of a state of Uyghuristan. Troops fired back and issued an ultimatum that the demonstrators depart by 9 p.m. in the evening or they would take further action and the demonstrators demanded that police who had opened fire be prosecuted.

On 25 April, the CCP (Chinese Communist Party), State Council and Central Military Commission ordered the Xinjiang CCP and Government and the Lanzhou and Xinjiang Military Regions to 'resolutely, thoroughly and rapidly put down armed rebellion organized by splittists and to resolutely crack down upon those organisations attempting dismemberment and those organisations masterminded and supported by foreign forces'. Twenty thousand troops of the thirty-third and forty-first divisions were dispatched by air and rail to the Ghulja region and put on a war footing. They imposed a curfew in Nilka, Qapqal, Xinyuan and Zhaosu and used armoured cars and cars with loudspeakers to demand the surrender of the insurgents. As many as 88 people may have been killed and 200 injured in fighting between local residents and Public Security police and People's Armed Police units. The insurgents fired rifle grenades stolen from military barracks against the police.

During the insurrection, two senior political figures from Beijing were sent to oversee the operations, Luo Gan, Secretary General of the State Council and Li Jing, Deputy Chief of the General Staff. Liu Jingsong, Xinjiang Uyghur Autonomous Region CCP Secretary and commander of the Lanzhou Military Region took command. The disturbances, evidently, were being treated as more than mere riots. A Chinese official at the Xinjiang Foreign Affairs Bureau in Urumqi, Liu Yusheng, is reported to have denied that any of these events occurred and there has been no independent verification to date.[21]

SEPARATIST ACTIVITIES INSIDE AND OUTSIDE XINJIANG

It is difficult to assess how far popular expressions of discontent such as occurred in Baren in 1990 and Ghulja in 1995 are spontaneous manifestations or how far they are influenced by underground and illegal Islamic or separatist organizations, both within and outside of Xinjiang. Accurate information on clandestine organizations operating inside Xinjiang is obviously difficult to obtain, but in 1988, the then Chairman of the Chinese People's Political Consultative Committee in Xinjiang, Ba Dai, identified a number of foreign organizations involved in separatist activities in the region: the Eastern

Turkish National Salvation Committee, the Eastern Turkish National Revolutionary Front, the Eastern Turkestan Charity Funds, the Kazakh Turk Peoples Charity Funds, the New Eastern Turkish Residents Association, the World Islamic Federation and the Eastern Turkestan, Mongolian, Manchurian and Tibetan Peoples' Federation Committee. The group associated with Isa Yusuf Alptekin, the Eastern Turkestan Foundation, was considered to be the most active, having forged links with Xinjiang people who go abroad on the *hajj* pilgrimage to Mecca or to visit relatives.[22] Alptekin, who was general secretary of the Xinjiang Provincial Government from 1947 to 1949 lives in exile in Istanbul, blind and 91 years old, but is still a focus of Uyghur national aspirations and his name is known to many young Uyghurs in Xinjiang.[23] A Xinjiang Justice Party was included in a classified list of 62 underground organizations prepared by the Ministry of Public Security and circulated in October 1992.[24] The authorities appear to have accepted that the activities of such groups are an inevitable consequence of the open-door economic policies that China has adopted since 1979.

Since the Baren rising the authorities in Urumqi have accused separatists of publicizing the history of East Turkestan, running Quranic schools, training 'East Turkestan backbone elements', developing an East Turkestan Islamic Party, sending agents into Xinjiang and subverting pilgrims on the *hajj*.[25] In April 1991, the Uyghur Liberation Organization registered as a legal political party with the Ministry of Justice in Almaty,[26] Kazakhstan and its support is expected to come from the 300 000 Uyghurs living in the CIS, half of whom are resident in Kazakhstan, although it is not clear what forces the ageing leadership, mainly veterans of the short-lived independent East Turkestan Republic of the 1940s might have at their disposal.[27] The organization appealed to the UN in November 1991 for immediate action on human rights in Xinjiang.[28] In June 1992, the creation of a new political party, For a Free Uyghuristan, was announced by Uyghurs living in Kyrgyzstan and an International Uyghur Union was formed on 16 January in Almaty at a meeting reportedly attended by 350 Uyghur delegates from Uzbekistan, Kyrgyzstan, Tajikistan, Turkmenistan and Kazakhstan. It claims to represent the interests of Uyghurs living in the CIS and to be working for democracy, human rights and self-determination for Uyghurs living in Xinjiang. Uyghurs in the CIS have also called for radio broadcasts to China in Uyghur, as the last were discontinued in 1979.[29]

Although Uyghur organizations in Kazakhstan are active and legal, they are clearly an embarrassment to the Kazakhstan Government which is attempting to maintain stable diplomatic relations with China while at least paying lip-service to Pan-Turkic sentiments in its own population. In practical terms, the Urumqi perspective of a Han-dominated, stable and economically successful Xinjiang coincides more closely with the interests of the Kazakhstan Government than the separatist Kashghar perspective. Scholars in Kazakhstan who are in contact with émigré Uyghur groups there do not have a very high opinion of their potential for achieving major political changes within Xinjiang.[30]

The number of terrorist incidents in Xinjiang or at least the number of reports of incidents has increased in recent years. A bomb attack on a bus in Urumqi in February 1992 was reported at the time to have injured at least 26 people and there were also reports of two other bombs the same day, in a cinema and on a second bus, although no injuries were reported in these other incidents. Bomb attacks were also reported in Ghulja (also known as Yining or Ili) in February and in Khotan, Kashghar, Kucha, Korla, Chochek and Bortala between 5 and 8 March 1992. The Front for the Liberation of Uyghuristan, based in Kazakhstan, has declared that it will carry out guerrilla warfare in Xinjiang.[31]

There was also a bomb attack in Kashghar in June 1993. Government buildings were damaged and as many as ten people killed or injured in what was seen as a calculated attack on the representatives of the provincial government in the city.[32] Émigré sources have reported that there were several bomb attacks in the Altıshahr region of southern Xinjiang during 1993 and that martial law had been declared in Kashghar city. There was a second explosion on 4 August and there were possibly bombings in five other cities. Leaflets calling for independence and the ending of Han migration into Xinjiang were distributed.[33]

The trial of eight men accused of carrying out the Urumqi bombing of 5 February 1992 was made public on 30 May 1995. Abdulimiti Talifu and Yidilisihan Wumaier were sentenced to death after having been found guilty of organizing and leading a counter-revolutionary group and engaging in counter-revolutionary sabotage. Maimaitiming Seyiti, Heilili Aletong and Abudula Maimaiti were sentenced to death for causing explosions, robbery and possession of explosives. The five were taken to the execution ground and executed immediately. It was alleged that Abdulimiti Talifu and Yidilisihan Wumaier were among the leaders of the Islamic Reformers Party, founded in October 1990. They financed their operations, *inter alia*, by robbing a bank in Xayar county on the northern fringes of the Taklamakan Desert and bought guns and ammunition with the proceeds. Two Urumqi buses, 01-16715 running on route 52 and 01-16786 running on route 30, were bombed on the evening of 5 February 1992. Three people were killed, four seriously injured and 11 others suffered minor injuries. Bombs planted at the same time in the Qunzhong Cinema and the balcony of a block of flats on Wenhua road failed to detonate. The trial took place in July 1993, but all eight appealed against their sentences. It was not until the appeals had been turned down in May 1995 that the details were made public.[34]

LI PENG'S 1994 SPRING TOUR OF CENTRAL ASIA

The Chinese Prime Minister, Li Peng, embarked on a major tour of the Central Asian republics of the former Soviet Union in April 1994. He addressed the Uzbek Parliament in Tashkent on 19 April and spoke of a new era in Chinese–Central Asian relations characterized by stable political relationships, economic cooperation, non-interference by China in Central Asian domestic affairs and the creation of a New Silk Road, the highly popular metaphor for cross-border economic cooperation. After talks with President Kerimov, agreements on bilateral trade and economic cooperation, air traffic control and material and technical aid were signed. China also agreed to grant Uzbekistan a loan but no details have so far been revealed.[35]

After the visit to Uzbekistan, Li Peng arrived in Ashkhabad on the afternoon of 20 April for talks with the President of Turkmenistan, Saparmurad Niyazov. Although Xinhua and ITAR–TASS reported that there had been 'discussions on regional and international issues of common concern', this was in fact just a courtesy visit.[36]

From Turkmenistan, Li Peng travelled to Kyrgyzstan on 22 April. China offered the Kyrgyz Government a loan, reported to be in the region of 50 million renminbi and signed agreements on economic and cultural cooperation. There is as yet no agreement on the delineation of the China–Kyrgyzstan border but both sides agreed that a convention would be drafted in the near future. Li Peng left Kyrgyzstan with presents of 'a thoroughbred horse, a snow leopard skin and a fur coat and traditional hat'.[37]

Prime Minister Li's visit to Kazakhstan was more significant. He arrived in Almaty on 25 April 1994, the first senior Chinese politician to visit Kazakhstan. After talks with President Nursultan Nazarbayev, the two signed a document defining the border between China and Kazakhstan and agreements on passenger and freight rail transport, business cooperation and the sale of iron and fertilizer to China. China also agreed to make available to Kazakhstan a state loan of 50 million renminbi and what was described as humanitarian aid to the value of 1.5 million renminbi.[38]

In return, President Nazarbayev affirmed that the Kazakhstan Government would not interfere in Chinese domestic affairs and in particular that there would be no support for East Turkestan separatists, an important consideration for Beijing. The Kazakhstan Government has also agreed to restrict travel to the areas bordering on the People's Republic of China, again a matter of some concern for Beijing which fears the spread of militant Islam and arms from its western neighbour.[39] During the discussions the question of the 1 million ethnic Kazakhs in China was raised and Li Peng is reported to have assured Nazarbayev that they would be allowed to travel to Kazakhstan and to settle there permanently if they wished to. Nazarbayev even spoke of the possibility of Kazakhstan opening a consulate in Urumqi to make it easier for Xinjiang Kazakhs to apply for visas.[40] Anecdotal evidence suggests that contact between Kazakhs in Xinjiang and Kazakhstan is now much closer than for over 30 years. Some Kazakhs in Kazakhstan, searching for a Kazakh identity to fit their post-Soviet society have identified Xinjiang Kazakhs as the only true Kazakhs because they were never Russified and scholars in Kazakhstan who are working on the history of the Kazakh nation take a particular interest in the Kazakhs in China.[41]

KAZAKHSTAN'S NUCLEAR WEAPONS AND CHINA

After the collapse of Soviet power in 1991, the west became increasingly concerned about the stockpiles of nuclear weapons remaining in the former Soviet republics, particularly in Kazakhstan where nuclear tests were carried out in an area some 2090 km southwest of Semipalatinsk from 1949 to 1990. It is less well known in the west that China was equally concerned about the proximity of weapons to its borders. This concern had existed since the Sino-Soviet dispute of 1960–1969 when border clashes had given rise to the fear of all-out war and even nuclear strikes from one side or the other.

This is the background to an extraordinary exchange of messages between Kazakhstan and China in the opening weeks of 1995. The government of the People's Republic of China gave an undertaking not to use or threaten to use nuclear weapons against non-nuclear weapons states or nuclear weapon-free zones, indicating clearly that this applied to Kazakhstan although at that time the status of nuclear weapons in Kazakhstan was still unclear. Beijing also reiterated its respect for the independence and territorial integrity of Kazakhstan.[42] President Nursultan Nazarbayev of Kazakhstan sent a personal message to the Chinese Prime Minister, Li Peng, thanking him for this pledge on Kazakhstan's security.[43]

China and Kazakhstan signalled their intention for closer ties with high level visits during 1995. Li Peng visited Kazakhstan in April and President Nazarbayev travelled to Beijing in September. A declaration signed by the two governments on 11 September proposed closer economic ties, including the development of an oil pipeline from Kazakhstan to China's Pacific coast and cooperation in the fields of energy, metallurgy, petrochemicals, mining, textiles and transport.[44]

XINJIANG AT 40: MID-LIFE CRISIS?

The fortieth anniversary of the establishment of the Xinjiang Uyghur Autonomous Region was celebrated on 1 October 1995 with a series of meetings and seminars and the construction of a 100-foot high monument to commemorate the arrival of the People's Liberation Army and the 'peaceful liberation' of Xinjiang in 1949. An 80-strong delegation of senior political figures from Beijing, several with Xinjiang connections, arrived in Urumqi on 29 September. The delegation was led by Jiang Chunyun, Deputy Prime Minister and member of the Politburo. It included Tomur Dawamat, now Vice-Chairman of the Standing Committee of the National People's Congress, but previously Chairman of the XJUAR (Xinjiang Uyghar Autonomous Region) Government, Ismail Amat, a member of the State Council, Vice-Chairman of the Committee of the Chinese People's Consultative Conference and Minister of the State Nationalities Affairs Committee and the veteran Seypidin Azizi (Saifuddin), the CPPCC (Chinese People's Political Consultative Conference) National Committee Vice-Chairman and founding titular head of the Xinjiang Uyghur Autonomous Region Government when it was established on 1 October 1955, all three of Uyghur nationality. Yu Yongbo, a member of the Central Military Commission and a member of the General Political Department of the People's Liberation Army was the other senior member of the delegation, reflecting the importance of the military in Xinjiang.[45]

At the meetings, the emphasis of the speeches was on the positive achievements of Xinjiang and the cooperation and common purpose of the various ethnic groups were emphasized. A communique issued by Xinhua (New China) News Agency also stressed the progress made in the previous 40 years and the glowing prospects for Xinjiang's economic development in view of the new opportunities opened up by the 'corridor of international trade between China, Europe and Central Asia which passes through Xinjiang'. However, it also pointed out the need for a stable political environment and the strengthening of 'solidarity among people of all ethnic groups from generation to generation', highlighting 'hostile forces abroad and separatists at home' as the main threats to this.[46] A second report compiled by journalists from Xinhua and *People's Daily* stressed the key role of the military in ensuring social stability.[47] Even at a time of great celebration, Beijing and Urumqi are keeping an eye open for the resurgence of the Kashghar phenomenon.

While the central government in Beijing and the authorities in the capital of the autonomous region in Urumqi wish to strengthen trade with Central Asia as part of the drive to develop what is seen as a backward part of China, there is concern that increased cross-border contact between Muslim communities, who are mostly speakers of related Turkic languages, will strengthen the sense of ethnic identity of the Uyghur, Kazakh and Kyrgyz people of Xinjiang. What the Chinese authorities are most anxious about is that this ethnic renewal will fuel the nascent separatist political movements already operating within the region, particularly in the southwestern part symbolized by the city of Kashghar, as well as outside China's borders and link them to nationalist or Islamic radical groups in the rest of Central Asia or Afghanistan.

Good relations with Kazakhstan and the other Central Asian states are vital to China's strategy and it is not in the interest of either Beijing or Almaty to permit the growth of nationalist, separatist or radical, politicized Islamic movements. In Xinjiang, time will show whether the politics of Beijing, Urumqi or Kashghar prevail.

NOTES

1. Earlier versions of this chapter were presented at the Symposium on the Caspian and Central Asia, University of Edinburgh, 9–11 July 1994 and ESCAS V, the Fifth European Seminar on Central Asian Studies, *Central Asia in Transition*, University of Copenhagen, 21–26 August 1995. A fuller analysis of Xinjiang and its relationship with Central Asia can be found in Michael Dillon 'Xinjiang: Ethnicity, Separatism and Control in Chinese Central Asia', *Durham East Asia Papers*, no. 1 (January 1995), p. 51. The author is grateful to the Department of East Asian Studies and the Staff Travel Fund of the University of Durham, the British Academy, the Economic and Social Research Council and staff of the Chinese Academy of Social Sciences in Beijing, the Xinjiang Academy of Social Sciences in Urumqi and the Kazakhstan Academy of Sciences in Almaty for assistance in the research for this paper.
2. Xinjiang Weiwuer Zizhiqu renmin zhengfu waishi bangongshi (Foreign Affairs Office of the Xinjiang Uyghur Autonomous Region People's Government) *Xinjiang gailan* (*Survey of Xinjiang*), Urumqi, 1988. The spelling 'Uighur' has been replaced in English language publications in China with 'Uygur' and this is closer to the spelling of the name in the Uyghur language, when written in the modified Latin script that was used during the 1960s and 1970s. Reinhard Hahn in *Spoken Uyghur* (Seattle: University of Washington Press, 1991) suggests

the spelling 'Uyghur', pronounced with the stress on the second syllable, as being the closest to the local pronunciation and that form has been adopted in this paper. The language has also been referred to in the past as Taranchi, Turki or Eastern Turki in late nineteenth and early twentieth century writings. Xinjiang, although a provincial-level administrative unit, is considered to be not a province but an autonomous region in deference to the non-Han majority of the population. Non-Han people in the region and émigré communities in Kazakhstan, Turkey and Germany try to avoid using the name 'Xinjiang' because of its imperial Chinese connotations and refer to the region instead as East Turkestan *Sharqi Turkistan*. Earlier studies of the region often use the spelling Sinkiang or the term Chinese Turkestan. Both 'Turkestan' and 'Turkistan' are used in English language publications. In this paper the former is preferred except when used for the title of the *Eastern Turkistan Dispatch*. However, the name Xinjiang has been used throughout for consistency and simplicity, even when it is anachronistic.

3. The term 'Han' is used to designate the majority population of China, whereas the term 'Chinese' can include both Han Chinese and non-Han citizens of China. 'Muslim' is used here rather loosely to indicate individuals and communities with an Islamic tradition. This obviously includes professed Muslims but it is very difficult to determine what proportion of the communities are believers.
4. *Xinjiang gailan*, 1988, p. 16.
5. 'Principles of Relations with the CIS', interview by Xinhua news agency correspondents, *Beijing Review* (14–20 December 1992). This lack of contact between Central Asia and China, in spite of their geographical proximity, was brought home sharply to me during a visit to the Academy of Sciences in Almaty, Kazakhstan in September 1994.
6. *BBC Summary of World Broadcasts (Far East)* 1338 (25 March 1992), hereafter referred to as FE.
7. FE 1284, 22 January 1992.
8. Liu Weiling 'Border Trade: a Boon for Xinjiang', *Beijing Review* (23–29 January 1995).
9. FE 1556, 5 December 1992.
10. FE 1569, 21 December 1992.
11. FE 1867, G2/2 citing Moscow Radio.
12. FE 1666, A1/5, 19 April 1993.
13. A. Rashid 'Caught in a Cleft' and 'With God on Their Side', 19 November 1992; 'Revival of Sufism', 17 December 1992; 'Forced to Flee: Civil Wars Start New Wave of Migration', 12 November 1992; 'Southern Savagery: Civil War Drives Tajik Refugees to Afghanistan', 28 January 1993, all *Far Eastern Economic Review*; H. Prysor Jones, *Newshour*, BBC World Service, 27 December 1992; A. Bennigsen and S. Enders Wimbush, *Muslims of the Soviet Empire: a Guide* and *Mystics and Commissars* (London: Hurst & Co., 1985).
14. There is very little reporting of clandestine political opposition in China in general and particularly in Xinjiang. Most information on the opposition activities in Xinjiang comes either from émigré supporters or by inference from statements of Chinese policy on the suppression of this opposition.
15. Seypidin Aziz (Saifuddin), quoted in FE 0214, 27 July 1988.
16. *Xinjiang Ribao*, 3 June 1991, 7 June 1991, 14 June 1991 cited in Joint Publications Research Service *China Report* JPRS-CAR-91-04; 21 July 1991 in JPRS-CAR-

91-049; Xinjiang Television, Urumqi, 1 February 1991 in FE 0988; FE 1100. *The Uyghurs* was serialized in the Uyghur language paper *Uyghur Avazı* (*Uyghur Voice*), published in Almaty in Kazakhstan in 1991, *Eastern Turkestan Information*, vol. 1, no. 2 (July 1991), p. 3.

17. Amnesty International, *Secret Violence: Human Rights Violations in Xinjiang* (November 1992). On the persistence of Pan-Turkic sentiments in Turkey and their revival in the 1960s and 1970s, see J. M. Landau, *Pan-Turkism in Turkey: a Study in Irredentism* (London: Hurst & Co, 1981).
18. He Pin, 'Why Do Rebellions Occur So Frequently in Xinjiang?', *Nanbeiji*, (Hong Kong, 18 November), cited in *China Report* JPRS-CAR-92-011, 18 December 1991.
19. FE 0491, 22 June 1989; Xinjiang Radio, 1 July 1989 in FE 0509, 15 July 1989.
20. He Pin, op. cit.
21. *Dongxiang (Trend)*, no. 118 (Hong Kong, 15 June 1995), pp. 13–14, in FE 2336, G/5-6, 22 June 1995. An Uyghur scholar who would normally have had access to classified information about such unrest had heard nothing by August 1995 (personal communication), but the degree of detail in the report and the features in common with previous outbreaks of anti-Han disorder make it impossible to disregard.
22. FE 0294, 28 October 1988.
23. Linda Benson, 'Uygur Politicians of the 1940s', *Central Asian Survey*, vol. 10, no. 4 (1991), pp. 91–3; report by Hugh Pope, *Independent*, 21 April 1990.
24. *Zhengming*, Hong Kong, cited in FE 1581, 8 January 1993.
25. Gao Chaoming, 'National Splittism is the Main Danger in Xinjiang', *Xinjiang Ribao*, cited in FE 0928, 22 November 1990.
26. The capital of Kazakhstan, formerly known as Alma Ata.
27. *Eastern Turkestan Information*, vol. 1, no. 2 (September 1991), p. 5.
28. *Yengi Hayat* (*New Life*) Almaty, 5 November 1991, cited in *Eastern Turkestan*, vol. 1, no. 4 (November 1991), p. 4.
29. *Eastern Turkestan Information*, vol. 2, no. 2 (March 1992); vol. 2, no. 5 (October 1992), p. 6.
30. Interviews with staff of Institute of Oriental Studies and Institute of Uyghur Studies, Kazakhstan Academy of Sciences, Almaty, September 1994.
31. For an account of the leadership of the front in Almaty, see Andrew Higgins, 'Tremors in the Chinese Empire', *Independent on Sunday* (19 April 1992). Uyghur organizations associated with Isa Yusuf Alptekin have condemned the bombings and have even suggested that they were a Chinese provocation to justify further repression, *Eastern Turkestan Information*, vol. 2, no. 2 (March 1992), p. 1.
32. FE 1724, citing Kyodo news agency.
33. *Eastern Turkistan Dispatch*, vol. 1, no. 5 (November 1993), pp. 1–3, citing in part *Der Spiegel*, 19 September 1993.
34. *Xinjiang ribao*, 31 May 1995 in FE 2330, G/7-8, 15 June 1995.
35. FE 1978, 22 April 1994.
36. FE 1983, 28 April 1994.
37. FE 1985, 30 April 1994.
38. The renminbi or yuan is the Chinese currency. This figure was worth over US$9 million at prevailing exchange rates.
39. FE 1985, 30 April 1994.

40. FE 1988, 4 May 1994.
41. For example, K.L. Siroezhkin Kazakhi v KNR: Ocherki Sotsialno-economicheskovo i kulturnovo razvitia (Kazakhs in the PRC: Studies in Social-economic and Cultural Developments), unpublished paper (Almaty, 1994). Additional material from interviews with members of the Institute for Oriental Studies and Institute of Uyghur Studies, Kazakhstan Academy of Sciences, Almaty, September 1994.
42. FE 2223, G/1, 9 February 1995.
43. FE 2225, G1, 11 February 1995.
44. *Beijing Review*, vol. 38, no. 40 (2–8 October 1995), p. 8.
45. FE 2423, G/16, 2 October 1995.
46. Xinhua News Agency, Beijing, 29 September 1995 in FE 2423, G/17-18, 2 October 1995.
47. Xinhua News Agency, 24 September 1995 in FE 2423, G/19, 2 October 1995.

Part III
Regional Cooperation and World Economy

9 CIS' Southern Belt: Regional Cooperation and Integration

M. Mozaffari

INTRODUCTION

There are four major cooperation networks to which the Central Asian and Caucasian newly independent states have committed themselves, each differing with respect to composition and objectives. None of these cooperation networks are purely Central Asian or purely Caucasian; not even merely Central Asian and Caucasian. In all these cooperation networks, there are always several extra-regional actors who are also part of the networks and generally the latter are the network initiators. The largest and most complex of them is the Commonwealth of Independent States (CIS) which embraces all eight independent states of Central Asia and Caucasus, the Russian Federation, the Ukraine, Belarus and Moldova.

The CIS (with a 'C' major) is composed of at least three subsystems: a political ('cis' with a 'c' minor), a military (The Tashkent Collective Security Agreement) and an economic and monetary structure (the so-called 'rouble zone'). In other words, the CIS constitutes a multidimensional cooperative network with multiple objectives. In fact, I regard the CIS as an integration construction. This does not mean that membership of the CIS automatically and necessarily leads to adherence to the above-mentioned military and/or economic arrangements. There is no obligation in this respect. As we will see later on, some countries have chosen to be members of the CIS without committing themselves to future engagements, while some other countries – in fact a significant majority – have demonstrated, though in different degrees and scopes, their will to elaborate a comprehensive, multidimensional cooperation network.

The three other cooperation networks are all regional organizations without any proclaimed or foreseeable integration objective. The largest of these, by number of adherents (11), is the Black Sea Economic Cooperation Zone (BSECZ). It encompasses all of the Caucasian states (Armenia, Azerbaijan and Georgia) but none of the Central Asian states are members. The objectives

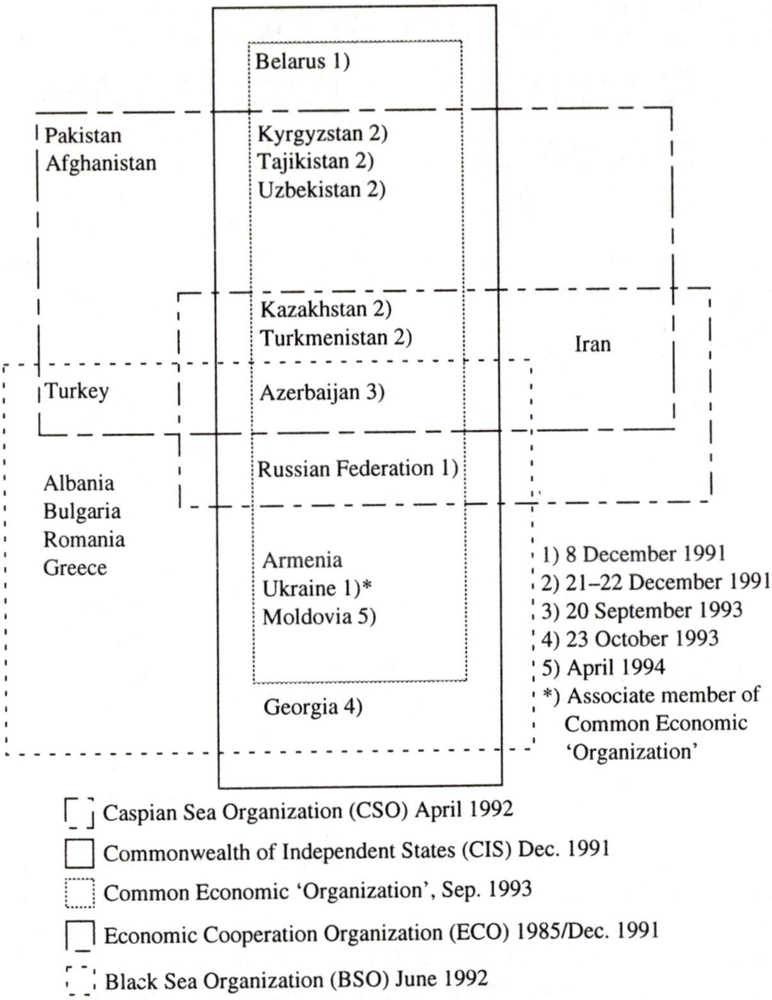

Figure 9.1 Diagram of Different Cooperation Networks (CIS and Regional Actors)

of the BSECZ – closer economic cooperation between the member states and the private sectors of the respective countries – are much more limited than those of the CIS.

The Economic Cooperation Organization (ECO), with its ten members, is the second largest of the regional organizations. Like the BSECZ, the ECO is designed to develop economic cooperation among its member states. The ECO differs from the other organizations in that all members are Muslim states. Consequently, the two Christian-dominated states of Caucasus (Armenia and Georgia), have not been invited to join the ECO, nor have they expressed any wish to do so. The third and last of the regional organizations is the Caspian Sea Organization (CSO) which counts only five members. Unlike the BSECZ, which embraces Black Sea littoral states as well as non-littoral countries, the CSO is composed exclusively of littoral countries. The specificity of the CSO is its primarily technical character, that is although economic cooperation figures in the framework of proclaimed objectives, it remains of secondary importance.

At the present time, and presumably for a long time to come, the CIS' construction as a whole and Central Asia and Caucasus's regions more specifically, represent a very interesting laboratory where almost all experiments are allowed, as long as they have to do with cooperation and integration. Still, the CIS laboratory has not produced any working product. It is still running experiments.

The aim of this study is to take a look inside this laboratory with the purpose of analysing the different experiments that are taking place in connection with cooperation and integration.

Such an analysis will allow us to provide a more qualified assessment of various future scenarios in the CIS and in the regional cooperation networks to which the Central Asian and Caucasian states have committed themselves.

ON INTEGRATION

Many authors from Mitrany (1943), the architect of functionalism over Haas (1958), the father of neo-functionalism and Deutsch *et al.* (1957), the inspirers of Transnationalism, to the contemporary school of liberal intergovernmentalism have contemplated the processes and modalities of integration (see Kelstrup, 1992). The purpose of this section is not to study these models *per se* but to apply them to the situation in the CIS. This confrontation between models and reality will implicitly be a test of their applicability to the CIS situation. I consider integration to be a political concept because, though it embraces both the economic and military dimension, it is in essence political. The two central aspects of integration are the integration process and structural integration. The integration process is a permanent state of matter, because integration is inherently dynamic. The experiences derived from the EU have demonstrated that the process of integration can stagnate, spill back, spill around, accelerate or spill over according to the prevailing state of affairs.

Thus, integration is not necessarily a smooth, linear process. Structural integration refers to a change, not only in degree, but also in the substance and quality of the integration process. Structural integration occurs when the integration process is so advanced that the concept of supranationality is established. This concurs with Haas' (1958) definition of integration as 'the process whereby political actors in several distinct national settings are persuaded to shift their loyalties, expectations and political activities towards a new centre, whose institutions possess or demand jurisdiction over the pre-existing national states' (p. 16). The High Authority of the European Coal and Steel Community and the ensuing Commission of the European Union are good examples of such transfers of loyalties from national to supranational bodies. Haas' (1958) definition refers to what could be called perfect structural integration. However, often structural integration is less than perfect, for example a situation in which structural integration is the proclaimed objective, but the supranational institutions are still very weak relative to the national institutions. Such a stand-by integration is characteristic of the case of the CIS.

Moravcsik (1993) has, in a more accurate manner, made the same analysis when identifying two different spill-over effects in the integration process: functional spill over and political spill over. The former

> occurs when incomplete integration undermines the effectiveness of existing policies, both in areas that are already integrated and in related sectors of the economy, thereby creating pressures for deepening and widening policy co-ordination. Functional spill over is economic ... [The latter] occurs when the existence of supranational organizations sets in motion a self-reinforcing process of institution-building (Moravcsik, 1993, p. 475).

Applied to the CIS, it is evident that with the establishment of the CIS I (8 December 1991) and CIS II (20–21 December 1991), a functional spill over (of a general character) was set in motion, whereas a political spill over still remained in the preliminary phase of formation. Perfect structural integration presupposes the simultaneous reunion of at least three elements: (1) the existence of transnational institutions, (2) the transfer of some loyalty and (3) the presence of a qualified and willing axis.

1. The existence of transnational institutions: not only must substantial transnational cooperation exist, it must be institutionalized in at least one effective supranational body, such as the Commission of the European Union. Furthermore, a transnational or supranational construction imperatively necessitates the pre-existence of nations. The establishment

of any integration construction presupposes nation building. This is because actors who seriously wish to commit themselves to as ambitious a task as integration must already be fully familiar with nation building and the consolidation of national ties. Thus, the construction of the nation state constitutes the first inevitable step in the process towards any other construction whose logic and dynamic surpasses the national framework. One could say that the pre-existence of the nation state constitutes the *sine qua non* condition for the realization of any supranational construction. The more consolidated a nation and the stronger its national institutions, the easier it will be for that particular nation to commit itself to a supranational cooperation network (that is, the EU). It is Utopia to believe that a reliable supranational cooperation, with integration as its final objective, could be built on the basis of actors with no solid experience in nation building. This is precisely why the CIS has had and will continue to have difficulties, particularly with regard to the newly independent states of Central Asia and Caucasus. These states are quite new and have little experience in nation-building. They are therefore faced with the task of building new national institutions, while at the same time cooperating with a supranational construction within the framework of the CIS.

2. The transfer of loyalty, which in reality is a direct consequence of transnationality, is the second necessary element in a successful integration. Without the transfer of loyalty, transnationality and supranationality have no real meaning. However, the transfer of loyalty is neither absolute nor all-encompassing (if it were, then we would be discussing some other construction such as a federation). Within the framework of integration, members conserve their sovereignty. It is precisely by virtue of this sovereignty that they are able and willing, on the basis of reciprocity, to concede specific parts of their sovereignty to mutually acceptable supranational organizations. An example of such a concession of sovereignty is the Treaty of Rome which led to the creation of the Commission. However, the transfer of loyalty is neither absolute nor complete, otherwise we would be talking about something other than integration (that is, merging). Following Article 157 of the Treaty of Rome, the Commission is recognized as a supranational authority which 'shall neither seek nor take instructions from any Government or from any other body'.

The metamorphosis that all Commissioners are required to undertake, from national politicians to public servants loyal exclusively to the Community, is remarkable and possibly unreasonable: what is even more

> remarkable is the extent to which past Commissioners have all been able to achieve this transformation, causing more than one government recently to complain that 'their' Commissioners had 'gone native' (Holland, 1993, p. 92).

In the case of the CIS, such an institution has not yet emerged. The only 'semi'-supranational instance in existence is the ambivalent, common military commandment of the CIS, which is in reality a Russian command.

3. The presence of an available axis is the third element in a successful integration. This element, despite its determinant importance, has not been given due attention by the scholars working on integration. The first two elements *per se* do not suffice on their own to establish an effective integration construction. An axis of able and willing actors is equally important. The axis must have capabilities (political, economic and military) of such a magnitude to allow it to be perceived as capable of undertaking the task of leader in the eyes of the other more 'junior' members of the cooperation network. The ability to act as an axis (*noyau dur*) is not enough. The will to undertake such a task must also be present. Japan, for example, possesses the necessary qualifications to be an axis, but for some reason it does not seem to want to play such a leading role at present. With respect to the EU, it is obvious that the French–German tandem has been and still is the pivot and pillar of European integration. The EU was originally conceived as a Franco–German project, and today, almost 40 years after the Rome Treaty, it is impossible to think of the EU without their presence. This is not the case with the other members of the EU, although they too have differing importance for the construction (the withdrawal of UK, for example, will probably have more repercussions for the EU than the withdrawal of, say, Portugal). Although the CIS construction still has a long way to go with respect to the development of its supranational institutions and the transfer of loyalty, it has a qualified and willing axis: the Russian Federation.

REGIONALISM, REGIONAL COOPERATION AND INTEGRATION

The notion of 'region' is originally related to the notion of 'frontier', 'delimitation' and 'country'. It refers to some comprehensive area *regio, regere*. 'Region' always relates to geography: Europe, North America, the Middle East and so on and so forth. Instead of region, one could talk of 'zone' ('zona' in Latin and 'zônê' in Greek), which literally means 'belt'. Thus, it seems that zone indicates the delimitation more adequately than region. The former appears more diffuse concerning its borders. We talk of 'zone franc', 'rouble zone' or 'zone d'influence' to indicate a specific geographic space where the franc or rouble is the dominating currency. The zone d'influence also indicates the geographical space where a specific country can easily exert its influence. But we do not talk about a 'US dollar zone' or a 'Coca-Cola zone', because the dollar is used almost everywhere and Coca-Cola is available worldwide without being limited to a specific geographical space. Despite the relative clearness of zone compared to the vague character of region, the latter is frequently used in the political jargon. The reason is that zone indicates either a clear political content (that is, zone d'influence) or it contains a quite specific connotation (that is, the zone of the franc); therefore the term region, despite the fact that it is vague. However, precisely because of this, it can indicate whatever one wants it to indicate (that is, 'security complex', a military alliance in the form of the North Atlantic Treaty, economic cooperation in the form of the Andean Trade Union, political cooperation, the Gulf Cooperation Council and so on). Some regions are geographically well defined, which is the case of the Persian Gulf Region or Europe. Europe is limited geographically to the Atlantic to the west, the Ural Mountains to the east, the Mediterranean Sea to the south and the North Pole to the north. Some other regions are not well defined (is the Middle East from Morocco to Afghanistan or from Egypt to Iraq?). The question will be raised especially when we try to politicize a region, adding to it some non-geographical substance (economic or political cooperation) for the purpose of differentiating it from other similar kinds of economic and political cooperation. In such cases we often need to use the geographical delimitation region. In the present study, region indicates three different cooperation networks, namely the ECO, the Black Sea Organization and the CSO. The CIS is not considered 'regional', because it cannot be characterized as a region. Therefore, some people use Eurasian when referring to both Slavic–European and non-Slavic and Asiatic parts of the CIS. The term Eurasian in itself indicates that the CIS is not regional (Eurasia is far from being a region).

I have chosen to use the term regional cooperation rather than regionalism. This choice is motivated by the fact that regionalism as a concept is ambiguous. Ambiguous because it refers simultaneously to regional cooperation and regional integration. Moreover, no distinction is made between economic cooperation/integration and political cooperation/integration. It is true that regionalism has traditionally been used to refer only to the economic dimension of cooperation/integration. Thus Grilli's (1993) definition of regionalism 'as the tendency of a certain number of countries to partially or totally liberalize trade among themselves, and therefore to do so on a discriminatory basis with respect to the rest of the world (the non-members)' (p. 2). This definition raises some questions. For example, can trade liberalization between a number of regional states take place without appropriate political harmonization? Certainly not and in particular not when regionalism is perceived in the sense of regional integration. This lacuna has been filled out by the so-called 'new' regionalism, which has the ambition of covering all aspects of regional cooperation/integration. As Hettne (1994) put it,

> New regionalism implies a stronger emphasis on the political dimensions. Regional organizations which emerged after the Second World War, whether economic or more security oriented, were usually organized from above and from outside the region. The new regionalism is emerging in a post Cold War context, in a situation where 'national' economies are outgrowing their national polities (pp. 1–2).

Adding the political dimension to the economic certainly makes regionalism more extensive, but it does so at the expense of precision. In other words, the new regionalism has not been able to offer any new clarification. In this context it should be noted that the alleged relationship between the collapse of the USSR and the sudden emergence of the new regionalism has not been certified. Moreover, the EEC (now the EU) existed long before this event and the construction of the NAFTA (North American Free Trade Agreement) also had no connection to the Soviet collapse. The same goes for the ECO. In fact, the only new regionalism related to the collapse of the Soviet Union is the CIS and the Black Sea and Caspian Sea Organizations. There is, however, a problem in viewing the emergence of the CIS as a sign of a new regionalism. It derives from the fact that new regionalism asserts that after the end of the Cold War, regional organizations were no longer 'created from outside' and 'from above' (that is, the superpowers). The new process is more spontaneous from within and 'from below' (in the sense that the constituent states themselves are the main actors). The statement is not *per se* incorrect, but with respect to the construction of the CIS, it merely describes the first phase. The ensuing evolution within the CIS contradicts the new regionalist assertion, considering the huge pressure that Moscow put on Azerbaijan and Georgia to ensure their adherence to the CIS. For the above-mentioned reasons, I believe that regional cooperation is more precise and provides better opportunities to operationalize the concept than regionalism, whether in its 'old' or 'new' guise.

Regional cooperation and integration represent two different concepts that sometimes but not always refer to two different phases of general evolution within a specific region or between several regions. There is no deterministic or causal relationship between cooperation and integration. That is, regional cooperation will not automatically lead to regional integration. However, regional integration cannot emerge without a network of cooperation between the regional actors. Cooperation is a necessary step towards integration. Some scholars believe that regional cooperation is a rather new phenomenon 'which started in the 1980s, after the decline of integration theory and praxis in the 1970s' (Hettne, 1994, p. 1). This assumption is based on the idea that regional cooperation and regional integration are not only two different concepts but also totally irreconcilable. This is not the case. Integration is not a *coup de foudre* emerging suddenly and spontaneously. Integration is a process during which the different partners involved get better acquainted so that a reliant and dependable relationship can develop.

A clear distinction between regional cooperation and integration will also help us distinguish between the different processes of cooperation in Central Asia and Caucasus. One interesting point about these areas is the fact that a number of processes (both cooperative and integration) co-exist side by side and interact or interfere with each other.

The Central Asian and Caucasian republics have committed themselves to two different kinds of cooperation: regional cooperation and integration cooperation. The difference between these two frameworks is concrete and substantial. While the former is intergovernmental, the latter is supranational. Intergovernmental cooperation is characterized by the fact that the participating states preserve their full sovereignty. In this particular case, no other authorities than the states themselves make decisions, because the only prevailing law is national. The NAFTA (USA, Canada and Mexico), despite its possible integration ambitions, is a typical example of regional cooperation. In contrast, states participating in the integration cooperation delegate part of their competence and sovereignty to some specific institutions or authorities. The best and perhaps the only real example of this is the EU in which the Commission plays the supranational role and the EU Court of Justice is recognized as the Union Court whose decisions can invalidate the national courts. So, by virtue of its supranationality, the EU is at the same time a regional and an integration entity *par excellence*.

MAIN DIFFERENCES AND SIMILARITIES BETWEEN THE EU AND THE CIS

There are five main differences between the EU and the CIS. First, when the integration process started in Europe, no European-wide centralized government, authority or hegemonic power existed. In the CIS case, the situation is very different. Until 1991 all the members of the CIS were submitted to the strongly centralized power structure of the Soviet regime and today, by virtue of its capabilities (economic, political and military), the Russian Federation stands as the unique, unrivalled hegemonic power. Moreover, the Russian Federation is not the *primus inter pares* within the CIS, it is simply the *primus*. The predominance of the Russian Federation in the CIS has produced asymmetrical relations between Russia and the other member states, particularly the less powerful and more dependent states of Central Asia and Caucasus.

Second, integration in Europe was originally an attempt to eradicate the roots of war from Europe, especially between France and Germany. Peace building was the main objective and was to be achieved through (1) economic reconstruction and development and (2) maintaining the balance of power, particularly between France and Germany. The situation within the CIS is very different, because it emerged from the collapse of the Soviet Union, that is the collapse of a mega-structure situated in Moscow. In other words, it was a disintegration of the different parts of the Soviet Union. Consequently, as opposed to the EU, which was not integrated at all before the Second World War, the disintegrated parts of the former Soviet Union are now attempting to reintegrate into a new construction. To succeed, they must go through a new integration process. During this process, they will be faced with a number of important dilemmas. Perhaps it is easier to build on virgin ground than on the ruins and semi-ruins of an old construction. Are the old structures and materials of the CIS – or at least some of them – good enough to be reused for a new construction? And, if so, how are the good parts to be used? Appropriate answers to these questions are absolutely necessary for the success of any new construction.

Third, in its present form the EU is composed of only western European countries whose cultures, religions and lifestyles are fairly similar. The civic cultures and values of all 15 EU members are essentially based on respect for the individual, human rights, freedom of speech and the equality of citizens in matters of law, justice and opportunities. Moreover, all the EU countries adhere to a democratic–pluralistic political system and their religious culture is predominantly Christian. It is worth noting that Spain, Portugal and Greece were not able to join the EU while they were undemocratic. Their membership was secured only after they converted to the values of democracy. In this respect, the CIS is very different. The CIS constitutes a large agglomeration of different cultures and religions. Moreover, although all the CIS states have adopted democracy in the post-Soviet era, democracy is still in its infancy and general elections often look more like a census than free voting. In short, whereas in Europe democracy rapidly became a routine, general framework for both citizens and governments, it is still to be fully implemented in the CIS democracies. Thus, from the perspective of a large part of the population of the member states, the CIS is not representative because the governments in question are not fully representative. So if the EU is characterized as fully democratic, the CIS can be characterized as semi-democratic.

Democratic integration corresponds to the liberal intergovernmentalist model in which the population participates actively (through elections, referendums and free debate) in the process, the degree and the speed of integration. Semi-democratic integration is characterized by the absence of public debate and governments that are elected in a not fully pluralistic political system.

The fourth and most important difference between the EU and the CIS relates to the fact that 'the European countries were already stable nation-states before their integration, and they were at more or less similar levels of economic development' (Vasiliev, 1993, p. 327), whereas this is not the case with the CIS. The CIS states' economic dependency on Russia has made the Russian authorities question the feasibility of integration. As Kozyrev *et al.* (1994, p. 14) put it, 'an important principle of integration demands that it really benefit all sides'. In other words, integration presupposes the pre-existence of a substantial reciprocity between the member states, as within the EU. However, today the subsidies still flow unilaterally from Russia to the other CIS states and 'not the other way round. Contrary to the earlier myth about some republics having all but fed Russia' (Kozyrev *et al.*, 1994, p. 13). The situation has been caricatured by Arbatov *et al.* (1994), the Director of the Centre for Strategic Studies: 'Our unquestionable goal is considered to be integration of the CIS ... It seems to me that this is not a strategy but is more like an Abkhazian wedding – anybody is welcome to it and free to eat what he pleases. But what about Russia's interests?' (p. 21). Furthermore,

> none of the states that are now members of the CIS were full-fledged nations at the time of the October 1917 revolution ... The present republics are early approximations of nation-states, still in need of geographic and institutional shaping ... How will these states, still lacking self-determination build their relationship with other states?
>
> (Vasiliev, 1993, p. 327).

Finally, although high politics (peace building and security issues) were the primordial motive for cooperation in both the EU and the CIS case, the context of the cooperation thus differs. European integration arose in the aftermath of war while the CIS emerged from the collapse of the USSR. The establishment of the European Coal and Steel Community in reality represents a political will on the part of France and [West] Germany to break with history, by abandoning the *status quo ante* and entering a new era. As opposed hereto, the CIS does not aim to create a new system but merely to rearrange the old system. In the words of Andrei Kozyrev, the former Russia's Foreign Minister,

> I believe, that we have done the important thing by stopping the 'flight' of republics that seemed inevitable at a certain stage, probably like the movement of a pendulum swinging away from an over-centralised and, moreover, ideologized state in which we lived before the CIS came into being ... Yes, the states in question are independent, but they belong to a commonwealth (Kozyrev *et al.*, 1994, p. 11).

Despite the many substantial differences between the EU and the CIS, there are some similarities. First, in both cases, the proclaimed goal is integration. In the case of the EU, integration has reached an advanced stage. Obviously, this is not the case of the CIS, which has just started on the integration process. Second, they both have approximately the same dimensions: political, military and economic. The relative cohesion and strength of these dimensions vary within the EU and the CIS. While the economic dimension is the predominant strength and focal point of the EU, it is the weakest element of the CIS. On the other hand, the military dimensions are still the weakest dimension in the EU (the West European Union) but the strongest in the CIS. The political dimension of the EU has developed considerably over the years. The progress is evident, considering the evolution in the cooperation since the 'Spirit of The Hague' (Dinan, 1994, p. 73) and Etienne Davignon's aborted proposal in 1970 to set up a permanent secretariat for the European Political Cooperation (EPC), to the procedural improvements (Title III) of the Single European Act (SEA) which dealt exclusively with the EPC and put an end to the distinction between foreign ministers' meetings in the 'EPC' and in the Council. Furthermore, it associated the Commission with the EPC fully, ensuring that the European Parliament was 'closely associated with EPC', 'creating a mechanism for convening the political Committee of Community foreign ministers within forty-eight hours at the request of at least three member states, and establishing an EPC secretariat in Brussels' (Dinan, 1994, p. 470). The SEA also stipulated that 'the external policies of the European Community and the policies agreed in Political Cooperation must be consistent' (Dinan, 1994, p. 470) and charged the presidency and the Commission with ensuring such consistency. The political and also the security ties between the members of the EU have been further improved by the Maastricht Treaty (Title V), which contains the Common Foreign and

Security Policy (CFSP) provisions, providing that on the basis of a unanimous decision, the Council may refer to the WEU (Western European Union) decisions and actions by the EU that have defence implications (Dinan, 1994, p. 472).

In the above comparison between the CIS and the EU, we did not consider the time factor, which is essential, as it explains why there are so many differences and so few similarities between these two integration processes and constructions. We compared the CIS with the EU as it is today and not as it was at the beginning of its construction in early 1950. There is a time difference of almost 40 years which differentiates the CIS from the EU. It would be interesting to compare the CIS in its present shape, processes, goals, institutions, ambitions and so on and so forth with the Coal and Steel Community in 1950. Such a vast and complicated task would be appropriate for a 'research programme'. I have not done research of this kind. Thus, a superficial comparison shows that, all things being equal, the CIS of 1995 (less than 5 years old) seems much better shaped than the Steel and Coal Community when it was the same age, although before the signing of the Treaty of Rome in 1957. At that time, the Steel and Coal Community was without any common structures with regard to military and security and it was also without a common political decision-making body and even without a common economic and monetary system. All these components were added later and took shape through the Treaty of Rome. The CIS already has these components, more or less formalized, but they are there. It is true that they are not all well-functioning, though they have been institutionalized. That means that to some extent the CIS is ahead of the present EU, if one considers the time factor.

After having reviewed the different aspects of integration, we shall now move on to study the different options for CIS in the future.

THE CIS' DIFFERENT OPTIONS

For the time being, integration within the CIS seems to be more a project than a reality. Despite the uncertainty surrounding the process of integration, the Central Asian and Caucasian republics are determined to maintain close relations with Russia, especially with respect to economic matters, for the simple reason that they are and will for a long time continue to be dependent on Russia.[1] The Russians, on the other hand, are split between affirmative action and caution. On the one hand, Russia would like to retain control over the internal components of its old empire, but, on the other hand, it finds itself constrained by the need to satisfy its own population's demand for rapid economic growth and development. Developing the infrastructure and the general level of know-how in Central Asia and Caucasus, necessary for effective integration, requires the dedication of a great amount of resources on the part of Russia that could have gone to realize the Russian aspiration/dream of reaching the European level of prosperity. The objective of accomplishing the European level of economic affluence is clearly not reconcilable with the aim of integrating the non-Slavic republics of the ex-Soviet Union. On the other hand, Russia is unlikely to accept being abased to a mere fourth power after the USA, Japan and the EU. The Russians will do all that is possible to retain their position as at least a political superpower. Moreover, if they were to abandon Central Asia and Caucasus definitely, a vacuum would emerge which would have to be filled by some other power, namely China, India or one of the Islamic countries. Such an eventuality would not be in accordance with the Russian ambition of rising in the ranks of nations. At present, Russia has not made any final decision as to the priority of its economic objective relative to its superpower objective. All the options are still open. In the following, I shall review some of the most important.

The EU model

Adopting a purely European integration model, implying the transfer of significant authority in the economic, financial and social domains to an autonomous supranational body similar to the European Commission, seems unrealistic in the foreseeable future mainly because of the very uneven levels of economic and social development within the CIS.

Yet another option would be to associate the Central Asian and Caucasian republics with the Slavic members of the CIS. This would correspond to the EU's relationship with Turkey and with the Maghreb countries.

The Payments Union

If the EU model nevertheless is to be pursued and all ex-Soviet territories (except the Baltic states) are to be kept inside the integration process, then the CIS will undergo the same process as the Europeans. The European integration process started with the Payments Union. The CIS could start out by rectifying 'the present system of foreign-economic settlements. The CIS countries could conclude agreements on settlements and payments within the framework of bilateral clearings for a period of nine to twelve months. At the same time work could begin on setting up a system of multilateral settlements which could rely on the ideas, tested in practice, of the European Payments Union (EPU)' (Petrakov and Shatalov, 1994, p. 9).

Academic Nikolai Petrakov and Professor Grigory Shatalof believe that the convertibility of currencies will only be achieved in the final stages of the Payments Union. Actually, the Payments Union's model was the model that the CIS leaders chose at their summit meeting in Kiev (26 May 1995). They agreed almost unanimously (with Turkmenistan abstaining from voting) to create the interstate currency committee to promote the mutual conversion to national currencies and to ease mutual payments.

The pragmatic model

The realization that there is a significant gap between the level of economic development of the various CIS countries could result in different speeds according to different alternatives 'because by virtue of certain aspects of its internal evolution, its geopolitical situation, and so on, the republics differ in pace of advance and interests with regard to integration, cooperation with Russia and one another' (Kozyrev *et al.*, 1994, p. 12). The task of a better cooperation for the purpose of integration in the future can be achieved in two different ways which will cross each other sometime in the coming years. The first way is the security path and the second is economic integration. The centre always remains as Russia. Precisely around Russia a 'security zone' will be erected by the countries who want to take part in it. Since the Ukraine and Belarus apparently are not willing to be members of a security zone, Russia has no other choice than to build it up with the participation of Central Asian republics at first, but also with the assistance of the Caucasian states. Parallel to this, Russia will reinforce its economic ties with the Ukraine and Belarus (and also Kazakhstan) who are welcoming the strengthening of economic cooperation, because the level of their economic development and the quality of their already existing infrastructure permit them to do it (see Tables 9.1 and 9.2).

This model corresponds roughly to what Kozyrev – the former Foreign Minister of Russia – has in mind. He left the door open to any qualified adherence to the Community, if the adherence goes towards a more close-knit commonwealth whose centre is undeniably Moscow. The advantage of this model is its openness and flexibility. Without rushing or pushing, the aim is to assure Russian supremacy and control over two vital issues: security and the economy. Another advantage of this model is that it permits a harmonious development towards integration. The peripheral economic group can concentrate on building up and consolidating their national structures before joining the centre while the centre is able to proceed rapidly towards an EU-like structure without being constrained by the less mature members of the peripheral group. In short, Kozyrev's advice to the ex-Soviet independent states is 'Take as much sovereignty as you can share with Russia!'

TABLE 9.1 *Economic growth in Central Asia*

	Kazakhstan	*Kyrgyzstan*	*Tajikistan*	*Turkmenistan*	*Uzbekistan*	*All Central Asia*
1992 GDP (millon roubles)	1 119 600	115 000	131 000	165 000	387 000	1 917 600
1992 GDP (millon dollars)	3 795	390	444	559	1 312	6 500
1992 GDP per capita	224	86	80	145	61	124
1992 GDP $ per capita (ppp)	3 786	2 062	1 220	2 510	1 925	2 510
1992 Population (millon)	16.9	4.5	5.6	3.8	21.4	52.3
1992 Local rouble/$ period average	295	295	295	295	295	295
Average GDP growth rate 1990–1992 (%)	–7.8	–9.3	–16.1	–6.1	–5.0	–5.3
Average inflation rate 1990–1992 (%)	214.5	164.4	229.0	178.1	146.8	188.0
Cotton production 1992 (000 metric tons)	247	50	420	1 289	4 128	6 134
Change on previous year (%)	–14.8	–19.4	–48.7	–9.7	–11.1	–18.0
Oil production 1991 (000 metric tons)	26.6	0.1	0.1	5.4	2.8	35.0
Change on previous year (%)	3.1	–	–	–3.6	0.0	2.3
Gas production 1991 (billion m^3)	7.9	0.1	0.1	84.3	41.9	134.3
Change on previous year (%)	11.3	–	–	–4.0	2.7	–1.0
Coal production 1991 (000 metric tons)	130 315	3 500	300	–	5 900	140 015
Change on previous year (%)	–0.9	–	–	–	–	–

SOURCES European Bank for Reconstruction and Development, The International Monetary Fund, World Bank, national sources, and The Economist Intelligence Unit in Apostolou, A., 'The Problems of Creating Economies in Central Asia' (Table 1, see Apostolou in References).

Table 9.2 *Agriculture, industry and trade in Central Asia*

	Kazakhstan	*Kyrgyzstan*	*Tajikistan*	*Turkmenistan*	*Uzbekistan*	*All Central Asia*
Land use 1990 (total area million ha)	271.7	19.8	14.3	48.8	44.8	399.4
Arable land (million ha)	197.6	10.1	4.3	35.8	26.6	274.4
Cultivated area (million ha)	35.2	1.2	0.8	1.2	4.1	42.5
Arable % of total area	72.7	51.0	30.1	73.4	59.4	68.7
Cultivated % of arable land (source: Narkhoz, 1990)	17.8	11.9	18.6	3.4	15.4	15.5
Share of total trade 1990 (%)	49.0	36.0	39.0	41.0	45.0	45.0
Russia	14.0	25.0	26.0	23.0	19.0	19.0
Rest of Central Asia, non-USSR	16.0	17.0	16.0	14.0	17.0	16.0
Origin of NMP by sector 1991 (%)	35.8	28.4	38.3	46.4	43.2	41.9
Agriculture	41.6	37.8	28.6	19.6	33.2	26.0
Industry	9.5	6.9	14.7	22.7	10.7	15.0
Construction services	13.1	26.9	18.4	11.3	12.9	17.1

Sources European Bank for Reconstruction and Development, the International Monetary Fund, World Bank, national sources, and The Economist Intelligence Unit in Apostolou, A., 'The Problems of Creating Economies in Central Asia' (Table 2, see Apostolou in References).
Note: GDP for Kyrgyzstan; 1990 figures for Tajikistan and all Central Asia.

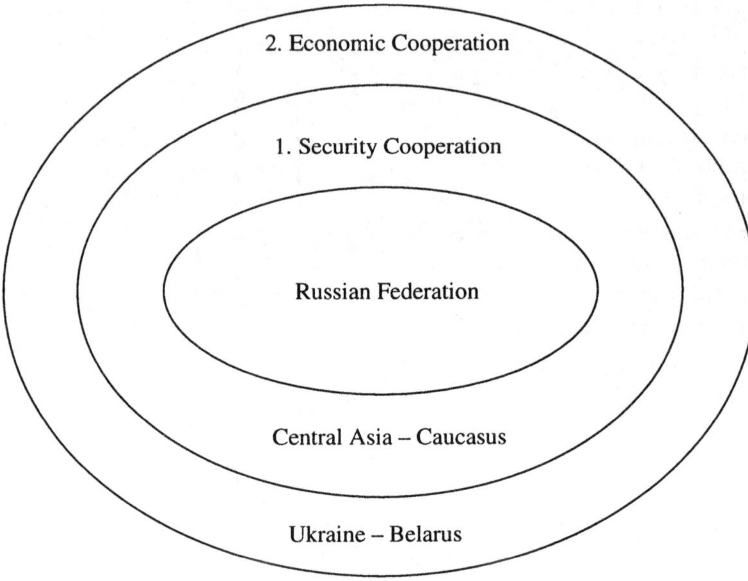

Figure 9.2 Kozyrev's View – Pragmatic Model. (This figure is the author's interpretation of Kozyrev's view)

The Slavic–Christian model

Another option would be to create a Slavic–Christian cooperation network without the Muslim republics. This corresponds *grosso modo* to the model set forward by Arbatov *et al.* (1994, pp. 21–3) but is contrary to the original philosophy behind the CIS, namely the multidimensional integration of the entire ex-Soviet Union. According to the Arbatov *et al.* (1994) model, Russia will choose its cooperation partners à la carte. In other words, Russia will only enter into institutionalized cooperation in those sectors and in those countries that correspond best to its interests. In essence it is a form of sectorial integration. Arbatov *et al.* (1994) holds the view that only two CIS states are comparable to Russia on the economic and political levels (as well as culturally), namely the Ukraine and Belarus. 'We may achieve economic integration with Ukraine but a military and political alliance with it is by no means a must. ... Ukraine is afraid of Russia, and Russia is occasionally apprehensive of Ukraine' (Arbatov *et al.*, 1994, pp. 21–3). Arbatov (1994) argued that this approach corresponds to the EU model according to which the economic integration and the military engagement of the members are not necessarily related. Some EU states are members of NATO while others are not (Sweden, Finland and Ireland). Arbatov *et al.* (1994) distinguished between the economic sector and the security and political sector. Security and political alliances can be formed with countries that have common adversaries or common military and political interests with Russia, namely Kazakhstan, Georgia and Armenia (Arbatov *et al.*, 1994). The Muslim states of the former Soviet Union are thus excluded from both the economic integration network and the military alliance, because their participation is not in the interest of Russia (Arbatov *et al.*, 1994). By excluding the Muslim countries from the military and economic cooperation, Arbatov *et al.* (1994) is contributing to realizing Huntington's theory on The clash of civilizations.

Figure 9.3 Arbatov's View – Slavic–Christian Model. (This figure is the author's interpretation of Arbatov's view)

Commonwealth à la British

The Soviet Union built an empire that perished just like the British Empire. If Great Britain was able to keep close relations with the disparate elements of its old empire, despite the very violent disintegration/decolonization process that put an end to the British Empire, so *a fortiori* can Russia, particularly because of the non-violent character of the disintegration of the ex-Soviet Union. The question is, however, whether this model over time has become obsolete and if, perhaps, it is not inappropriate in the context of the CIS.

Russian Jamahiriya

This model has been advocated by the famed ophthalmology professor Svyatoslav Fyodorov within the frame of the Russian Federation itself. Inspired by the Libyan Colonel Muammar al-Qaddafi, he dreams about a Jamahiriya where 'there is no bureaucratic apparatus in the country. Everything is being decided by the people's committees of streets, settlements and cities' (*Moscow News*, 9–15 June 1995, p. 2). By some extension and imagination, the Jamahiriya model could maybe be applied to the whole CIS system. However, in the end, this model looks more like an ophthalmological imagination than a political solution.

THE DIMENSIONS AND INSTITUTIONS OF THE CIS

The CIS constitutes an international multigoal and multidimensional cooperation network. Its first goal is the building of a new political entity based essentially on the old and traditional ties, established through history between Russia on one side and the different parts of the ex-Soviet–Russian empire on the other. In this respect, it is a question of sharing the same destiny and being in the same boat. As Kozyrev *et al.* (1994) expressed it, the CIS is something more than just a 'community' as it is more than a process of interaction and integration. 'We needed a word connoting friendly ties, something warmer' (Kozyrev *et al.*, 1994, p. 11). Connected precisely to the common (or imagined) political destiny, the second goal of the CIS can be resumed in assuring and preserving the security of the members of the CIS. 'Security' must here be understood as the safeguard of the territorial integrity and independence of each member; 'security' also means the conservation of internal peace insofar as it concerns the internal peace of the non-Slavonic members. Obviously, the possible internal turbulence inside the Russian Federation, as well as the political struggle between the different parties and political fractions in Russia are realistically out of the control of the other CIS members, for the simple reason that these states are not able to intervene in Russia's internal concerns. This is also true of the Ukraine and Belarus, which have always demonstrated an extraordinary sensitivity *vis-à-vis* any Russian attempt to interfere in their respective national matters. If they are sensitive to Russia, they are *a fortiori* sensitive to any intervention from other states. We may also add the fact that the Ukraine and Belarus are not facing the same problems concerning both internal and regional security as the non-Slavic states of the CIS. The multiple Russian interventions in Tajikistan and in Caucasus illustrate very well the asymmetrical relations inside the CIS with respect to the security issues. The war in Chechnya is a good example which demonstrates the very cautious and highly prudential attitude of the CIS member states *vis-à-vis* Russia. The fact is that no member of the CIS had publicly criticized the Russian military intervention in Chechnya.

The third goal of the CIS is to achieve an economic and consequently a monetary union whose shape and intensity are not yet defined. Nevertheless, the idea behind constructing such a union is quite simple and is coherent with the logic behind the CIS. In short, the question is that 'if we are, *nolens volens*, sharing the same political destiny and if our security matters are closely related to each other, then is it the same for our welfare and prosperity?'. However, the Russian élites are still questioning the opportunity of an economic and monetary union with the non-Slavic members of the CIS; some of them are also expressing serious doubts about the inevitable linkage between political and security matters, on the one hand and economic and monetary matters, on the other.

The achievement of these goals necessitates formal and appropriate institutions, which have been created in 'record time', if one considers the huge and multiple problems and difficulties that the collapse of the Soviet Union produced. It is quite astonishing that in a span of only 6 months – from December 1991 to May 1992 – the political and security institutions of the CIS were in place, were institutionalized and functioned. Then the Common Economic Space and the Common Monetary Zone were established 1 year later (August 1993). Considering the high speed which characterized the institutionalization of the CIS, there is no doubt that a large part of the problems which the CIS is facing during its young age is undoubtedly due to the work being done in a hurry and without real preparation. Nevertheless, the CIS is today more than a simple project: it already has its own institutions and officials at different levels meet regularly. However, difficulties, particularly in the economic and monetary field, still constitute a real obstacle to the establishment of an all-encompassing integration system. In the following, I shall try to analyse the three vital components (political, military and economic) of the CIS.

The political dimension of the CIS

The political dimension embodying the accord of a group of states to cooperate with each other in order to achieve explicitly agreed upon objectives is the founding pillar of every security system. If all goes well, other objectives may ensue (spill over) in the course of cooperation. Obviously, every international political organization has one or more vectors of common, agreed upon objectives. These objectives may be explicit or implicit. NATO's common objective was to 'safeguard the freedom, common heritage and civilization of [members] peoples, founded on the principles of democracy, individual liberty and the rule of law' (Preamble of the Treaty). The Warsaw Pact had no proclaimed political aims, being merely a 'system of collective security in Europe based on the participation of all European States, *irrespective of their social and political structure*' (Preamble of the Treaty, emphasis added). It is worth emphasizing that the political, jointly agreed objective of the CIS resembles that of NATO's, when it is explicitly proclaimed that the aim is 'seeking to build democratic, law-based states' (Preamble of the Agreement).

Originally, the idea behind the CIS was to exclude the southern republics rather than to integrate them into the new arrangement. One could argue that the CIS was originally an attempt to resurrect the old idea of Pan-Slavicism. At that time, nobody in Moscow cared about the destiny of the 'archaic', 'underdeveloped', 'Asiatic' republics of Central Asia and Caucasus. On the contrary, it seemed that almost everybody in the Kremlin was happy to get rid of this 'burden'. It was only when the CIS was secretly born on 8 December 1991 in the Bieloviezha forest between Minsk and Brest that the idea of possibly extending the CIS to include the southern republics came up. During the Bieloviezha meeting, the presidents of Russia (Yeltsin), Belarus (Sushkevich) and the Ukraine (Kravchuk) signed an agreement containing 14 articles (see Appendix 1). None of the heads of the other republics had been consulted. Therefore the announcement of the creation of the CIS came as a shock to the Central Asian and Caucasian republics which had already proclaimed their independence. Later, on 20–21 December of the same year, at a summit meeting held in Alma Ata (now Almaty), the CIS was extended by eight members, among them all the Central Asian republics plus Armenia, Azerbaijan and Georgia. Azerbaijan and Georgia ratified the agreement on 20 September and 24 October 1993, respectively. Apparently, the two weeks between 8 and 21–22 December 1992 were critical to Russia's perception and policies towards the southern republics. This change was the first and the most crucial step towards integration. However, the agreement was too general and too vague to be considered a treaty or a framework for interstate cooperation. It looked more like the 'death certificate' of the USSR[2] than the 'birth certificate' of a new federation or commonwealth in that the contracting states could not agree on the security issue, because the Ukraine, Moldova and Azerbaijan wanted to reserve the right to establish their own national military units. The events in Tajikistan showed the necessity of such security arrangements. The intervention of Russian, Kazakh and Uzbek troops in Tajikistan was negotiated between these states. Nevertheless, the most significant article may be Article 5 in which the parties 'recognise and respect each other's territorial integrity and the inviolability of existing frontiers within the framework of the Commonwealth'. Article 7 encourages the 'coordination of foreign-policy activities'. And finally Article 14 stipulates that the official residence of the coordinating bodies of the Commonwealth is the city of Minsk.

Despite the vague and ambiguous character of the CIS Agreement, it has been perceived and interpreted as a significant step towards the construction of a system equivalent to the EU. Zagorsky (1993), who is pro-rector of the Moscow State Institute of International Relations, strongly recommended the CIS to follow the EU model, by aiming to 'create and strengthen the common institutions of the Commonwealth, which will have an ever wider range of powers delegated to them in time. Then we will be keeping in step with the EC [EU]' (p. 46). He also felt that the success of the EU is essentially due to two factors: the 'existence of a formidable, general external threat [from Stalin] to the welfare and security of West European nations' (Zagorsky, 1993, pp. 42–3) and the existence of 'poles' able to balance each other in economic and political terms (French–German tandem). The problem is that these two essential factors are not present in the CIS arrangement; there are no signs at all of a 'formidable general external threat' against former Soviet republics, nor are there any poles to balance Russia. The CIS is therefore largely built vertically, that is between Russia on one side and the other states of the Commonwealth on the other. Consequently, some states such as the Ukraine, Turkmenistan and Moldova for a time searched to escape from this verticality preferring 'to build their relations with the former republics of the USSR on a bilateral basis' (Zagorsky, 1993, p. 48). However, such widespread bilateralism could be a serious threat to a cooperation network hoping to construct something like the EU. Kozyrev *et al.* (1994) are apparently in favour of a combination of bilateralism and multilateralism when they say that 'I see nothing terrible in the fact that Ukraine and, say, Turkmenistan give increasingly outspoken preference to bilateral relations. I believe we ought to try more than one alternative of approaching the formation of relations inside the CIS' (p. 4). The military staff considers the CIS agreement as 'part of a tightly integrated alliance with common defence interests'. Something not unlike the former Warsaw Pact. A draft of a military doctrine was published in the general staff journal *Voernaya mysl* (May 1992).[3] This interpretation at least partly reveals the existence of two different approaches in Moscow: a political approach (which at the time was uninterested in

Central Asia and Caucasus) and a military approach (favouring an ongoing commitment on the part of the Russian army in Central Asia and Caucasus).

The purely Atlantic–European approach, which was essentially formulated by Andrei Kozyrev, gave first priority – as mentioned above – to Western countries (far abroad) at the expense of the near abroad. This approach was later changed after pressure from two factors. The first was due to the hard criticism from the opponents of the Atlantic line. They criticized Kozyrev on the following points.

1. Russia's lack of a coordinated approach towards the near abroad, and, first of all, neglect of Russia's geostrategic and security interests in the ex-Soviet republics.
2. A failure to develop a well-defined policy for defending the rights of Russian nationals left in the near abroad.
3. A one-sided concentration on developing relations with the West and neglect of Russia's 'legitimate and historic' interests in Asia ... (Shahshenkov, 1993, p. 11).

The second factor was the explosion of political turbulence in Tajikistan during the autumn of 1992. The Tajik question leads us to the military dimension of the security system.

The military dimension of the CIS: the Tashkent Collective Security Treaty

Russia's reaction to the dramatic events in Tajikistan is interesting. In the beginning, Moscow hesitated to take part in the internal conflicts of Tajikistan. However, since approximately 300 000 Russians live in Tajikistan, Yeltsin and Kozyrev could not afford to ignore the turbulence. Therefore, Yeltsin ordered a military intervention which resulted in a consolidation of the old communist leaders and a marginalization of both the Democratic Party (whose leader, Dr Shadman Yousef, has since fled to Iran)[4] and the Islamic movement in Tajikistan. These two events as well as the proliferation of interstate military conflicts in Caucasus and the uprise of separatist movements in northern Caucasus (Chechnya's self-proclaimed independence) led to a revision of Russia's attitude towards the southern republics. As a result, a security treaty was signed in Tashkent on 15 May 1992 (see Appendix 2). This treaty was signed by the Russian Federation, Kazakhstan, Kyrgyzstan, Uzbekistan, Tajikistan and Armenia. The absence of both the Ukraine and Belarus should be noted. The absence of these two important Slavic actors as co-signers of the Tashkent Treaty was a clear sign of Moscow's changing policy regarding security issues. Slavicism was abandoned and Moscow reaffirmed its determination to establish a balance between Atlanticism, Slavicism and Eurasianism. Currently this line seems to be prevailing in Moscow. It is also noticeable that Turkmenistan did not adhere to the Tashkent arrangement. This is due to the fact that Turkmenistan is the only financially independent ex-Soviet republic and, consequently, it is able to stand up to Russia's pressure better than others. Rich Turkmenistan fears that adherence to the Tashkent security system will bring about regional troubles, namely in Tajikistan. Being a free-rider fits well with Turkmenistan's policy, but it must be accepted by its partners, Russia first of all. Otherwise, Turkmenistan risks jeopardizing its own security (that is, the southern borders with Iran). The price that Turkmenistan had paid to be an 'outsider' was to assure Russia of its loyalty to Moscow. It did this in two different ways. First, Turkmenistan signed an accord with Russia on dual citizenship (December 1993) whose aim was to protect Russian minorities, a great concern for Moscow. Secondly, a bilateral, military agreement was signed by Turkmenistan and Russia (also in December 1993) giving the Russian troops a special status in Turkmenistan, which shares a border of some 900 km with Iran. Therefore, in view of Turkmenistan's double engagements *vis-à-vis* Russia, there is no doubt that despite Turkmenistan's non-commitment to the Tashkent security arrangement, this country still remains and will remain in the foreseeable future in Russia's grip, most probably within bilateral arrangements. The negative impact of the dramatic events in Chechnya on the improvement of political and security issues within the CIS also became apparent during the CIS Summit meeting in Minsk (May 1995). On this occasion, four countries (the Ukraine, Moldova, Azerbaijan and Turkmenistan) refused to sign agreements on the closer political and military integration championed by Moscow.[5]

What does the Tashkent Treaty contain? It is composed of a preamble and 11 articles. The most important clauses of the treaty are summarized below.

1. The right of members to have their own armed forces (Preamble).
2. The obligation to refrain from the use of threat of force in interstate relations involving members of the treaty (Article 1).
3. The obligation not to enter into military alliances or participate in any groupings of states, nor in any actions directed against states participating in the treaty (Article 1).
4. If one participating state is subjected to aggression by any state or group of states, this shall be perceived as an act of aggression against all states participating in the treaty (Article 4).

5. The treaty does not affect any rights or commitments under other bilateral or multilateral treaties or agreements in force concluded by participating states with other states directed against third countries (Article 8).
6. The treaty is open to all interested states which share its aims and principles (Article 10).
7. The treaty is valid for five years with a subsequent renewal clause (Article 11).

By studying the Tashkent Treaty, one observes that (even though 'Russia has no probable adversaries' as Pavel Grachev the former Russian Minister of Defence stated on 2 November 1993) it is a defensive arrangement open to new members.

On 2 November 1993, 18 months after the proclamation of the Tashkent Treaty and almost 1 month after the dramatic events in Moscow (October 1993), the Russian defence doctrine was announced in Moscow by General Pavel Grachev. According to the new doctrine, Russia abandons the 'no first use' of nuclear weapons as well as the use of nuclear weapons against non-nuclear states unless they are allied with a nuclear power. For the first time since the Cold War, the role of the armed forces is also specified. On this point, it seems that the new doctrine is constructed not primarily to defend the CIS against possible external threats, but to provide protection for Russia and other CIS countries in case their internal security is threatened by nationalists, separatists or other illegal, armed groups. It is precisely in this perspective that Russia unilaterally reserves the right to station its military forces and equipment outside Russian territory. In other words, Russian troops can be stationed on all the territories of the Tashkent Treaty. As one military analyst, Major General (res.) Gennedy Dmitriev, puts it, 'the more Russian military bases have been deployed on their territory, the more quickly will the single economic and military union be restored'.[6]

It is clear that the military dimension is the most important issue of the new security system and that it constitutes a vehicle for Russian 'neo-expansionism'. At present, the main security objective of Russia is undoubtedly to assure its military presence everywhere in Central Asia and Caucasus. Russian officials argue that Russia's military presence in ex-USSR is not only in the interest of Russia and the other CIS countries, but also in the interest of the world as a whole. Russia has, in its view, been vested with a 'peace-keeping' or 'policing' mission in the regions which, by virtue of history, have been put under their 'responsibility and authority'. Thereby, it is argued, the 'Yugoslavian scenario' is avoided and peace and stability are assured. Thus, Russia's new mission 'should be recognised by the West and sanctioned by the UN' (Arbatov, 1994, p. 30). However, as many Russian observers have noticed

> If Russia does not see 'potential enemies' around itself, the foreign policy section of its military doctrine will hardly reassure the countries near and far abroad, which are accustomed to seeing it as a potential threat. Another notion of the military doctrine is the provision on the possibility of using army subunits 'for assisting the bodies of internal affairs'. Since the document does not stipulate in what cases such 'assistance' is permitted, the possibility of this norm being freely interpreted is great. In effect, it sanctions the army's use in domestic political conflicts.[7]

In the future, the world may not tolerate Russia's 'neo-imperialistic' policy. The Central Asian and Caucasian states may be suspicious and even apprehensive of Russia's intentions. However, for the time being, because of the lack of any credible alternative (at the global level as well as at the regional level), Russia has the opportunity to carry on, despite the criticism and the suspicion. Azerbaijan's President Heidar Aliev described the reality of the situation very well when he said 'Russia is our neighbour. It is one of the most powerful countries in the world. It's been connected with the fate of Azerbaijan for 200 years. So what should we do – have a state of hostilities with it?'[8]

The war in Chechnya, which began in December 1994, had a direct effect on the CIS security system, even though this war was considered an internal matter of the Russian Federation. The Chechnya effect was almost negative, meaning that instead of encouraging the CIS members to consolidate their security ties with each other for a better and stronger collective security system, the drama in Chechnya caused suspicion and fear among a great number of the members of the CIS *vis-à-vis* Russia. It was for that very reason that the CIS Summit in Almaty (10 February 1995) did not provide any substantial progress in security domains. On the contrary, the summit clearly demonstrated the limits of willingness and commitment of the CIS members concerning security issues. These limits were reached very quickly. Of the 13 documents submitted by the Council of Collective Security, only three were adopted. The discussion of ten other documents has been put off until the next summit. Moreover, the summit failed to settle two main questions: one on the joint protection of the CIS external borders and another one on the installation of a single air defence system. The Almaty Summit was also an occasion to observe the growing differences between two main tendencies among the members. On the one hand, there is the so-called 'tripartite union', consisting of Russia, Kazakhstan and Belarus, which called for deeper commitments concerning security and economic integration. These three countries were naturally in favour of a joint protection of the CIS external borders as well as the single air defence. On the other hand, is the refusal bloc, led essentially by the Ukraine and Azerbaijan. They refused to engage in the Yeltsin–Grachev security projects. The meagre results of the CIS summit in Almaty in the security matters demonstrated the ongoing uncertainty and tumult which still exist among the CIS members on a number of very important issues which touch the heart of the collective security, for instance whether they might have a system based on the joint protection of the CIS external borders or whether this issue should be left to the individual initiatives and responsibility of the states. The answer to this question will shape the future of the CIS as a collective security system. Some CIS leaders did express a pessimistic assessment. This was the case with President Leonid Kuchma of the Ukraine, who said that 'I am clearly and fully aware that a shapeless organization like the CIS has no future'.[9]

The economic and monetary dimensions of the CIS

There is no automatic relationship between the existence of economic affinities and the emergence of a security system. Nevertheless, the emergence of a security system is generally assumed to be more likely when a group of countries possess strong economic affinities with one another than if they do not. Thus, it is difficult to imagine that countries with divergent economic visions and principles (for example, Marxist versus Capitalist) would agree to form a security system. Economic affinity does not imply full economic concordance or economic interdependence between the participating parties of the security system, but that the basic economic philosophy be the same. In other words, it is not a question of a vector of countries with a similar degree of development, but with similar economic ideologies. Hence, a country with an advanced economy (Germany) may be in the same security system (for example, NATO) as a country with a less developed economy (Turkey) as long as their underlying economic ideology is similar (capitalist market economy) or at least not incompatible. However, two countries with divergent, underlying economic ideologies will not form a security system regardless of the convergence in their respective level of development. NATO and the Warsaw Pact are prime examples. All NATO members have adopted a market economy and all Warsaw Pact countries had adopted a centrally (state) planned, socialist economic philosophy. Not much is left to coincidence in the formation of security cooperations. In any case, one should not be surprised to find such a relation. After all, economic affinities are a reflection of political correspondence. And political vision to a large extent determines one's perception of the world as a whole and the geographical proximity in particular.

In the former Soviet Union, Central Asia, Caucasus and the Russian Federation constituted a single political and military entity and were integrated into the same socialist economic system. Later, after the disintegration of the USSR, they all decided to opt for market economy. Until now, however, this resembles more of a project than a reality. Everyone is aware of the fact that the economic situation in several of the former Soviet republics is distressing and chaotic. Because the bewilderment is so great and general, the economic and monetary dimension of the security system seems most exposed. Thus, in July 1992, the Russian Central Bank decided to distinguish between roubles circulating within Russia and those circulating in the other former Soviet republics, in an attempt to reduce hyperinflationary pressures by reasserting control over the money supply. Thereby, the rouble zone, *de facto*, ceased to exist,[10] despite the CIS Agreement of 14 February 1992, which stipulated that 'for the purpose of mutual settlements between the entrepreneurs, credit and other financial operations in the framework of the CIS, the parties shall use the common monetary unit (the ruble)'. Anyhow, the *de facto* and temporary extinction of the rouble zone meant that, for instance, 'the Kazakhstan ruble grew weaker with each passing day; in nine months of this year [1993] inflation reached about 800%, budget deficit nearly 700 billion [roubles]'.[11] Precisely for the purpose of improving this disastrous situation the heads of states of Russia, Kazakhstan and Uzbekistan met in the Kremlin (6–7 August 1993) in an attempt to reach an agreement. They agreed to develop the Common Economic Space and to set up a Common Monetary Zone. A month later (Moscow, 7 September), representatives of the governments and national banks of Armenia, Belarus, Kazakhstan, Russia, Tajikistan and Uzbekistan signed an agreement 'On practical measures to establish a new-style rouble zone'. The final decision was made in Moscow on 24 September by Yeltsin and his colleagues from Armenia, Azerbaijan, Belarus, Kazakhstan, Kyrgyzstan, Moldova, Tajikistan and Uzbekistan. It soon became apparent that the other participants would not accept the conditions that the Russians put forward. The Russians argued that new bank notes be given in the form of a state debt to avoid the possibility that the republics export inflation to Russia. Moreover, the non-cash money currently in circulation should also be registered as state credit at the interest rates prevailing in Russia. Finally, Russia insisted on the control over export–import operations of the gold and hard currency reserves of the republics.[12] The rouble zone, as a single currency market, collapsed once again in November 1993. The majority of the Central Asian and Caucasian republics introduced their own currency. Kyrgyzstan and Turkmenistan had already circulated their own currencies, the som and the manat.[13] This future monetary cooperation within the CIS looks rather uncertain. A definitive Russian withdrawal from such cooperations (perhaps due to internal difficulties) would eventually endanger the whole CIS network and seriously question the full establishment of the new security system. If the republics were to become disillusioned about Russia's economic engagement and goodwill, it would not be unthinkable for them to change priorities not only in economic terms but also in political terms. According to 'the law of the pendulum', they would then swing from their great northern neighbour to the south (that is, the Economic Cooperation Council in which Iran, Turkey and Pakistan play a pivotal role). Thus, it may not simply be the Russian rouble that is withdrawing from Central Asia and Caucasus, but Russia itself.[14] The former Soviet republics may, in this case, take their frustrations out on the large Russian minorities of the regions.[15] Early signs of such irritation are already appearing. Andrei Kozyrev, the former Russian Foreign Minister, got a taste of this during his visit (November 1993) to Kazakhstan and Uzbekistan (which are traditionally among the most pro-Russian republics). President Nazarbayev of Kazakhstan not only refused to receive Kozyrev, but compared Russia's concerns for the Russian minorities of the region to Hitler's concerns for the ethnic German minorities of Sudet (Czechoslovakia). Kerimov, the president of Uzbekistan, reacted almost in the same way when he vigorously protested against Russian demands to accord dual citizenship to ethnic Russians, while Asiatic residents of Moscow are treated with gross prejudice (for example, the introduction of a special tax on citizens of Central Asia and Caucasus residing in Moscow).

The real and so far dramatic dilemma that all the CIS states are presently facing is whether to create a rouble zone with all its costs, which are enormous, especially for the non-Slavic states or to leave the zone and create their own monetary units. In this respect, Apostolou (1993) described this dilemma very well. If the Central Asian and Caucasian states remain in the rouble zone, it would mean that 'Russia, with roughly 80% of rouble zone output, would dictate policy. Whatever the political implications of this, in the short term it will not slow inflation significantly' (Apostolou, 1993, p. 4). On the contrary,

> leaving the rouble zone could ... mean that the Central Asian republics are stranded and isolated economically. [Also], leaving the rouble zone would mean losing Russian markets (some 45% of total trade ...). Furthermore, Kazakhstan and Turkmenistan might have rapidly appreciating currencies because of hard currency inflows from oil and gas exports, which might well damage the competitiveness of other export

> sectors. The only way to prevent these non-oil and non-oil non-gas sectors from closing down would then be to embark on a programme of extensive subsidies. This might be ruinous for Turkmenistan (whose agricultural sector and the textile industry together accounted for 53% of Turkmenistan's NMP in 1991 (Apostolou, 1993, p. 4).

Another example is Belarus, whose National Bank's deputy chairman (Pavel Kalladur) said the bank is considering withdrawing its share of equity capital from CIS Inter-State Bank, which was set up 2 years ago for work in the rouble zone. It will not be capable of multilateral clearing and has not even begun to operate (20 March 1995).

Despite the fact that the economic integration is still far away in the CIS's horizon, some progress is noticeable here and there. For example, at the end of May 1995, Belarus and Russia signed an agreement to remove all customs barriers, effective immediately. However, such positive events are rare and almost sporadic.

This review of the economic and monetary dimension of the security system has demonstrated that it is the weakest dimension of the cooperation and its Achilles' heel. The lack of any alternative, both at present and in the foreseeable future, has once again left Central Asia and Caucasus with no other realistic choice but to cooperate with Russia. At the CIS Summit in Almaty (10 February 1995), only the Ukrainian proposal concerning the creation and maintenance of common scientific space was approved. This was almost all the CIS leaders could agree on concerning economic and monetary matters. Thus, the economic ties between three countries – Russia, Kazakhstan and Belarus – were consolidated and intensified in January 1995, with the establishment of a tripartite customs union. Later on this agreement was extended to Kyrgyzstan. In the same spirit, a treaty was signed between Russia, Belarus, Kazakhstan and Kyrgyzstan on 29 March 1996 which will lead to even deeper economic and social integration. The closer relations between these four countries will probably lead to the emergence of a hard core (*noyau dur*) within the CIS, which in the future will be capable of bringing other members a step further in the integration process.

REGIONAL ORGANIZATIONS

The term 'regional organization' refers first to those organizations whose membership is restricted on the basis of geographical contiguity and second to those whose structures embody institutionalized forums of periodic diplomatic interactions, based on formal agreements among independent governments. (Kim, 1992).

There are three different regional organizations of interest for the Central Asian and Caucasian states.

The ECO

Geographically, the ECO does not really represent a typical regional organization. Some member states belong to Central Asia, some others, like Turkey, are situated between Europe and Asia and the third group is Asiatic, though from different parts (Azerbaijan from Caucasus, Pakistan from the south-west and Iran between the Middle East, Caucasus and Central Asia!). The ECO is actually the result of an accumulated series of attempts during different time periods with the ultimate goal of creating a successful, regional economic cooperation. In this respect, the ECO is really a resurrection of the old Regional Cooperation and Development (RCD) which was created on 20–21 July 1964 as the regional economic dimension of the Central Treaty Organization (CENTO). The CENTO itself was established in 1959 as the successor to the Baghdad Pact (concluded in 1955). Thus, except for Iraq (which left after the revolution of 1958), the members of the Baghdad and CENTO pacts were the same (Iran, Turkey, Pakistan and Great Britain – with the USA as observer). The RCD consisted of Iran, Turkey and Pakistan. Economic and cultural ties between RCD members were improved after the signing of the Treaty of Izmir (signed on 12 March 1977). The treaty, however, remained largely inactive as a consequence of the Iranian revolution which started in 1977 and ended with the fall of the Shah and his regime in 1979. Only after the 8 year Iran–Iraq war could the RCD members reactivate the Izmir Treaty. Representatives from Iran, Turkey and Pakistan proceeded to review and amend the Izmir Treaty at two separate meetings (1 June 1990 and 28 November 1992) in Islamabad. Their deliberations resulted in the creation of a new organization, namely the ECO.

With the disintegration of the Soviet Union, the ECO faced new challenges. Suddenly, eight new independent states – five in Central Asia and three in Caucasus – emerged in the immediate neighbourhood of the ECO. To confirm their independence, the newly emerged states had a strong inclination to adhere to a number of international organizations. The ECO was the obvious and most natural choice, particularly because of its non-military character. Thus, by joining the ECO, the Central Asian republics were able to confirm their independence, not only *vis-à-vis* the Russian Federation, but also China, without provoking any of them. The adhesion of the five Central Asian republics (Uzbekistan, Turkmenistan, Tajikistan, Kyrgyzstan and, to a lesser extent, Kazakhstan) and Muslim Azerbaijan of Caucasus was largely perceived as a return to the family. By analogy, Christian Armenia and Georgia have not adhered. In sum, the ECO is currently composed of ten states (Turkey, Iran, Pakistan, Afghanistan, Azerbaijan, Kazakhstan, Kyrgyzstan, Uzbekistan, Turkmenistan and Tajikistan), representing 300 million people over an area of 7 million km^2. In recent years, the ECO has developed horizontally by setting up some new bodies. On 15 March 1995 at an ECO summit in Pakistan, the leaders of ten Muslim countries decided to set up four regional institutions: (1) a trade and development bank, (2) a shipping company, (3) an airline with capital of $300 million and (4) a reinsurance company also with capital of $300 million.[16]

The CSO

In contrast to the ECO, the CSO represents a typical regional organization which is composed exclusively of the Caspian Sea littoral states (Russia, Kazakhstan, Turkmenistan, Azerbaijan and Iran). The CSO was officially established at a meeting between representatives of the said states in the Iranian port of Nowshahr (29–30 April 1992). Cooperation within the CSO is essentially limited to technical matters relating to shipping, transport, tourism and the environment. According to the five-point resolution document issued at the end of the Nowshahr meeting, the member state agreed to harmonize the shipping rates. One of the main objectives of the new maritime cooperation network was to establish sound and reliable links between the ports of the Caspian Sea and the Iranian ports of the Persian Gulf. Specifically, it was decided that the ports of Anzali, Nowshahr, Bandar Abbas and Bandar Shah (now Bandar Imam Khomenei) in Iran, Baku in Azerbaijan, Akatu in Kazakhstan, Krasnovodsk in Turkmenistan and Astrakhan in Russia should be used as transit ports for the littoral states of the Caspian Sea. Kazakhstan has announced that Iran will be allowed to use the port of Akatu for exports to the Far East. In this connection, Kazakhstan has introduced plans to link the national Kazakh railway tracks to the port of Akatu. In exchange, Kazakhstan would like to use Iran's Caspian Sea ports as well as its roads and railways for the transportation of goods to and from the Persian Gulf, Europe and other parts of the world. Despite the predominantly technical character of the CSO, the implicit economic and political aspects of the cooperation cannot be ignored. If they succeed in implementing their plans, the commercial flow to and from Central Asia could be altered dramatically. At present, Central Asian imports and exports almost exclusively go through Russian territories. However, by linking Central Asia to the Persian Gulf, through the CSO, new opportunities will be opened up for Kazakhstan and Turkmenistan. The other Central Asian republics that are not members of the Caspian Sea littoral states (Uzbekistan, Kyrgyzstan and Tajikistan) are also bound to benefit from the CSO states and Iran's position as an economic partner and transit country for Central Asian goods will consequently increase. The new opportunities offered by the CSO explain why Russia has had so many reservations towards this new cooperation network.

The BSECZ

The BSECZ arose as a direct reaction, on the part of the Turks, to the Iranian initiative in April 1992 to create the CSO.

It was founded in Istanbul on 24 June 1992 on the basis of the 'Istanbul Declaration' signed by the heads of state and governments of 11 countries from the Black Sea region. The proclaimed aim of the organization is to assure the free movement of goods, services and capital between member states as well as to implement large-scale economic cooperation. The BSECZ secretariat has (against the wishes of Greece and Bulgaria) been situated in Istanbul. For the time being, Turkey has taken on all the charges of the secretariat and the data centre. At the Varna meeting (in 1993) it was decided to create the Black Sea Trade and Development Bank (BSTDB) with a subscribed capital of $715 million. Greece, Turkey and Russia are each to contribute 165.5 per cent, Bulgaria and the Ukraine 13.5 per cent each and the remaining members 2 per cent each.

The private sector Black Sea Economic Council is another Turkish-inspired initiative within the BSECZ framework. It has been assigned to identify possible joint projects, particularly in the areas of maritime, land and air transportation, infrastructure, energy and telecommunications.

The BSECZ represents almost 400 million people. Cooperation with the EU has also been initiated. On 6 June 1994, the European Commission and the BSECZ agreed to set up a Black Sea regional energy centre to be located in Bulgaria.

After reviewing the different regional cooperation networks, it is time to ask ourselves about the future of these networks. In this connection, if we take into account the similar experiences, we have to admit that the prior experiences of those regional cooperations which were deprived of having an appropriate axis are not particularly encouraging. These are so-called 'autonomous', regional cooperations, although those established among the Third World countries in the absence of any industrial power among the most advanced countries were either complete failures or merely remained on paper and at the formal stage.[17] The main reason for failure 'has been often identified in the similarity of economic structures and national endowments of member countries, from which derives the limited potential for specialization and traditional (inter-industry) trade along comparative advantages' (Grilli, 1993, p. 5). These regional arrangements were also more attempts from some Third World countries to increase their collective bargaining in dealing with industrial countries than efforts to create workable and durable cooperation structures. Concerning the Central Asian countries, they had tried – at least on five occasions – to construct an 'autonomous', regional cooperation network. They failed, partly because of the similarities between their exports of cotton, metals and minerals, which make them competitors rather than complementary partners, but also because they do not trade enough with each other to form a viable, free trade bloc (Apostolou, 1993, p. 4). Even the best cases of well-functioning regional cooperation among the Third World countries do not lead to integration. One reason may be that the 'economies are less complex, which makes spill-over from one technical, economic task to another less likely to occur' (Ray, 1995, p. 393).

CONCLUSION

In this study, I first made a clear distinction between two key concepts: regional cooperation and integration. Then I analysed the commitments of the new, independent Central Asian and Caucasian states to regional cooperation and integration. In this connection, it has been demonstrated that these states are vehemently interested in pursuing two track policies. Immediately after obtaining independence, they committed themselves to regional cooperation networks like the ECO. Later on, they joined all the other regional arrangements (the Caspian Sea and Black Sea organizations). By doing this, they intended to demonstrate solemnly and firmly their newly obtained autonomy *vis-à-vis* Moscow. At the same time, they were very aware of the limited capacities for regional networks with their neighbours, particularly Turkey and Iran. These networks could in any case be considered credible alternatives to their cooperation with the Russian Federation, on which they remain dependent in more than one way. Therefore, the Central Asian and Caucasian republics simultaneously tied their fate with Russia and, thus, with other Slavic states within the CIS. We also observed that the commitment of these states to cooperation with Russia has been a matter of individual choice. Not all countries have the same needs nor the same goals. In this respect, we registered some significant variations with regard to the attitude of each newly independent republic. Viewed by Moscow, the CIS constitutes a compact arrangement, a kind of 'menu' which embraces the political, economic and security components. This view was not always shared by the Central Asian and Caucasian republics. They preferred to open the CIS package to choosing 'à la carte'. In this way, the preference of one was to strengthen the security dimension (Tajikistan), while another one focused on economic cooperation (Belarus) and the third one liked to have all dimensions together (Kazakhstan). This situation reminds us in a way of the difference between the 'Euro enthusiasts' versus 'Euro sceptics' within the EU. Thus, while 'Euro realists' dominated in the EU, the CIS did not succeed in prevailing in a clear way. Therefore, the present confusion characterizes the whole destiny of CIS.

What can be said about the future of these regions? How will the regional cooperation and integration processes look in – let us say – the year 2000? Despite some confusion and significant uncertainty which at the moment dominate the regional relations, it seems that the regional cooperation will continue and even they will see – in the future – some improvement. Nevertheless, this kind of cooperation will be predominantly technical and commercial, without any substantial political or military significance. Following this path, the Central Asian and Caucasian republics will develop their cooperation with Turkey, Iran, Pakistan, India, the Arab countries and Israel. On the contrary, since the cooperation within the CIS is related precisely to the political and military questions, its evolution seems more problematic and making predictions in this matter is more hazardous. Yet, some factors are permanent 'à la longue durée' and can help us make some plausible predictions. For instance, the character of Russia is among these independent variables. Russia is a territorial power; Russia is and presumably will remain to be for a long time a great power. Russia as a territorial great power can never be indifferent to the future of its near abroad like Central Asia and Caucasus. By virtue of geography, history and politics, these regions are situated within the Russian territorial zone d'influence. Therefore, Russia's interest in these areas stands inalterable and this is regardless of who is in power in Moscow and what political colour they have. Faced with this fact, the Central Asian and Caucasian republics have little room to manoeuvre. It will take them quite a long time before they become totally independent of Russia. It is a long way to go from formal independence to a real and effective one. But there is no evidence at the moment that complete independence for these countries from Russia figures among the first priorities that the Central Asian and Caucasus states have fixed for themselves.

NOTES

1. In 1992, Russia accounted for 68 per cent of the total imports of Kazakhstan, 58 per cent of Uzbekistan, 51 per cent of Kyrgyzstan and 48 per cent each of Tajikistan and Turkmenistan. Russia imported 61 per cent of Uzbekistan's exports, 54 per cent of Turkmenistan's exports, 53 per cent of Kazakhstan's exports, 51 per cent of Tajikistan's exports, and 39 per cent of Kyrgyzstan's exports, Goskomstat (The State Committee of Statistics), Russian Federation.
2. The preamble of the CIS Agreement states that, 'We ... state that the USSR as a subject of international law and a geopolitical reality, is ceasing to exist'.
3. J. Lough, 'The Place of the Near Abroad in Russian Foreign Policy', *RFE/RL Research Report*, vol. 11, no. 2 (12 March 1993).
4. *Tehran Times*, 30 September 1993.
5. *Financial Times*, 27–28 May 1995.
6. See A. Zahlin's (1993) article on 'Military Policy and a War on Politicians', *Moscow News*, 26 November 1993.
7. Ibid.
8. *Financial Times*, 14 March 1994.
9. *Herald Tribune*, 11–12 February 1995.
10. *The Economist*, 20 November 1993.
11. *Moscow News*, 5 November 1993.
12. Ibid., and *Le Monde*, 21–22 November 1993.
13. Kazakhstan has introduced the tenge, Armenia the dram and Moldova the lei.
14. *Moscow News*, op. cit.
15. *The Economist*, 20 November 1993.
16. *Financial Times*, 16 March 1995.
17. In 1992, at least 32 major regional trading organizations existed around the world, with ten each in Africa and America, five in Asia or the Pacific, four in the Middle East and three in Europe. See E.H. Fry, 'Regional Economic Integration: North America', International Political Science Association, Berlin, 21–25 August 1994; and J.L. Brand, 'The New World Order of Regional Trading Blocs', *The American University Journal of International Law and Policy*, no. 8 (Autumn 1992) p. 157.

REFERENCES

A.A. Apostolou, 'The Problems of Creating Economies in Central Asia'. Paper presented at the Symposium on The Gulf and the Central Asian Republics (University of Exeter, Centre for Arab Gulf Studies, 12–14 July 1993), p. 4.

A.G. Arbatov *et al.*, 'Russian Interests in the CIS', *International Affairs*, no. 11 (1994), pp. 11–30.

K.W. Deutsch, Burell, S.A., Kann, A. *et al.*, *Political Community and the North Atlantic Area* (Princeton: Princeton University Press, 1957).

D. Dinan, *Ever Closer Union? An Introduction to the European Community* (London: Macmillan, 1994).

Financial Times, 16 March 1995, p. 4.

E.H. Fry, 'Regional Economic Integration: North America', International Political Science Association (Berlin, 21–25 August 1994).
E. Grilli, 'Regionalism and Multilateralism: Conflict or Coexistence?' paper presented at European Association of Development Institutes (Berlin, 15–17 September 1993), pp. 1–21.
E. Haas, *The Uniting of Europe: Political, Social and Economical Forces* (London: Stevens, 1958), p. 16.
Herald Tribune, 11–12 February 1995.
B. Hettne, 'The New Regionalism: Implications for Development and Peace', *The New Regionalism* (Hettne, B. and András, I.) (Japan: The United Nations University, 1994), pp. 1–49.
M. Holland, *European Community Integration* (London: Pinter, 1993).
S. Huntington, 'The Clash of Civilizations', *Foreign Affairs* (Summer 1993), pp. 22–49.
M. Kelstrup, 'Europe Integration and Political Theory', in M. Kelstrup (ed.), *European Integration and Denmark's Participation* (Copenhagen: Political Studies Press, 1992), pp. 31–44.
S.S. Kim, 'Regional Associations: Political', in M. Hawbesworth and M. Kogan (eds), *Encyclopedia of Government and Politics* (London: Routledge, 1992), pp. 982–1001.
A. Kozyrev, *et al.*, 'Russian interests in the CIS', *International Affairs*, no. 11 (Moscow: 1994), pp. 11–30.
Le Monde 21–22 November 1993, p. 18 (Jan Kreuze).
J. Lough, 'The Place of the Near Abroad in Russian Foreign Policy', *RFE/RL Research Report*, vol. 11, no. 2 (12 March 1993), pp. 21–9.
D. Miltany, *A Working Peace System* (London: Royal Institute of International Affairs, 1943).
A. Moravcsik, 'Preferences and Power in the European Community: a Liberal Intergovernmentalist Approach', *Journal of Common Market Studies*, vol. 31, no. 4 (December 1993), pp. 473–524.
N. Petrakov and Shatalov, G. *Moscow News*, no. 51 (23–29 December 1994), p. 9.
J.L. Ray, *Global Politics* (Boston: Houghton Mifflin, 1995).
M. Shahshenkov, 'Russian in Central Asia', paper presented at the Symposium on the Gulf and the Central Asian Republics (University of Exeter, Centre for Arab Gulf Studies, 12–14 July 1993), p. 11.
The Economist, 20 November 1993.
S.A. Vasiliev, 'Russia' in J. Williamson (ed.), *Economic Consequences of Soviet Disintegration* (Washington, DC: Institute for International Economics, 1993), pp. 323–333.
A. Zagorsky, 'The Commonwealth: One Year On', *International Affairs*, no. 2 (Moscow, 1993), pp. 45–62.
A.Z. Zahlin, 'Military Policy and a War of Politicians', *Moscow News* (26 November 1993), p. 3.

10 Transition in Central Asia: Role of the EBRD

M. Babaev*

In this chapter I shall discuss the role of the European Bank for Reconstruction and Development (EBRD) in the dramatic process of transition of Central Asian countries, unfolding in front of our eyes.

Structurally, I would like to start with a brief description of the purpose of the EBRD ('the Bank') by analysing some aspects of economic and political transition in general and, specifically, with regard to the Central Asian region. Then, the Bank's operational strategies and pipeline of projects in Central Asian countries will be discussed. Finally, I will touch upon the evolution of the Bank itself since its establishment in 1991 and the effects on the role the Bank plays (and will play in the future) in the region of Central Asia.

The purpose of the Bank is defined in Article 1 of the Agreement Establishing the Bank as follows.

> In contributing to economic progress and reconstruction, the purpose of the Bank shall be to foster the transition towards open market oriented economies and to promote private and entrepreneurial initiative in the Central and Eastern European countries committed to and applying the principles of multiparty democracy, pluralism and market economics.[1]

The twofold purpose of the Bank 'to foster transition towards market-oriented economies' and 'promote private entrepreneurial initiative' is to be carried out in the Central and Eastern European ('CEE') countries committed to and applying the principles of multiparty democracy, pluralism and market economics.

The provisions of Article 1 in conjunction with paragraphs 1 and 2 of Article 8[2] of the Agreement Establishing the Bank establish the legal basis for the Bank to determine whether a recipient country is eligible from the economic (transition towards market economy) or political (transition towards multiparty democracy and pluralism) perspective.

Let us now deal with questions relating to economic transition in the countries of operations. How to assess the progress made by a country

* The views expressed are those of the author, and do not reflect the official position of the EBRD.

towards a market economy? Where do the countries of Central Asia stand in this process?

This year saw the publication of the *Transition Report* which developed indicators for a number of dimensions of the transition process.[3] It showed that significant advances had been achieved in most of the Bank's countries of operations. However, it also brought out strongly the diversity among the countries of operations in their stages in transition.

The transition indicators[4] capture the stage which the economy of a recipient country[5] has reached in its move to a market economy. According to the report, the Central Asian countries are in the early (Tajikistan, Turkmenistan) or middle (Uzbekistan, Kazakhstan and Kyrgyzstan) stages of transition. Using the flexibility of the financial instruments available to it, the Bank has learned over the years to tailor its activities to the stages of transition. Both experience and analysis have shown that the opportunities for Bank financing vary over the transition process.

At the early stages of transition the demand for EBRD financing is rather modest. The private sector is small and the primary emphasis is on critical infrastructure projects and the development of financial institutions and natural resources. To the extent possible, the Bank seeks to work with local financial intermediaries to provide financing for small and medium sized enterprises (SMEs).

As the reform process progresses and the country moves from the early into the intermediate stages of transition, the private sector begins to emerge and, therefore, a sustainable demand for private sector financing develops. In addition to the larger private sector, a larger economy, creates favourable conditions which are more likely to satisfy 'sound banking principles'.[6]

This analysis clearly indicates that the Central Asian countries (together with most countries of operations) are moving into and through the medium phase of transition over the coming years. This movement will be associated with an accelerating expansion of the demand for Bank services.

Before continuing, I would like to highlight an important point discussed in certain detail in the Transition Report 1994.[7] It draws a clear distinctive line between the concepts of 'transition' and 'development'. The latter concept is a summary term which generally refers to a command over resources, education and health. There are many possible indicators along these major dimensions: literacy, infant mortality rates, life expectancy and wealth, income and consumption. Clearly, if a country embarks on transition it believes that it will advance development. However, it is also clear that transition is associated with sacrifices to be made on the way. This distinction is especially relevant in the Central Asian context. One can hear an extensive debate along the same lines (not necessarily using the same terminology), say, in Turkmenistan. Is it worthwhile embarking on transition by accepting certain (sometimes, rather painful) sacrifices to reach a higher level of development? Is a market economy (being a destination point on the way of transition) worth the pain and difficulties, associated with the transition process? The report gives a positive answer to this important question. It argues that 'on balance, a market-based economy has overwhelming advantages over central planning'.

The unique character of the transition in the countries of the Central and Eastern Europe, in general and the Central Asian region, in particular, is that the countries are simultaneously confronted with two sets of challenges: economic and political. The issues relating the slower pace of political transition, the development of political institutions and democracy building in Central Asia are quite often are the subject of debate in the international community at large. Where does the EBRD stand with regard to the assessment of progress towards multiparty democracy, the rule of law and respect for human rights? How does one measure the progress in the political sphere? What are the mechanisms to implement the respective provisions of the Agreement Establishing the Bank?

The political conditionality under the Agreement Establishing the Bank stems from the same provisions as economic conditionality, that is the combination of Articles 1 and 8 (paragraphs 1 and 2). These provisions establish the legal basis for political conditionality, while leaving it for the governing bodies of the Bank (Board of Directors and the Board of Governors) to determine the precise contents and means of implementation. Such guidance with regard to the interpretation and implementation of the political aspects of the Bank's mandate was given in a policy document, adopted by the Board of Directors in 1991.[8]

The document emphasises the critical link between the economic and political aspects of the Agreement. It also underlines that that the appropriate way to assess the progress in countries of operations towards multiparty democracy, pluralism and market economics is vital to the Bank's successful fulfilment of its mandate. The paper identifies a number of reference points (some comparisons can be drawn with the transition indicators discussed above) against which to assess progress in the political reform process.[9] In analysing the political aspects of the mandate of the Bank I would like to underline that the respective provisions of the Agreement should be narrowly construed. The interpretation of these provisions should be carried out in such a way, which reflects the will of the Founders of the Bank. In this regard, it is not accidental that Article 1 does not mention human rights *per se*, but refers to multiparty democracy and pluralism. Moreover, commitment to multiparty democracy is placed in the text of the Agreement next to the commitment to the market economics. In other words, the Bank is concerned with political reform to the extent that favourable conditions for transition to a market economy are created.

Such a strict reading of the Agreement does not exclude the issues of the rule of law and human rights. The Preamble of the Agreement contains a specific reference to respect for human rights and the rule of law. It says that the contracting parties are 'committed to the fundamental principles of multiparty democracy, the rule of law, respect for human rights and market economics'. Although the Preamble of the Agreement is an integral part of the Agreement, the drafting technique avoiding a reference to 'human rights' in the main text of the Agreement, namely in Article 1, confirms the understanding that only those political factors, which are related to the transition towards market economics, are considered by the Founders of the Bank to be of relevance for the purposes of the Bank. The Bank's policy paper also stresses that 'only those [human] rights which, in accordance with international standards, are essential elements of multiparty democracy, pluralism and market economics should be considered when evaluating a country's progress. Such a reading of the Agreement focuses primarily on civil and political rights.'[10]

Working in close cooperation with other international organisations (and, in particular, with the Organisation for Security and Co-operation in Europe (OSCE), of which all Central Asian countries are members), the Bank closely monitors political developments in these countries. According to the Agreement, the Board of Directors, at least annually, reviews the Bank's operations and lending strategy in each recipient country to ensure that the purpose and functions of the Bank are fully served. It is within the framework of these discussions that the directors express concerns over the slow pace of political reform, lack of progress towards multiparty democracy and pluralism and human rights conditions, which are fundamental elements of multiparty democracy. The Bank's management ensures that the Board's reaction is conveyed to the countries concerned.

As I have outlined the general parameters for the assessment of economic and political transition from the Bank's point of view, let me now turn briefly to the Bank's operational strategies and pipeline of projects in Central Asia. Strategy papers identify the Bank's priorities in an individual country.

An analysis reflects a pattern for the Bank's priorities in the countries of the region, which is similar across the countries. This is the development of the financial and banking sectors and support extended via the local financial intermediaries to SMEs. For the land-locked countries of Central Asia a high priority is attached to the development of a critical infrastructure, roads and telecommunications. In Central Asian circumstances, natural resources (oil, gas, gold and so on) are a 'natural' priority for Bank activities. The Bank's financing in this area is primarily through joint ventures, where the local companies are supported by a strategic foreign partner. Agribusiness throughout the region, with cotton processing (in Uzbekistan and Turkmenistan), as well as the development of tourism in the Uzbek and Kyrgyz case, are also identified among the Bank's main priorities.

By the end of 1996, the total amount of Bank-approved projects for Central Asian countries is approximately US$680 million. Most financing to date has been channelled into Uzbek projects US$270 million, followed by Kazakhstan US$220 million, Kyrgyzstan US$110 million and Turkmenistan US$70 million. The only country of the region, where the Bank has not until very recently developed investment projects is Tajikistan. In fact, it was only in June 1995 that the operational strategy for this country was approved by the Bank's Board of Directors. In 1994 the Bank activities in Tajikistan were limited a technical cooperation projects. A first investment project for Tajikistan of US$9 million was approved in December 1996.

These figures look impressive. The engagement of the Bank in Central Asia is a *fait accompli*. However, I wanted to reflect on the very first days of the Bank's entrance into Central Asia and on the evolution of the Bank itself with regard to understanding the needs of the region and the ways to address them. I recollect the first mission of the EBRD to Central Asia in February 1992, when we arrived to negotiate membership of these countries in the Bank. Starting from scratch, the newly independent states were then at the very beginning of the process of nation building. New, post-Soviet constitutions, were still to be adopted, first post-Soviet parliaments still to be elected and new business opportunities yet to be identified. Located at the crossroads between Europe and Asia, the region did not operate as a functional political whole. Being subject historically to conquest from outside it had not seen much consolidation from within. After many decades of the Soviet era, Central Asians were rediscovering their national identity and place in the wider world. Fifty five million people of mostly Turkic origin, inhabiting a huge landmass in the 'middle of the world', were displaying the wide spectrum of an ethnic mix. In some areas this mix was of a dangerously explosive nature.

The states of Central Asia were advocating a gradual path of cautious pragmatism in their transition to democracy. They argued that 'genuine democracy' needs a substantial economic basis with a developed class of private owners. In the circumstances arising from more than seven decades of command economies, they argued for a cautious approach towards the decentralisation of political power. Even the most democratically advanced country of the region, Kyrgyzstan, was clearly supportive of a strengthened role of the state in order to maintain control over the direction of the political and economic transformation. The Russian example, with a deepening constitutional crisis and deteriorating living conditions, which many Central Asians attributed to an uncontrolled democratic process, was a frightening prospect for most of the Central Asian states.

The concepts of economic and political transition, reflected in the Bank documents, were new and, as such, treated with caution. It was evident that a gradual approach towards economic and political reform would be likely. Moreover, from the Central Asian perspective, it was not totally clear, whether an economy, based on market principles, was preferable as a vehicle to achieve economic prosperity. The same doubts, even more acute, were related to the applicability of the rather unfamiliar 'Western' concepts of multiparty democracy, rule of law and respect for human rights.

Faced with this tremendous challenge in the middle of Asia was the European Bank. Having limited staff resources and confronted with an enormous need for critical infrastructure projects (roads, pipelines, ports, airlines, telecommunications and railroads) and encountering an undeveloped private sector and uncertain and unpredictable legal and regulatory framework, the Bank accepted the challenge by embracing the countries of the region. In 1992 and 1993 the Bank developed operational strategies for the countries of the region.

The Bank has also started to invest in the region. The first EBRD private sector loan to a Central Asian country was made in 1993. A loan of US$105 million to the Zarafshan–Newmont Joint Venture to finance a heap leaching facility near the Muruntau mine in Uzbekistan, was approved in 1993. This was not only the first loan extended by the Bank to a Central Asian country, but it also represented the first mining project finance for the Bank, the first syndicated financing for the former Soviet Union and the first limited recourse private sector loan for Uzbekistan in any of the capital markets. The EBRD, being a lender of the record for the full amount of the loan, attracted the participation of 13 commercial banks, such as Barclays Bank, Chase Manhattan Bank, Chemical Bank, Credit Lyonnais, Credit Suisse, UBS and other banks. During 1993 the Bank completed studies to outline the basis for its activities in the transport and communications sector in five Central Asian republics (and the three Transcaucasian republics).

In a regional context, as part of the concept to develop the so-called Euro-Asian corridor, the Bank initiated the Euro-Asian Trade Facilitation Project in order to identify high priority projects directed at eliminating major current bottlenecks, the rehabilitation and modernization equipment and opportunities for privatization and commercialization. Another important regional project is worthwhile mentioning here. It was a regional bank training centre in Tashkent, in short referred to as the Banking School. The

Banking School, established by the Bank in conjunction with the EU and the Banks Association of Turkey, is providing practical training in banking operations for the banking community of three countries of the region – Kyrgyzstan, Tajikistan and Uzbekistan. A number of other investment and technical cooperation projects were launched.

The critical upsurge in the activities of the Bank in Central Asia is linked to the evolution of the organizational structure of the Bank itself. A reorganization, carried out by the end of 1993, has achieved the goal of a wider geographic distribution and diversification of the Bank's portfolio. The country focus was significantly sharpened. Two country teams, working specifically on the countries of Central Asia within the Bank,[11] as well as sector teams, have significantly increased the output of investment projects.

In addition, the increase of the pace of lending operations is also directly related to the evolution of the region itself. Today's picture of the region drastically differs from the 1992 scene, which I attempted to describe earlier. The progress achieved is momentous. The significance of the changes increases even more when we consider the point of departure of the countries of Central Asia. Most of the countries have embarked on market reforms – privatization is picking up in Uzbekistan, Kyrgyzstan and in Kazakhstan. The transition indicators (price and trade liberalization, growth of the private sector and so on) of Uzbekistan, Kyrgyzstan and Kazakhstan have reached a level, which allows us to put them into the intermediate category in the transition process. Lagging behind in the process are Turkmenistan and Tajikistan. In general terms, the Central Asians have come to terms with understanding the necessity to accelerate market reforms. In comparison with 1992, much ground has been covered. The private sector is emerging and taking ground. The state of confusion, prevailing at the dissolution of the USSR, has been clearly replaced by distinct objectives leading to economic market-oriented reforms. For me the most important factor in this process is the acceptance by these countries of the concept of a market as a viable, however painful, path to future economic prosperity.

The pace of political transformation of Central Asia is slower. Relatively advanced in Kyrgyzstan, it is still slow in Kazakhstan and Uzbekistan and even slower in Turkmenistan. Tajikistan, emerging from the aftermath of the civil war and economic and political disruption, is making some progress towards national reconciliation and the building of new institutions. Significantly, there is a growing realization within the countries of the region of the link between the rapid economic growth and proper functioning democratic institutions.

The development of democracy, pluralistic civil societies, with an established rule of law and respect for human rights is a long and a complex process. It is very difficult to build a democratic society within the very short period of 5 years since the Central Asian countries became independent. What is more important is to move in the right direction, to make progress towards democracy, pluralism and the market economy.

With the local presence increasing,[12] a competent and highly dedicated staff, a growing pipeline of projects and the countries of the region entering the intermediate stages of the transition process, the European Bank stands ready to meet the ever increasing challenge coming from Central Asia.

NOTES

1. The Agreement Establishing the European Bank for Reconstruction and Development, 29 May 1990. The Agreement entered into force on 28 March 1991.
2. Paragraphs 1 and 2 of Article 8 state the following:

   1. The resources and facilities of the Bank shall be used exclusively to implement the purpose and carry out the functions set forth, respectively, in Article 1 and 2 of this Agreement.
   2. The Bank may conduct its operations in countries from Central and Eastern Europe which are steadily proceeding in the transition towards market oriented economies and the promotion of private and entrepreneurial initiative, and which apply, by concrete steps and otherwise, the principles set forth in Article 1.

3. Transition Report 1996: Infrastructure and Savings. European Bank for Reconstruction and Development, London, 1996.
4. The *Transition Report* uses such indicators as the size of the private sector, large-scale privatization, small-scale privatization, enterprise restructuring, price liberalization, trade and foreign exchange system, competition policy, banking reform and interest rate liberalization, securities markets and non-bank financial institutions, extensiveness and effectiveness of legal rules on investment.
5. The Bank has 58 member countries, plus the EU and the European Investment Bank (EIB), while 26 of them are recipient countries, officially referred to as 'countries of operations' (including Kazakhstan, Uzbekistan, Kyrgyzstan, Tajikistan and Turkmenistan).
6. Article 13(i) of the Agreement Establishing the Bank establishes that 'the Bank shall apply sound banking principles to all its operations'.
7. Transition Report 1994. The European Bank for Reconstruction and Development. London, 1994.
8. Procedures to Implement the Political Aspects of the Mandate of the European Bank for Reconstruction and Development – Doc. BDS91-16 (Final).
9. They include free elections, a representative government in which the executive is accountable to the elected legislature or the electorate, the duty of the government and the public authorities to act in accordance with the constitution and law and the availability of redress against administrative decisions, separation

between the state and political parties, independence of the judiciary, equal protection under the law, including minorities, fair criminal procedures, freedom of speech, including the media, of association and of peaceful assembly, freedom of conscience and religion, freedom of movement, the right to private property and the right to form trade unions and strike.

10. See Procedures to Implement the Political Aspects of the Mandate of the European Bank for Reconstruction and Development.
11. Two country teams respectively comprise (1) Kazakhstan and Uzbekistan and (2) Kyrgyzstan, Turkmenistan and Tajikistan. This team also includes Azerbaijan.
12. To date the Bank has functioning resident offices in Tashkent, Almaty and Bishkek.

11 The Oil and Gas of the Caspian Sea: Regional Cooperation and Competition

M. Mozaffari

INTRODUCTION

The Caspian Sea, the world's largest inland body of water, is generally known for its caviar. To the delight of consumers of the exclusive caviar, the caviar production will be able to continue as long as the sturgeon is not threatened by pollution. However, the situation remains alarming because the supply of sturgeon in the Caspian Sea has dropped from 200 million tons in 1990 to no more than 60 million tons today. By the year 2000, the Caspian Sea will not only be known merely for its caviar but also for its gigantic oil and gas deposits. The latest tests performed by Western experts after the collapse of the Soviet Union show that the Caspian Sea, with more than 68 billion barrels (= 9092 billion tons) of oil, has the world's third largest oil deposits, only surpassed by the Persian Gulf and Siberia. Everything indicates that the deposits are even larger than the preliminary evaluation has shown. According to the technical jargon, the oil deposits in this region belong to category A + B + C1, almost equivalent of 'proven-plus-probable'. The amount of gas deposits is just as impressive as the amount of oil deposits. Kazakhstan alone has natural gas deposits of approximately 1.5 trillion m^3. In addition, both Turkmenistan and Uzbekistan possess large gas deposits, however not as large as those in Kazakhstan. A true eldorado! (see Table 11.1).

So this means that in the next century, the Caspian region will be one of the most strategic and vital areas for the industrialized world. The possibility of new, violent conflicts and intensified power struggles on all levels cannot be excluded. The power struggles and the conflicts have already started, after the collapse of the Soviet Union in 1991. The drama in Chechnya is probably the most obvious, but far from the first and maybe not the last conflict. The struggle takes place not only on a regional level but also between Russia on one side and the USA on the other. For example, in June 1993 the Russian infantry (Divisions 104 and 107) headed for Baku, when Azerbaijan's then anti-Russian Government wanted to sign a 30-year contract with a US consortium. A couple of days later, Azeri's Nationalist Government fell and President Elchibey had to flee Baku. That same year, Russia prevented Baku's Government from signing another contract with a US company for the construction of oil pipelines for oil transport through northern Nagorno–Karabak to Georgia and on to the Mediterranean via Turkey. In 1994, Russia interfered again – this time to stop oil transport through Iran. Russia supported Armenia's invasion of the Fizuli region near the Iranian border. After these events the Americans, who are trying to diversify their oil supply sources, started to feel that their right to trade with any independent state – in this case Azerbaijan – was threatened.

TABLE 11.1 *Oil and gas deposits of the Caspian region*

	1993		*1994*	
	Million tons	*Billion barrels*	*Million tons*	*Billion barrels*
Azerbaijan	470	3.50	1 000	7.50
Kazakhstan	2 137	16.00	6 612	49.60
Turkmenistan	210	1.60	698	5.24
Uzbekistan	117	0.90	587	4.40
Russia	195	1.50	195	1.50

SOURCE *The Middle East* (October 1994).

However, the struggle for control of the Caspian eldorado started years ago – right after the Soviet Union's collapse in 1991. The struggle has three dimensions: (1) who owns the oil, (2) participation in production and (3) oil transportation problems.

WHO OWNS THE OIL RESERVES?

The issue of ownership has come up because the five countries bordering on the Caspian Sea (Russia, Azerbaijan, Iran, Turkmenistan and Kazakhstan) still have not agreed on how to establish their respective maritime zones. Unofficially, each country's national maritime zone is 12 km, but beyond this zone nothing has been settled. There was no problem under Soviet rule because the sea was common property except for the Iranian part whose border was established in the nineteenth century. Russia has let the three former Soviet republics by the Caspian Sea know that it wishes to continue the earlier *de facto* joint property rights. Furthermore, Russia argues that the Caspian Sea is a lake and a closed water space and, as such, it cannot be subjected to the international law of sea concerning its partition. The Iranian Government supports – at least implicitly – Russia's position. Consequently, the Caspian Sea has to be regarded as the common property of the littoral states. Of course Russia's thesis has been met with strong protests from Azerbaijan, Turkmenistan and Kazakhstan. They have flatly rejected the Russian thesis. The three republics and Uzbekistan know very well what is behind the Russian demand: Russia wants supremacy over the Caspian resources. Their rejection is also founded in consideration of Western investors. Western oil companies will not invest their capital in a network which is controlled completely by Russia. The oil and gas reserves are just about the only effective symbol of the new republics' independence, a unique tool to execute their development projects and also their only means to possibly distance themselves from Russia. Determined to solve the legal dispute over the partition of the Caspian Sea, Russia proposed, in October 1996, to increase the national offshore border, already increased from 12 to 20 miles, to 40 miles. The proposal, if adopted, could cost Azerbaijan billions of dollars, as Chirang, one of Azeri's richest oil field, is situated beyond the 40 mile limit. Nonetheless, the Russian proposal is backed by Iran and has found favour in both Kazakhstan and Turkmenistan. In fact, only strong vocal support from the USA can break Azerbaijan's isolation.

THE PRODUCTION ISSUE

Even though the question of property rights still has not been solved, the Caspian republics have begun to establish connections to Western oil companies. Azerbaijan has taken the lead, partly because of the war with Armenia over the disputed enclave Nagorno–Karabak, which gave the Azeri Government the impression that Russia supported Armenia and partly to demonstrate that they are serious about independence and feel that they have a right to act as a sovereign state, also – in particular – when it concerns oil. After several riots and crises, internally as well as in relations with Moscow, a consortium including a number of Western companies, led by BP, was finally created in November 1994. The total investments are estimated at between $6 and 8 billion and the intention is to produce 4 billion barrels of light oil a year. It is interesting that the now-privatized Russian oil company LUKoil is also a member of the consortium with a 10 per cent share. The Russians were furious when Azerbaijan announced that the Iranian national oil company would also be a member of the club with a 5 per cent share. The Iranians were therefore offered to 'buy' one-quarter of Azerbaijan's share (a total of 20 per cent). The Iranian oil minister has announced that Iran will invest between $300 and 350 million. Later on, because of strong US opposition to the Iranian participation in the consortium, the Azerbaijan Government cancelled its deal with Iran.

A similar model was used in connection with Kazakhstan's gas and oil reserves – particularly in Tengiz and Karachganak. Since June 1992, British Gas and the Italian company Agip have had exclusive rights to negotiate with other companies about the production of Karachganak's gas. However, because of the difficulties in negotiations with the state-controlled Russian gas company Gazprom, nothing positive came out of the negotiations. Kazakhstan, which needs cash badly and which wants to export its gas reserves to the world market, could no longer accept that the negotiations were not moving forward. Therefore Kazakhstan's president, Nazarbayev, threatened British Gas and Agip in November 1994 with cancelling their exclusive negotiation rights, unless a settlement with Gazprom was reached soon. Apparently the threat worked and the negotiations started in December. Observers think that a treaty will be signed soon. They are talking about a $6 billion investment. On the other hand, Chevron, a US oil company which has already invested $1 billion of high-risk capital in the development of the Tengiz field, faced a strategic obstacle concerning oil transportation. Since Chevron is not a member of the Caspian Pipeline Consortium (CPC), it was obliged to accept the Russian LUKoil's participation, along with Omanis, with the result that Chevron had to concede its 20 per cent share in the Tengizchevr oil deal (November 1995).

THE PIPELINE CONFLICT

One thing is certain: all the pipelines must transport oil and gas to the Western market and Japan. There are four options, each with advantages and disadvantages. The most talked-about option is of course running the pipelines through Russia (1) because the Central Asian and Caucasian republics now are all members of the Commonwealth of Independent States (CIS) together with Russia and still have close economic ties to Moscow and (2) because part of the pipelines from the Soviet period are already there. Azerbaijan's oil can be transported through Chechnyan territory (not far from Grozny) to Tikhoretsk and finally to Novorossiisk by the Black Sea. If Azerbaijan wanted to avoid Russia, it would be technically possible to transport Azerbaijan's oil through Georgia to Poti by the Black Sea. That would be the shortest route. However, because of the conflict between Georgia and Abkhazia (where Poti is located), this option is not realistic in terms of security. Kazakhstan's oil can be transported via different routes depending on where the oil is produced. The oil from the Tengiz oil field could be transported through Atyrau, Astrakhan (in Tatarstan) to Grozny, where it can be led into the pipeline from Azerbaijan. An alternative would be to transport the oil directly from Astrakhan to Novorossiisk. Turkmenistan's oil could be transported through Uzbekistan and Kazakhstan territory along the Caspian Sea to Russia and further on to Europe through Poland. The route through Turkey goes through Georgia (to avoid Armenia) to Ceyhan, the Turkish harbour by the Mediterranean. This route presents two main problems, both security related. The first problem is Armenia who is engaged in an armed conflict with Azerbaijan. According to the project, the pipeline will run along the Armenian border which means that Armenia could threaten the transport. So could the Kurds in Turkey, since the pipeline will pass Anatolia where a large majority of the population is Kurds fighting for independence. The third option is Iran, which is a great geostrategical location and which presents more options. One option is to lead the pipeline from Baku through Iranian territory and on to Turkey. Another option is to transport the oil from the Caspian Sea to the Persian Gulf. The advantage would be that the Caspian republics would avoid Russia and would thus be able to trade directly with the world market. The disadvantage would be that they would become dependent on the Islamic Republic. Furthermore, it would be so expensive to build a 1200 km pipeline from the Caspian Sea to the Persian Gulf that the republics would have a hard time financing it. However, there is one interesting alternative: the Caspian republics could transport their oil to Tehran's and Tabriz's refineries; in return Iran could sell the oil on behalf of the Caspian republics – a kind of oil barter. The fourth and least realistic transport option – in particular concerning Turkmenistan's gas reserves and Kazakhstan's oil and gas reserves – is through China or Afghanistan to India, Japan and the other Asiatic countries.

Azerbaijan offered Iran to join in the exploitation of the gas-rich Shah Deniz field as compensation for being ousted from the Caspian pipeline project, but the Iranian Government rejected this offer.

All these projects are technically possible. According to experts, running the oil through Turkey and Iran would create the greatest economical advantage. However, there are security-related conditions of a political and military nature which could threaten the execution of such a project (fundamentalism and ethnic conflicts). It is precisely for these reasons that Russia still holds the best hand. The war in Grozny is not only a fight against 'bandits', as Russia claims. The war in Grozny is first and foremost a fight for control over the world's third largest oil reserves.

Recently (October–November 1995), the Azeri Government – after obtaining President Clinton's agreement – chose to build two pipelines through Russia and Georgia, finally eliminating the Iranian option. Following the Azeri decision, Kazakhstan, which would like to be a leading energy producer in the early twenty-first century, started feeling nervous, fearing that Azerbaijan would capture an important slice of the world market. Therefore, the Kazakh authorities urged Chevron to deal with LUKoil with the purpose of having access to the CPC. The projected pipeline will start in the Tengiz oil fields, crossing Komsomol on the Caspian littoral and will reach Tikhoretsk and finally Novorossiisk at the Black Sea. It seems that this deal is now almost settled.

ACTORS' STRATEGIES

By 'actor' I here mean the 'states', excluding the multinational companies which play a very important role in the Caspian region. Since the interests of these companies are often identical with the main state behind them, the choice of state as actor seems to be accurate. Many states are interested in this region and not all of them belong to the region. It is, however, possible to classify the actors as follows: (1) oil producers, (2) oil transporters, (3) oil consumers, and (4) some countries which are both oil producers and oil transporters – this is the case of Russia and Iran.

Oil producers' strategy

Temporarily excluding Russia and Iran from this category, four other countries remain: Kazakhstan, Turkmenistan, Uzbekistan and Azerbaijan. All of these countries obviously have huge interests in producing and exporting as much oil and gas as they are able to. With their strong and urgent need for hard currency, oil and gas are at the present time the only tangible resources which can provide them with the necessary hard currency. Another benefit that they can extract from their natural resources is political advantages. In fact, these resources – once produced and exported – will be the most efficient instrument for the purpose of their newly acquired independence, in particular *vis-à-vis* Russia. Along this path they are facing a number of difficulties, beginning with the dispute over the legal status of the Caspian Sea as well as a lack of investments both in the technical renovation of the petroleum industry, which is far from being in a good shape and also investments in the production of oil and gas. These difficulties have been aggravated by the problems concerning the construction of new pipelines and the transportation of oil and gas.

Actually, there are three main options open to them. First, to follow their individual, national interest and to deal alone and directly with international oil companies. This policy could succeed if these countries had geographical, direct access to the international market; this is not the case. Another necessary condition of success is political stability and the possession of an appropriate and operational army capable of dissuading any attempt on their respective oil and gas industry. These conditions are not fulfilled at the moment. The second option is the establishment of a regional cooperation network, well structured and well functioning. The only cooperation of this kind is the Caspian Sea Organization (CSO) of which both Russia and Iran are members (but not Uzbekistan). The CSO is an infant regional organization which was created in April 1992. This organization is also limited to technical matters relating to shipping, transport, tourism and the environment. Concretely, this means that there is no regional cooperation network among the Caspian oil-producing countries. The third option is based on an alignment with Russia – which is able and willing to provide security, access to the international market and technical assistance. Apparently, this is not the option that the Caspian countries are willing to choose. On the contrary, they prefer to avoid it for the simple reason that a complete alignment with Russia would result in the transfer of an essential part of their sovereignty to Moscow.

Faced with these options, the Caspian states opted for an eclectic strategy, based on a mixture of the first and the third options. Each of them pursuing their individual national interests whilst respecting Russia's political and economic interests. Respecting Russian political will, they adhered to the CIS. By accepting LUKoil's participation in different deals they made with Western oil companies, they satisfied Moscow's economic interests.

Oil transporters' strategy

There are four states in this category: Russia, Iran, Turkey and Georgia. The two first countries are also giant oil producers themselves. Although the financial interests related to transport royalties are common to all of these four countries, their political objectives are different. Russia and Iran are pursuing almost the same goal: political control of oil transportation to the international market, with the difference that Russia is also seeking domination, while Iran is trying hard to break down its own isolation. Turkey's interest is strategy rather than domination. If the Caspian oil goes through Turkey's territory, it will undoubtedly provide Ankara with a new opportunity to stress its geopolitical importance before the USA and in particular the EU which Turkey is desperately seeking to join as a full member. Georgia has the same interest as Turkey but at a more modest level. The Georgian authorities hope that oil transportation through their territory will improve their catastrophical economic situation and that the pipelines will contribute indirectly to preserving Georgia's territorial integrity.

Oil consumers' strategy

The international market is dominated by the Western countries and Japan. The strategic goal of these countries comprises three points which must be in place simultaneously. These points are the diversification of the energy resources, the safety of production and transportation and low prices. In fact, the Caspian oil and gas resources stand as a new and quite important energy resource for the West. Therefore, the giant international oil companies rushed into this region. These companies are still facing two main obstacles which are political stability at the national and regional levels and the safety of transportation. Concerning political stability, it seems that the central Asian region is more safe and more stable than Caucasus. The conflicts in Caucasus remain unresolved despite the relatively low tension currently prevailing. Political and violent struggles within the Republic of Azerbaijan, the dispute between Armenia and Azerbaijan about Nagorno–Karabak, the Abkhazian conflict in Georgia and the war in Chechnya symptomatically illustrate the risks of instability in the Caucasian region. Paradoxically, oil can have a beneficial impact on reducing the intensity of tensions in this region. And it is no exaggeration to say that oil has already had such an effect on the conflicts. For example, Azerbaijan, which expects that oil revenues will remedy its economic situation and indirectly lead to political stability in the country, has changed its political orientation from 'national chauvinism' under President Elchibey to 'national pragmatism' under President Aliev. The same political change has happened in Georgia: from President Gamsakhurdia to President Shevardnadze.

Oil producers and transporters

This is the case of Russia and Iran. These two countries share similar interests and seek almost the same objectives. Of the Caspian states, Iran is the only member of OPEC and its main oil fields are located in the Persian Gulf. Russia's situation, without being a member of OPEC, is to some extent the same as Iran's: the main Russian oil fields are in Siberia, far from the Caspian region. Russia and Iran also share the same view on the question of ownership of the Caspian Sea and its legal status. Both consider the Caspian Sea a closed sea. Furthermore, both countries have direct access to open sea: Iran has the Persian Gulf and Russia has the Pacific Ocean as well as the Barents and Black Seas. This means that neither of them is dependent on the Caspian oil resources. It also means, in terms of energy supplies, that they have merely a secondary attachment to and interest in this region. All these factors indicate that Russia and Iran have no vital interests around the Caspian Sea. It makes a huge difference if we compare their self-sufficiency with the total dependency of other Caspian states on their natural resources which are situated either directly in this region or near it. In political terms, Iran's and Russia's advantageous geographical situation combined with their energy independence (from the Caspian region) provide them with the luxury of playing their political game in a more relaxed manner than all other states in this region. Focusing on the similarities between the Russian and Iranian interests and objectives in the Caspian region does not mean that this element alone necessarily leads to similarity in terms of their output. It is no secret that Iran, despite its highly favourable geopolitical position, has only limited space to manoeuvre. Because of the nature of its political regime, Iran actually lives in a kind of quarantine, facing the containment imposed by the Clinton administration. As a result, the Iranian Islamist regime cannot make many moves in the south (the Persian Gulf) and has only a limited liberty of action in the north (the Caspian region). The American *de facto* veto on the transportation of Azeri oil through Iran was one of the measures which clearly demonstrated the sharp limitation of Iran's possibilities. In this respect, Russia is incomparably placed in a much better situation. Moscow not subject to any containment; on the contrary, the USA and other Western countries are ready to assist Moscow in overcoming its political and economic crisis precisely with the purpose of avoiding Russia's possible isolation. Therefore, we have to conclude that – at the present time and probably in the near future – Russia is the actor with the brightest opportunities in the Caspian region.

12 Uzbekistan's Place in the World Economy

S.M. Kasimov

The topic of my study is a novelty in itself, both for me as well as for most other Uzbekistan scholars, inasmuch as for more than 70 years not only could they not make reports on such topics, they could not even do research on them. The issues concerned were the exclusive prerogative of the Centre and the way the economy was organized assigned to Uzbekistan the role of a source of agricultural raw materials, with cotton the king in a one-crop system. That is all now past.

Uzbekistan's economy may be said to have truly begun to integrate with the world economy in 1991, when the republic acquired political and economic independence and became a member of the UN. My report, therefore, will concentrate on developments since that time and specifically how Uzbekistan has fared in its efforts to establish a socially oriented market economy in conformity with its own needs and possibilities.

THE STATE OF UZBEKISTAN IN CENTRAL ASIA

Uzbekistan has inherited one of the most favourable natural and geographical environments in Central Asia. It is located in the middle of Central Asia between the two big rivers of Amu-Darya and Syr-Darya. It is totally landlocked and extends 1425 km from west to east. Its population is over 22 million, with an average annual increase of 450 000–550 000, which is a relatively high growth rate. The country's area far exceeds that of the UK, Belgium, Denmark, Switzerland and Austria together. Uzbekistan has the largest population of all the former Central Asian Republics of the USSR and ranked third after Russia and the Ukraine in the USSR as a whole. Of this total number 71 per cent are Uzbeks, 9 per cent are Russians, 4 per cent are Tajiks and Kazakhs, 2 per cent are Tatars and Karakalpaks and the others are Koreans, Persians, Turks and other minor peoples. Archaeological evidence traces human activity back 45 000 years.

The peoples who inhabited the area have had ties with many countries of the West and East and can boast of major achievements in building irrigation systems, developing irrigated agriculture and promoting industry, trade, science and art. Uzbeks can be traced back to the tenth and eleventh centuries as an identifiable ethnic group on the territory of Turkestan; they became a nation (in Soviet terminology) with the establishment of the Uzbek SSR. Before that time, peoples living in what is now the territory of Kazakhstan, Turkmenistan, Uzbekistan and Kyrgyzstan were called Turks and the land was called Turkestan. In 1876 the territory was conquered by Russia in a typical act of colonial seizure. Russia needed Central Asia, above all as a market for Russian goods and a source of raw materials for Russian industry, while Uzbek merchants had their sights set on Russia markets. Uzbek goods, cotton, silk and dried fruits, were in demand in Russia and the West, while textiles, silk, metal articles and metals were needed in Central Asia. However, the Russian Government permitted Turkestan to develop only those branches of industry involved in primary goods processing. Thus, in 1913, these branches accounted for 83 per cent of all production, while heavy industry accounted for only 2 per cent.

During the years of Soviet Power (1924–1990) Uzbekistan's economy grew considerably: its industrial production by 245-fold, agricultural output by 20-fold and volume of retail sales by a factor of 80. At the same time light industry as well as the food industry began to develop, along with electric power, fuel, metallurgy the chemical industry, engineering, instrument making and so on. However, most stress was laid on agriculture, irrigation, land reclamation and the development of virgin soil. The agricultural output was high enough to cover the republic's own needs, with the surplus being shipped to the rest of the Union. Uzbekistan's cotton output covered the needs of almost all the countries of the former Soviet bloc (East Germany, Poland, Romania, Bulgaria, Hungary and Czechoslovakia).

However, Soviet rule, with its administrative–bureaucratic, overly centralized system of government, left Uzbekistan and its autonomous regions with many problems, stemming above all from flawed planning, such as the programmes to develop and localize industrial capacity, the ensuing one-sided, hypertrophied specialization of industry and one-crop agriculture (cotton) and the relegation of Uzbekistan to the role of a source of raw materials. More than 80 per cent of the republic's exports were raw materials, primarily cotton. Industrial branches that provided for Union-wide needs enjoyed a high rate of growth and development, to the detriment of the vital needs of the republic, despite the fact that favourable conditions objectively existed for this. The result was that more than 50 per cent of the goods consumed in the republic were imported from the other republics, along with approximately 50 per cent of the manufactured garments, although the raw materials originated in Uzbekistan. Despite the many slogans heralding

Uzbekistan's becoming a mixed industrial and agrarian republic, it remained a source of raw materials. Ninety per cent of the exports of cotton, silk, oil, gas and precious and non-ferrous metals were in raw material form rather than in the form of finished products.

The republic's topography is varied and marked by plains and mountains. Mountains including foothills make up one-third of the republic's territory. Between them are wide and vast valleys. There is a high level of seismic activity in Uzbekistan, with tremors reaching 8–9 on the Richter scale. There is abundant sunshine – an average of 2700–2980 hours per year in the north and 2800–3130 hours in the south.

The climate in Uzbekistan is continental, with cold winters (January –30–38° C) and hot summers (July +42° C). Water is a vitally important resource. Therefore, making rivers deeper and creating artificial lakes assume a crucial significance. The republic has few lakes, but one of the biggest of them is the Aral Sea. Over the last 30 years the water level has fallen by 12–14 m. Uzbekistan also has a variety of medicinal mineral waters. The mineral and raw materials of the Republic of Uzbekistan are rich in several kinds of minerals: there are more than 100 kinds of mineral resources. Uzbekistan is among the world leaders in deposits of copper, silver, gold, lead, zinc tungsten and natural gas and some other minerals. Uzbekistan is the world's fourth biggest producer of gold and has huge energy resources in the form of natural gas, coal and oil. It should in the future become self-sufficient in oil and petroleum products, with even a surplus available for export.

From 1 September 1991 Uzbekistan began to make its own decisions on how to exploit and distribute its natural resources with an eye to its own socioeconomic development and raising the living standards of the population.

THE ECONOMY AND INFRASTRUCTURE OF UZBEKISTAN

Between 1988 and 1991 production declined sharply, particularly in 1991 (see Table 12.1). Most of the decline in 1991 was prior to the economic reform. The share of agriculture in the total production increased steadily, reaching 36 per cent in 1991 (Table 12.3), while that of industry fell to 21 per cent in 1990, after which it began again to rise (28 per cent in 1991).

The percentage of the labour force employed in agriculture has remained constant since 1985, while that of industry has risen, reaching 15 per cent in 1990. The public sector is still the biggest employer, although its share has declined since 1985. Cooperative enterprises, self-employment and commerce and services, have partially absorbed some of the decline in public sector employment. The total spending rose considerably between 1987 and 1991. Personal consumption, public consumption and capital investments increased between 1987 and 1990 (in per cent of GNP) from 58 to 61 per cent, from 21 to 26 per cent and from 29 to 32 per cent, respectively. The year 1991 saw a decline in the last two indices from 26 to 19 per cent and from 32 to 26 per cent, respectively, while personal consumption remained at 61 per cent of the GNP (Table 12.3).

TABLE 12.1 *Key macroeconomic indices for 1988–1991*

Characteristic	*1988*	*1989*	*1990*	*1991*
Production (real rate of growth)				
GDP	10.2	3.7	1.6	4.3
Net national product	9.6	3.1	4.5	0.91
Balance of trade	–6.3	–13	–16.4	–3.0
(in per cent of GDP)				
between republics	–5.7	–11.4	–11.4	–0.7
external state	–0.6	–1.6	–5.0	–2.3
Prices and wages*	–2.0	0.8	4.0	98.2
indirect net national product deflator	0.0	0.9	8.8	83.1
retail prices	–1.0	7.2	11.2	51.0
Core prices	7.3	6.5		51.2

* State commission by statistic and forecasting.

TABLE 12.2 *The structure of the employed population (in per cent)*

Characteristic	*1985*	*1990*	*1991*
Per cent of population			
Employed	97	39	40
Pensioned	11	12	12
Employment in branches			
Industry	15	15	14
Construction	6	9	8
Agriculture	38	39	42
Transport and communication	4	3	3
Trade and related branches	7	6	6
Others	28	28	27
Employment according to type of enterprise			
Public sector	72	66	65
Cooperative	18	20	18
Others	10	15	17

TABLE 12.3 *The structure of production and spending (per cent GMP)*

Characteristic	*1987*	*1988*	*1989*	*1990*	*1991*
Branches					
Industry	29	26	22	21	28
Agriculture	26	28	31	33	36
Construction	11	11	11	11	11
Service sector	35	36	36	36	37
Spending for					
Personal consumption	58	58	59	61	61
Public consumption	21	20	23	26	19
Capital investment	29	27	32	32	26
Left over from balance	–8	–6	–13	–19	–5

Uzbekistan's economy today is multisectoral, the principal industries being gas, ferrous and non-ferrous metallurgy, mechanical engineering (mainly for agriculture), cotton processing and textiles. Uzbekistan leads the Central Asian republics in economic potential. Its industrial and agricultural indicators are high. Natural and climatic conditions as well as traditional skills benefit the development of such sectors as silkworm breeding, stock raising, viniculture, apiculture and fruit growing (including melons). Approximately 40 per cent of Uzbekistan's net material product is agriculture production. The main crop is cotton: Uzbekistan is fourth in the world in cotton production and third in cotton exports. The republic was also one of the biggest producers of fruit and vegetables in the former USSR. More than 30 million ha is devoted to agriculture and two-thirds of that area is for cattle raising. At the present time 90 per cent of the gross agriculture product is accounted for the by non-public sector. Uzbekistan has economic treaties with 70 countries of the world. One hundred and sixty products are exported. Formerly, external business was conducted by the Centre. Eight million out of a population of 22 million are employed in the public sector, including 24.6 per cent in heavy industry and construction, 38.4 per cent in agriculture, 5.1 per cent in transport and communication, 6.0 per cent in commerce, public catering, material and technical supplies, sales and purchases and 25.9 per cent in the other branches of the national economy. Above over 8500 schools provide general education, including over 50 institutions of higher learning, 147 secondary and specialized schools and so on. Uzbekistan played a major role in the development of the overall national economy of the former USSR. It produced 100 per cent of the Soviet cotton-picking machines, 90 per cent of the cotton gins, 66 per cent of the cotton fibre, 47 per cent of the raw silk, 27 per cent of the spinning machines, 20 per cent of the electric cranes, 100 per cent of the kenaf, 38 per cent of the astrakhan, 19 per cent of the rice, 15 per cent of the vegetable oil, 9 per cent of the vegetables and 8 per cent of the fruit and grapes. The structure of Uzbekistan industry is currently in a process of readjustment. Its traditional sectors, light industry and the food industry, are also well developed. Among recently built large projects in these sectors are the Bukhara cotton mills and the Khiva carpet factory. The energy and fuels sector (natural gas and oil) is the leading industrial sector. The Mingbulac oil fields will soon begin production. Non-ferrous metallurgy, another important industry, is located mainly in the Angren–Almalik mining and industrial region. The gold-mining industry is represented by the Muruntau Mining and Concentrating Works. Other large enterprises are the Chirchik Electrochemical Works, the Samarkand superphosphate factory, the Navoi chemical works and the Namangan chemical plant. Mechanical engineering is well-developed and is the basis of the technological progress of all sectors. Dozens of enterprises and associations are operating in this sector. One of the former USSR's largest aircraft companies is located in Tashkent. It produces the passenger and freight aircraft AN76, AN10 and so on. Uzbekistan is rich enough in raw materials to be able to satisfy all of its own needs with a surplus left over for export.

Agriculture production is represented by cotton, rice, grain, grapes, vegetables, melons and cattle. By 1996 the republic will fully meet its own needs for grain. Finally, silkworm breeding, Uzbekistan's oldest agricultural sector, should be mentioned.

Exports should grow. In 1995 the export volume was $1.5 billion, compared with $677 million in 1990. The share of finished products in total exports grew from 30 per cent in 1990 to 43 per cent in 1993. The share of cotton in the total exports decreased from 82 to 51 per cent, while machinery exports grew from 2 to 4 per cent of all exports. The present economic reforms are affecting all sectors of the national economy. Whereas formerly state ownership dominated in the economy, now there are many forms of ownership: collective, personal, private and mixed. There are more than 1000 joint ventures, with numerous foreign firms, for example the American Newmount, the German Mercedes Benz and Siemens, the South Korean DAEWOO and Samsung, the Japanese Mitsubishi and the French Elf Aquitaine. The South Korean firm DAEWOO is engaged in a joint venture to build an automobile plant offering vehicle maintenance. A joint venture in Samarkand is producing LIAZ buses with a capacity of 120 passengers. A joint venture with Mercedes Benz in Khorezm will produce the first freight-carrying buses. Joint ventures with Turkey, Germany, China, the USA and other countries are already in operation. The serial production of the IL-144, a splendid long-distance passenger plane, is about to commence. The development of new forms of international collaboration will produce new decision-making structures that can deal with regional problems, of which there are many, for example the Aral Sea problem, the problem of the use of water resources in Central Asia and the Tedzhen–Sarakhs–Mashhad railway.

UZBEKISTAN'S FOREIGN ECONOMY RELATIONS

Uzbekistan's foreign trade has undergone a wholesale change since 1991. The country has gained independence and has been admitted to the UN and other international organizations, thus enabling it to conduct its own foreign policy, to find its own ways to enter into the world community and to determine its own international relationships. Foreign policy is practically virgin territory for the new republic. Under the old totalitarian system Uzbekistan had no possibility of operating directly on the international arena, had no foreign trade institutions and very few experienced diplomats and foreign trade specialists. However, the development of foreign trade is a must if Uzbekistan is to retain its independence and maintain a stable economy. It is difficult to imagine a country, extending over a vast territory, with a population of millions and rich in resources, that could maintain a propitious development without constant and intense economic links with other countries. International trade is indispensable to economic growth. According to calculations, the volume of international trade at the present time is 16–18 per cent of the GNP for the USA, 36–39 per cent of the GNP for Germany and 110–135 per cent of the GNP for Belgium, Hungary and Singapore. The share of foreign trade in the Uzbekistan GNP has been fluctuating within the range of 10–12 per cent (cf. Table 12.4).

TABLE 12.4 *The role of foreign trade in Uzbekistan's economy by years (in per cent)*

Characteristic	*1980*	*1985*	*1990*
Indexes			
Share of exports in proceeds from national production	6.2	4.6	4.9
Share of imports in consumed national income	–	–	–
Export volume per population	67.4	54.4	80.3
Import volume per population	–	–	114.1
Relative share of foreign trade turnover in GNP	–	–	10.0

The structure and composition of foreign trade partners has undergone many changes since the reforms began and more than 1200 firms now have the right to engage in foreign trade. Foreign trade grew from 1986 to 1990, largely due to growing imports. Between 1987 and 1990 imports increased by 45 per cent at constant prices. In 1990 the total volume of imports declined by 12 per cent compared with 1986. Exports have declined, however, owing to the economic crisis and to a decrease in the volume of cotton fibre exported. Considering that according to various estimates Uzbekistan had mined more than one-quarter of all Soviet gold this can safely be said to be a good starting basis for the country to develop its own foreign economy policy. The strategy for the development of foreign trade envisages a steady rate of growth.

By the year 2000, exports should account for 10 per cent of the GNP compared with 4.5 per cent at present. The development of Uzbekistan's foreign trade may be broken down into several stages. The first stage, 1992–1993, saw a rationalization of imports, which consisted mainly of new equipment for light industry, the food industry and machinery construction, chemistry and non-ferrous metallurgy and the creation of a basis for export industries. The second stage, 1994–1995, involved the completion of the modernization of the export base and the establishment of a new foreign trade profile, as well as the creation of a free enterprise zone and the development of international tourism. In the third stage, from 1996 to the year 2000 and beyond, Uzbekistan should be transformed from an exporter of raw materials to an exporter of mainly finished products. For economic, geographical and historical and cultural reasons, the strategic orientation of Uzbekistan's foreign trade policy must be Asia. The Asian countries are experiencing sustained economic growth, they are near and while Western firms are interested in supplying modern technology to these countries, it is questionable whether they can do so competitively without considerable financial incentives and privileges.

ECONOMIC REFORM AND ITS PROGRESS

As an independent state, able to conduct its own foreign and domestic policy, Uzbekistan is now ready to take its place in the international division of labour. The transition to a market economy entails a broad range of complex social and economy tasks, such as eliminating the defects of the totalitarian system, rectification of the negative consequences of the command and administrative methods of the government and planning by directive and ensuring economic and financial stability. The transition to the market can be either forced, as in Russia or gradual and evolutionary, as in Uzbekistan. The former requires immediate and radical reforms, a complete demolition of the former system and the establishment of new economic relations. This is the so-called shock treatment. In the latter case, the old economic and administrative relations are remoulded step-by-step to conform to the requirements of the market. Already, reform in the Commonwealth of Independent States (CIS) countries shows that the evolutionary path causes fewer social shocks and the effects are more solid and permanent. Because the evolutionary path is gradual and more methodical, each country may test out its own models for regulating the market in accordance with national peculiarities and transitions. For example, South Korea, Germany, Poland and Turkey have approached economic growth and development each in their own distinctive way and each can probably offer Uzbekistan some valuable suggestions.

Because of its own special history Uzbekistan is in some respects unique. A general programme for restructuring and reforming Uzbekistan's economy, therefore, should be based on the following five key principles.

1. Economics should take precedence over politics.
2. The state should be the principal agent of reform, and set priorities.
3. The law should be supreme and obedience to it and the constitution unconditional.
4. The welfare of the population must be safeguarded.
5. The transition to the market should be evolutionary and steered by the state.

Economic stability requires a restructuring of the economy and the promotion of free enterprise. There are six spheres of problems relevant to these ends.

1. The reprofiling of production to increase the output of industrial and food goods, decrease the deficit and develop the service sector with due consideration given to the needs of the different ethnic and social groups.
2. Diminishing economic dependence on other states, eliminating the irrational territorial division of labour and restructuring the specialization of production of different economic complexes.
3. Moving away from the export of raw materials to the production and export of finished goods.
4. High capital investment in all economic branches, with a full and effective employment of labour.
5. Renewal of equipment and machinery and the introduction of new technology throughout the economy, the state sector, as well as the mixed, private and corporate sectors.

6. Training and retraining of specialists and businessmen for all branches of national economy, as the market requires.

The economic reforms have been furthered by a series of presidential decrees, for example 'On guaranteeing private ownership'. The next stage of the economic reforms provides for an acceleration of the privatization process. More than 50 000 enterprises have now changed their form of ownership: of these, 22 000 have become sharehold companies, more than 8600 collective enterprises, 18 000 private enterprises and 700 leased enterprises. This enables everyone to take part in privatization, if the work collective agrees. The republic stock exchange is functioning: shares in enterprises in industry, construction and the service sector are now being traded. As of the end of 1993 there were more than 13 000 small and medium sized enterprises in operation, employing 174 000; of these 2500 were state enterprises employing 43 000 people. A fund has been established to develop small and medium sized businesses. Small and medium sized enterprises at present fall into the following categories: private, individual, family, collective and state owned. There are also consultancies and broker agencies.

To close we propose the following recommendations for furthering Uzbekistan's integration with the world economy.

1. Uzbekistan is situated at the crossroads of Europe and Asia, linking west with east and south with north. It is in a key position in the long term to contribute to the building of economic, scientific and cultural bridges between Europe and Asia, like the Great Silk Route.
2. Uzbekistan produces one-quarter of the world's cotton fibre and thus is poised to play a leading role in supplying all kinds of cotton goods (cotton fibre, fabrics, clothes and so on) to the countries of the world.
3. Uzbekistan produces 25 per cent of the world's gold; jewellery and gold items could be major export products.
4. Uzbekistan can export fresh tinned vegetables and fruits to Western European countries.
5. Uzbekistan is an exporter of non-ferrous metals and could develop this industry in accordance with Western European countries requirements.
6. Uzbekistan could make a valuable contribution to research into the uses of solar energy, space research, the establishment of international monitoring stations. It could broaden cooperation with international and regional financial organizations and banks to ensure secure investments in promising perspective branches of the economy. It is obviously centrally placed for research into Central Asian history and for international tourism to numerous historical sites (Samarkand, Bukhara and Khiva) and so on.

Appendix 1

AGREEMENT ON THE CREATION OF A COMMONWEALTH OF INDEPENDENT STATES

We, the Republic of Belarus, the Russian Federation (RSFSR), and Ukraine, as founder states of the USSR who signed the Union treaty of 1922, designated below as the High Contracting Parties, state that the USSR as a subject of international law and a geopolitical reality, is ceasing to exist.

Basing ourselves on the historical community of our peoples and the ties that have formed between them, taking into consideration the bilateral treaties concluded between the High Contracting Parties, seeking to build democratic law-based states, intending to develop their relations on the basis of mutual recognition of and respect for state sovereignty, the inalienable right to self-determination, the principles of equality and noninterference in internal affairs, a rejection of the use of force, economic or any other methods of pressure, the settlement of disputes by means of conciliation, and other generally recognized principles and norms of international law, considering that the further development and strengthening of relations of friendship, good-neighbourliness and mutually advantageous cooperation between our states answers the fundamental national interests of their peoples and serves the cause of peace and security, confirming their adherence to the goals and principles of the United Nations Charter, the Helsinki Final Act, and other documents of the Conference on Security and Cooperation in Europe, pledging to observe the generally recognized international norms on the rights of man and of peoples, have agreed on the following:

Article 1

The High Contracting Parties are forming the Commonwealth of Independent States.

Article 2

The High Contracting Parties guarantee their citizens, regardless of their nationality or other differences, equal rights and freedoms. Each of the High Contracting Parties guarantees the citizens of the other parties, and also stateless persons living on their territory, regardless of their national affiliation or other differences civil, political, social, economic, and cultural rights and freedoms in accordance with the generally recognized international norms of human rights.

Article 3

The High Contracting Parties, wishing to promote the expression, preservation, and development of the ethnic, cultural, linguistic, and religious distinctiveness of the national minorities living on their territory and of the unique ethno-cultural groups that have formed there, take them under their protection.

Article 4

The High Contracting Parties will develop equal and mutually beneficial cooperation between their peoples and states in the spheres of politics, the economy, culture, education, health care, environmental protection, science, trade, and in the humanitarian and other spheres, promote a wide-scale exchange of information, and strictly observe mutual obligations.

The parties consider that it is necessary to conclude agreements on cooperation in these spheres.

Article 5

The High Contracting Parties recognize and respect each other's territorial integrity and the inviolability of existing frontiers within the framework of the commonwealth.

They guarantee the openness of frontiers and freedom of movement of citizens and the transfer of information within the framework of the commonwealth.

Article 6

The member states of the commonwealth will cooperate in ensuring international peace and security and the realization of effective measures to reduce armaments and military expenditures. They will strive for the elimination of all nuclear weapons and for general and complete disarmament under strict international control.

The Parties will respect each other's desire to attain the status of nuclear-free zones and neutral states.

The member states of the commonwealth will preserve and maintain under joint command a common military-strategic space, including single control over nuclear weapons, the manner of implementing which will be regulated by a special agreement.

They also jointly guarantee the requisite conditions for the stationing, functioning, and material and social well-being of the Strategic Armed Forces. The parties undertake to conduct a coordinated policy as regards the social protection and pension arrangements for military personnel and their families.

Article 7

The High Contracting Parties acknowledge that the sphere of their joint activity, realized on an equal basis through common coordinating institutions, includes:

- coordination of foreign-policy activity;
- cooperation in the formation and development of a common economic space, of all-European and Eurasian markets, and in the sphere of customs policy;
- cooperation in the development of transport and communications systems;
- cooperation in the sphere of environmental protection, participation in the creation of an all-embracing international system of ecological safety;
- questions of migration policy;
- the fight against organized crime.

Article 8

The parties recognize the global nature of the Chernobyl catastrophe and undertake to unite and coordinate their efforts to minimize and overcome its consequences.

For these purposes they have agreed to conclude special agreements that take account of the seriousness of the consequences of the catastrophe.

Article 9

Disputes regarding the interpretation of the norms of the present agreement are subject to solution by means of talks between the appropriate bodies, and, when necessary, at the level of heads of government and state.

Article 10

Each of the High Contracting Parties reserves the right to suspend the operation of the present agreement or its individual articles having notified the participants in the agreement a year in advance.

The provisions of the present agreement can be supplemented or changed by mutual agreement of the High Contracting Parties.

Article 11

The application of the norms of third states, including those of the former USSR, is not permitted on the territory of the states signing this agreement from the moment of its signing.

Article 12

The High Contracting Parties guarantee the fulfillment of the international obligations ensuing for them from the treaties and agreements of the former USSR.

Article 13

The present agreement does not affect the obligations of the High Contracting Parties as regards third states.

The present agreement is open to accession by all member states of the former USSR, and also by other states sharing the goals and principles of the present agreement.

Article 14

The official residence of the coordinating bodies of the commonwealth is the city of Minsk.

The activity of agencies of the former USSR on the territory of the member states of the commonwealth ceases.

Accomplished in the city of Minsk on 8 December 1991 in three copies, each in Belarussian, Russian, and Ukrainian, the three texts having identical force.

For the Republic of Belarus	S. Shushkevich. V. Kebich
For the RSFSR	B. Yeltsin. G. Burbulis
For Ukraine	L. Kravchuk. V. Fokin

SOURCE *RFE RL Research Report.*

Appendix 2

CIS: TREATY ON COLLECTIVE SECURITY

Text as published of 'Treaty on Collective Security' signed by representatives of Armenia, Kazakhstan, Kyrgyzstan, the Russian Federation, Tajikistan and Uzbekistan at the 15th May session of the Council of CIS Heads of State in Tashkent. The states participating in the present treaty, hereinafter referred to as 'participating states', guided by the independent states' DECLARATIONS of sovereignty, mindful of the creation by the participating states of their own armed forces, taking coordinated actions in the interests of ensuring collective security, recognizing the need to fulfil strictly the treaties which have been concluded with regard to the reduction of arms and armed forces and the strengthening of confidence-building measures, have agreed as follows:

Article 1

The participating states confirm their commitment to refrain from the use or threat of force in interstate relations. They pledge to resolve all disagreements among themselves and with other states by peaceful means. The participating states shall not enter into military alliances or participate in any groupings of states, nor in actions directed against another participating state.

In the event of the creation of a system of collective security in Europe and Asia and the conclusion of treaties on collective security to that end – for which the contracting parties shall strive unswervingly – the participating states shall enter into immediate consultations with each other for the purpose of incorporating the necessary intentions in the present treaty.

Article 2

The participating states shall consult with each other on all important questions of international security affecting their interests and coordinate their positions on these questions. In the event of the emergence of a threat to the security, territorial integrity and sovereignty of one or several participating states or of a threat to international peace and security, the purpose of coordinating their positions and taking measures to eliminate the threat that has emerged.

Article 3

The participating states shall form a collective security council consisting of the heads of participating states and the commander-in-chief of the CIS joint armed forces.

Article 4

If one of the participating states is subjected to aggression by any state or group of states, this shall be perceived as aggression against all participating states to this treaty.

In the event of an act of aggression being committed against any of the participating states, all the other participating states shall give it the necessary assistance, including military assistance, and also give support with the means at their disposal by way of exercising the right to collective defence in accordance with article 51 of the UN Charter.

The participating states shall immediately inform the UN Security Council of any measures taken on the basis of this article. When implementing these measures, the participating states shall abide by the corresponding provisions of the UN Charter.

Article 5

The collective security council of the participating states and the bodies to be created by it shall undertake the coordination and ensuring of joint activities by the participating states in accordance with this treaty. Until the aforesaid bodies have been created, the activities of the armed forces of the participating states shall be coordinated by the High Command of the commonwealth of joint armed forces.

Article 6

Any decision to use armed forces for the purpose of repulsing aggression in accordance with article 3 of the present treaty shall be adopted by the heads of the participating states. The use of armed forces outside the territory of the participating states may be effected exclusively in the interests of international security in strict compliance with the UN Charter and the legislation of participating states in the present treaty.

Article 7

The location and functioning of installations in the collective security system on the territory of participating states shall be regulated by special agreements.

Article 8

The present treaty does not affect any rights and commitments under other bilateral and multilateral treaties and agreements currently in force and concluded by the participating states with other states and it is not directed against third countries.

The present treaty does not affect the participating states' right to individual and collective defence against aggression in accordance with the UN Charter.

The participating states pledge not to conclude international agreements that are incompatible with the present treaty.

Article 9

Any questions arising between the participating states in connection with the interpretation or application of any provision of the present treaty shall be resolved jointly in the spirit of friendship, mutual respect and mutual understanding.

Amendments to the present treaty may be incorporated on the initiative of one or several of the participating states and adopted on the basis of mutual agreement.

Article 10

The present treaty is open to all interested states which share its aims and principles.

Article 11

The present treaty is concluded for five years with a subsequent renewal. Any of the participating states has the right to withdraw from the present treaty if it notifies the other parties of its intention at least six months in advance and fulfils all the commitments resulting from withdrawal from the present treaty.

The present treaty is subject to ratification by each of the signatory states in accordance with its constitutional procedures. The ratification documents shall be handed to the government of the Republic of Belarus which is thus appointed depositary.

The present treaty comes into force immediately the ratification documents have been submitted by the participating states which have signed it for safekeeping.

Done in the city of TASHKENT on 15th May 1992 in one authentic copy in the Russian language. The authentic copy shall be kept in the archives of the government of the Republic of Belarus, which shall send certified copies to the states that have signed the present treaty.

SOURCE BBC Monitoring Service, Summary of World Broadcasts, 25 May 1992.

Index